BILL EDRICH

BILL EDRICH

THE MANY LIVES OF ENGLAND'S CRICKET GREAT

LEO McKINSTRY

BLOOMSBURY SPORT
LONDON • OXFORD • NEW YORK • NEW DELHI • SYDNEY

BLOOMSBURY SPORT
Bloomsbury Publishing Plc
50 Bedford Square, London, WC1B 3DP, UK
29 Earlsfort Terrace, Dublin 2, Ireland

BLOOMSBURY, BLOOMSBURY SPORT and the Diana logo are trademarks of
Bloomsbury Publishing Plc

First published in Great Britain 2024

A catalogue record for this book is available from the British Library

Library of Congress Cataloguing-in-Publication data has been applied for

ISBN: HB: 978-1-3994-0784-7; eBook: 978-1-3994-0780-9

2 4 6 8 10 9 7 5 3 1

Typeset in Adobe Garamond Pro by Deanta Global Publishing Services, Chennai, India
Printed and bound in Great Britain by CPI Group (UK) Ltd, Croydon CR0 4YY

To find out more about our authors and books visit www.bloomsbury.com
and sign up for our newsletters

To my dear friend and fellow historian Ian Redman,
whose lifelong devotion to Hartlepool United shows
a heroic detachment from reality.

CONTENTS

Edrich the cricketer

'Edrich brought into the England team two qualities which had been lacking for so long. One was a thoroughly sound technique of meeting the new ball. The other was a fighting, almost fierce, courage such as has characterised his whole career.'

Reg Hayter, Pardons news agency cricket correspondent

Edrich the lover

'He just kept falling in love. He had a twinkle in his eye and laughed easily. I think women loved him because he made them feel like they were the only person in the room.'

Peter Hayter, Mail on Sunday *cricket correspondent*

Edrich the tumultuous

'He spent so much of his time battling with various demons and never reached the stage where he was truly contented. Dad got his pleasure from short-term highs rather than overall fulfilment or peace.'

Justin Edrich

Edrich the pilot

'I cannot believe that a braver man than W.J. walked on to a cricket field. He showed his courage time and again during his wartime bombing missions when he continually cheated death.'

Denis Compton

INTRODUCTION

A mood of suppressed excitement and nervous anticipation hung in the air as the crowd began to fill The Oval. Every ticket had been sold for this final, climactic day. International cricket's greatest prize lay tantalisingly within the grasp of the England team, but the closeness of victory only heightened the tension after so many years of disappointment. The iconic ground, flanked by the colossal, wrought-iron gasholder which was the largest in the world at the time of its construction in 1853, had witnessed many milestones in the history of the game, including the very first Test match in England in 1880, played against Australia. England won by five wickets and W.G. Grace became its first centurion, scoring 152. Two years later, a nail-biting Australian victory by just seven runs had provoked the *Sporting Times* to publish a mock obituary 'in affectionate remembrance of English cricket', declaring that 'the body will be cremated and the ashes taken to Australia'. That winter an England side led by the aristocrat Ivo Bligh undertook a successful tour of Australia. Their triumph inspired a group of Melbourne ladies, one of whom became Bligh's wife, to present him with a tiny wooden urn said to contain the ashes of a burnt bail. It was only meant as a romantic, whimsical gesture but its resonance in the imagination of the Victorian public put the fight for the Ashes at the heart of the long rivalry between England and Australia.

Now on Wednesday 19 August, 1953, a century since The Oval's famous gasometer had gone up, England stood on the threshold of winning back the urn. For the last 19 years the Ashes had been in Australia's hands, a period of unparalleled ascendancy that partly reflected the dominance of Don Bradman, the most prolific batsman the world has ever seen. But since his retirement, Australia had become a less formidable opponent, while England had revived, especially through the advent of a new generation of fast bowlers. Traditionally, The Oval was the venue for the final, often decisive, contest in every five-match

Ashes series in England, and the 1953 Test had been preceded by four draws, in two of which England had come perilously close to defeat. Through sheer tenacity and luck, they had survived and, as the Oval Test entered its last day, they had a clear advantage, though the weight of the nation's expectations put tremendous pressure on England's captain Len Hutton.

For all his shrewdness as a tactician and classical brilliance as a batsman, Hutton was regarded with suspicion in parts of the cricket establishment because of his novel position as the first professional player to lead England since Arthur Shrewsbury's Ashes tour of 1886–87. Until his appointment in 1952, this post had always been held throughout the late Victorian age and the twentieth century by amateurs, based on the theory that those who earned their living from the sport could not exercise sufficient authority over their fellow players. Much of this attitude was nothing more than snobbery, but it meant that Hutton often felt he was on probation. Critics further alleged that his leadership lacked the dynamism needed for an Ashes fight because of his excessive caution and dourness. Those characteristics were said to be typical of Yorkshire cricket, whose unforgiving culture was encapsulated in the famous warning from Wilfred Rhodes, the county's greatest all-rounder, to a lackadaisical young colleague: 'We don't play for fun, you know.' In Hutton's case his reserved, pessimistic nature may also have had roots in his family's upbringing in the Moravian Church, a Protestant sect that settled in Yorkshire from Bohemia in the eighteenth century. Some figures in the press had even argued that Hutton should be displaced as skipper for the Oval Test, given the pivotal importance of this encounter. One potential alternative was the veteran batsman and Middlesex captain Bill Edrich who, despite a chequered international career, had the assets of his status as an amateur and his reputation as a battler. In the mass-circulation *Daily Mirror* the influential chief sportswriter Peter Wilson said that he 'would rather see Bill Edrich leading England than Len Hutton', a view endorsed by several of his readers. 'Edrich possesses that fighting spirit which Hutton seems to lack,' wrote one. 'Bill Edrich is the man for the job, a fighter all the way,' wrote another.

Twice in the interwar period, in 1926 and 1930, the selectors had changed the England captain for the last Test at The Oval in the hope of winning the Ashes, but there was no chance of changing the skipper in 1953. Such a move would be both an unnecessary sign of panic and a gross injustice to Hutton. Nor, despite Wilson's agitation, was there any public demand for a new leader. As the match unfolded, it looked as if Hutton was about to succeed where six previous amateur leaders had failed since 1934. Having bowled out Australia cheaply in their second innings, England had been set just 132 to win the series and the Ashes. With 50 minutes to survive on Tuesday night and the partisan crowd hushed in nervous anticipation, Hutton had gone out to open England's second innings with Edrich, who might have led his country years before had he not been so wayward in his turbulent personal life or so willing to challenge the authorities. Yet, for all the official gripes about his indiscipline away from the playing arena, Edrich had proved the ideal partner for Hutton, as he had used his long experience and sound defensive technique to repulse the deadly Australian pace attack of Ray Lindwall and Keith Miller. 'Bill Edrich is a lion of a cricketer,' the former Australian captain Bill Woodfull had once written, and even in the twilight of his international career the diminutive England batsman was reinforcing the wisdom of that comment.

It had been Hutton, not Edrich, who had produced the shock that suddenly undermined England's hopes. Just ten minutes before the close of play, he had called Edrich for a single despite hitting the ball straight to the fielder at square leg. His desperate charge down the pitch had turned into a suicide mission, and he was run out by yards. 'This was nothing more or less than a mental blackout – the snapping of tension that had been highly strung all season,' recorded Jack Fingleton, the distinguished journalist and former Australian Test cricketer. 'A deplorable mistake' was the verdict of Neville Cardus.

There had been no further alarms that evening. In the tense Oval atmosphere, Edrich had remained astonishingly calm. When play resumed the following morning in front of a packed house, England needed just 94 runs with nine wickets left. It was an indicator of the match's importance that the BBC, then the monopoly provider of television programmes, suspended their normal schedule to provide a live, uninterrupted broadcast of the day's play, with the irrepressible Brian Johnston as the chief commentator. Earlier in 1953, British television had received an enormous boost through the decision by Winston Churchill's government, strongly backed by Prince

Philip, to show the coronation. At the beginning of the 1950s, there were only 350,000 television sets in Britain, a figure that rose to 2.5 million by the summer of 1953. Like the crowd at The Oval, the audience at home was about to witness one of the most memorable passages in the story of the England Test side. Accompanied by the elegant young Surrey batsman Peter May, Edrich was the epitome of resolution as he hauled England towards the target, particularly in the cool way he handled Lindwall's short-pitched bowling. The hook was always Edrich's trademark shot, and at one point he delighted the spectators by hitting successive bumpers from Lindwall to the leg-side boundary. 'If I were asked to pick a side from post-war cricketers, Bill Edrich would be among my first choices. He is a great fighter at all times, never better than in a crisis,' Lindwall later said. Edrich's own England teammate Trevor Bailey, a player who was also renowned for his defiance, recalled that 'seeing this little man hooking Ray Lindwall was one of the most exhilarating sights I ever witnessed on a cricket ground.'

Edrich ensured there was no crisis at The Oval. He had only been recalled to the England side halfway through the 1953 series after an absence of three years from the Test arena, but he had fully justified the selectors' faith in him. Reg Hayter, the cricket correspondent at Pardons news agency, wrote that 'Edrich brought into the England team two qualities which had been lacking for so long. One was a thoroughly sound technique of meeting the new ball. The other was a fighting, almost fierce, courage such as has characterized his whole career. In the last three Test matches he has met all the speed and fury of Lindwall and Miller with an unconcern amounting to disdain.' The longer he remained at the crease, the closer he brought the Ashes, though the runs came slowly as he concentrated on the avoidance of any risks. In the *Daily Mirror*, Peter Wilson described how Edrich 'inexorably gnawed' his way to the target. Without giving a clear chance, he and his Surrey partner put on 64 before Miller had May caught at short fine leg. This dismissal was the cue, not for an Australian fightback, but for the uplifting climax to England's run chase. The new batsman was none other than Edrich's long-serving Middlesex colleague Denis Compton, a fellow conqueror of bowling attacks and connoisseur of intoxicating or intimate liaisons. So aligned was their outlook, so compelling their batting partnership and so close their relationship that they were known as the 'Middlesex Twins' or the 'Terrible Twins', though they were very different in appearance and style. Dashing, charming and carefree, Compton had the looks of a film star and the most famous face of any sportsman in England, thanks not just to his exploits as a cricketer and an Arsenal footballer, but also to his advertising of Brylcreem hair products. In contrast, Edrich was short and stocky, with 'an upturned nose that gave him a vaguely feral air', in the vivid words of the author Christopher Sandford. One of Edrich's ex-wives described him as 'like a randy mole'. Where Compton promoted hair cream, Edrich made commercials for cricket boots and concrete pitches.

Their approaches to batting were also dissimilar. Compton was gloriously unconventional and creative, regularly using strokes that were not in any coaching manual. Touched by genius, he was often called a 'Cavalier' because of his sense of freedom at the crease. Edrich was much more of a Roundhead, with an emphasis on sure defence and an attacking repertoire that favoured the leg side. 'Bill was a hard worker with his cricket, but with Denis it just flowed,' recalled Fred Titmus, the Middlesex off-spinner who played alongside them both in the 1950s. The renowned commentator Henry Blofeld, who was in the Norfolk team captained by Edrich after his retirement from first-class cricket, told me that, 'Bill knew more about cricket than almost anyone I ever met. He had a terrific understanding of the game. He understood it in a way that his great partner Denis never did, probably because Denis was such an instinctive player.' One professional who witnessed them at close hand during the peak of their careers in the late 1940s was the Middlesex opener Jack Robertson, who wrote in 1984[1] that: '. . . their batting was a contrast in styles and very entertaining. I saw Bill wielding his bat like a broadsword of his Viking ancestors – driving, cutting, hooking – with a natural ferocity. The only mercy he showed to the ball was with a leg glance and late cut, both strokes performed to perfection. Denis, with his hair always giving the lie to the hair cream advert that he adorned, despatched the ball to all parts of the ground with a lazy majesty, mixed with the cheek of the unorthodox, which had the crowds roaring and the bowlers staring in disbelief.'

---

[1] From a brochure entitled *Fifty Years On* published for the anniversary dinner held at the London Hilton to mark 50 years of Bill Edrich and Denis Compton's association with Middlesex.

Even as bowlers they had opposing methods. With his tearaway slinger's action, not unlike Jeff Thomson's in the 1970s, Edrich focused on pace and for a brief spell after the war was perhaps the fastest bowler in England. Commentating on radio during the 1948 Ashes series, John Arlott offered this description: 'One of these days I am convinced that Edrich will burst on the way to the crease. As it is he merely explodes when he gets there. It is an amazing action. He leans forward, goes up on tiptoes and gradually, with a heel swung gallop, he flings one down at Bradman.' No such exhausting dynamism was displayed by Compton, whose brand of occasional slow left-arm wrist spin was often distinguished by its inaccuracy.

They had first batted together almost 20 years earlier, but now at The Oval in 1953 this was the most significant partnership of their lives. Edrich continued to accumulate steadily, and Compton, after an erratic start, grew more secure. By lunch they were in command on 101 for 2, needing just 31 for victory. 'Bill had been batting magnificently and it seemed plain that as long as I could stay there with him we could easily get the runs together,' recalled Compton. When the afternoon session began, the spectators became quieter and their applause for scoring strokes was strangely truncated, as if they did not want either to tempt fate with premature celebrations or to slow down the march towards the target, when the real ecstasy could be released. As John Arlott recalled, 'The prospect of winning the Ashes after 19 years had been so distant that we had become like a small boy who has looked forward to a special treat for so long that he fears something will happen to stop it – or is himself so sick with excitement that he cannot enjoy it.' Even when Edrich passed 50, the cheering was not prolonged. By then, victory was in sight. At ten to three the Australian captain Lindsay Hassett effectively conceded defeat by bringing on himself and Arthur Morris, both part-timers. In fact, Edrich was almost stumped off Hassett, but the wicket-keeper Gil Langley missed the chance. Then, with the fourth ball of Morris's over, Compton seemed to have hit the winning run as he imperiously swept down to deep square leg, only for the fielder Alan Davidson to pull off an athletic stop. The fifth ball, another slow long-hop from Morris, was almost a replica of the previous one. This time Compton made certain by hitting it harder and wide of Davidson. There was a moment of near silence as the crowd waited to see the ball cross the boundary. When it did so, an explosion of relief and delight sounded in every part of the ground. 'It's the Ashes! England have won the Ashes!' yelled Brian Johnston into his BBC microphone. Out in the middle, Compton and Edrich had crossed as the ball sped across the turf. In Compton's recollection, Edrich was 'whooping like a boy opening his presents on Christmas morning'. Soon the pair were engulfed by the fans who swarmed over the outfield towards the pitch, impeding their return to the pavilion. 'I cannot remember seeing such a crowd on a cricket field,' wrote Peter Wilson of the *Daily Mirror*. The Australian commentator Bernard Kerr, broadcasting at the time as a guest on BBC radio, told listeners, 'I can see Denis Compton and Bill Edrich being embraced, being kissed by girls and women. I think they'll be bruised by the time they get in.' According to the Queensland newspaper the *Brisbane Courier-Mail*, 'The English are not only on top of the world after this Fifth Test – they are halfway to Mars. Their elevation is prodigious, their exultation phenomenal. El Alamein did not lift spirits this far.' Watching from the balcony of the England dressing-room was the wicket-keeper Godfrey Evans, who recalled how Compton and Edrich almost disappeared as 'congratulating hands grabbed them and laughing faces cheered them. At one stage I saw stocky Bill Edrich holding his bat like a chopper above his head and clearing a way for himself through the crowd.'

Once both of them were back in the pavilion, the party started. 'Boy did we celebrate,' said Edrich, whose exuberant conviviality was legendary in the cricket world. 'The champagne was coming out of our ears. Denis and I had dreamed of this moment from when we first started out as lads at Lord's and we deserved that drink.' The Australians also joined in the mayhem. 'We were drowning our sorrows but were happy for the England boys. It was a helluva party and continued long into the night,' said Keith Miller, a hedonistic soulmate of Compton and Edrich. As the pile of empty bottles grew around him, the Australian star was suddenly gripped by an impulse to move from consumption to propulsion. He picked up one bottle, then hurled it through an open window into the members' seating area. Others followed his example, and soon fusillades of breaking glass could be heard inside and outside the nineteenth-century building, matched by raucous laughter from players, selectors and officials. One bottle even smashed into the Australians' dressing-room clock, stopping its hands, but no one seemed to care.

Time was a matter of supreme indifference to Compton and Edrich, who were eager to carry on celebrating once The Oval supplies ran low. 'I have only a hazy recollection of what happened after we left The Oval. We went on the town and just everywhere people were queuing up to pat us on the back and buy us drinks,' said Compton. 'Even the hangovers the next morning were a joy,' wrote Edrich. Late in his life, in a letter written to a friend in 1980, he said that this was 'the most enjoyable Test' he ever played. The sense of euphoria among the England cricketers and the public lingered for weeks. A Coronation summer that had been marked by outstanding achievements of physical endeavour, including the conquest of Everest by Sir John Hunt's expedition, the pulsating victory in the FA Cup by the Blackpool team that featured Stanley Matthews, and the win in the Derby by Sir Gordon Richards in the week that he was knighted, had been given the perfect end by the return of the Ashes. It was appropriate that Compton and Edrich were at the crease in this memorable moment. For 15 years they had been battling against Australia as faithful servants of the Test side, always determined but never rewarded with a series success despite their individual heroics. Now they had helped English cricket to reach its own summit.

Churchill had heralded the arrival of the new Queen on the throne as the start of a second Elizabethan age, and Dudley Carew, writing in *The Times*, hailed Edrich for his 'natural Elizabethanness of spirit', as shown by the 'quality of eagerness and vitality' in his cricket. For Len Hutton, Edrich's batting at The Oval brought particular pleasure. As captain, he had been one of the architects of Edrich's return to the Test side in the summer of 1953 after several years in the wilderness, due mainly to accusations of poor discipline. Hutton's faith had been vindicated, as he later wrote: 'The measure of the part played by Bill Edrich was that he withstood their blistering attack for three hours and a half in scoring 55 not out – an innings that to me was worth more than a century in easier circumstances. Iron nerves as well as top-class skills were needed to combat the Australian attack. And I felt very pleased that my claim for his inclusion had borne fruit.' Like Hutton and Compton, Edrich had always seemed destined for greatness from his youth. In July 1937, *The Cricketer* magazine had written that 'there is no mistaking the class of Hutton, Compton and Edrich, the three discoveries of a generation'. Bradman himself, on his first tour of England as captain in 1938, had been moved to remark that 'Australia does not possess three young players of such collective strength as Hutton, Compton and Edrich. They are a formidable trio.' As a schoolboy from a cricket-mad farming family in Norfolk, Edrich's precocious talent won him a place in the county XI and attracted attention far beyond the Fens. 'Many years must pass before we can hope to see his equal,' reported his school magazine on his last season there in 1933. Before Edrich had even joined Middlesex, the *Daily Mail* columnist Geoffrey Simpson described him in July 1935 as 'the farmer's boy cricketer who may play for England'. Simpson dared to draw a parallel with the Australian giant: 'Like Don Bradman, Edrich was practically born with a bat in his hand and has been coached from his earliest days by his father.'

Edrich never quite lived up to that initial billing. Rich periods of success were matched by troughs of failure and friction with the authorities. Nevertheless, he remained one of the most fascinating cricketers of his era, adored by the public for his tough-minded resilience, and by the press for his vivid personality and ability to generate controversy. Although 'neither a stylist nor a poet,' wrote Neville Cardus, 'he was always the right cricketer for the crowd, who love a fighter always and a man who, small of inches, gets to the top by determination as well as by skill.' The most striking element of Edrich's cricket was his bravery, both in his refusal to give up any cause and in his ability to stand firm against the most hostile bowling. In his diary of the 1954–55 Ashes tour, the England fast bowler Frank Tyson wrote, 'Never have I met a more courageous individual. He appears almost indifferent to his own safety. No bowler is too fast to hook, no score too large to defy challenge.' At the Brisbane Test of the 1946–47 tour, Edrich batted for almost two hours on a rain-affected pitch, taking repeated blows to his body, that was left covered in bruises. 'Edrich scored only 16 but his was one of the finest batting displays that I have ever seen. It was better than many hundreds,' wrote Norman Preston, the Reuters Agency correspondent. Miller, who was responsible for many of those bruises that day in Brisbane, once described Edrich as 'the gutsiest cricketer that ever lived'.

Edrich's courage also shone through his admirable record in the Second World War as a pilot in RAF Bomber Command. When he joined up at the start of the conflict, he was offered, like many other professional sportsmen, a position as a physical-training instructor. 'Not likely. If I am good enough to play cricket for England, I am good enough to fight for England,' he responded. Once he had completed his training as a pilot, he carried out some of the most dangerous RAF missions of the conflict, among them the celebrated low-level attack on the major power station at Cologne in August 1941, during which more than 20 per cent of the British aircraft were lost. But Edrich was never one to be daunted by the odds against him, as reflected in the gallantry medal he won and the confidence he inspired in his men.

After losing six years to the war, Edrich was at his peak as both a batsman and a bowler in the late 1940s. Yet for all the magnificence of his achievements for England and Middlesex, he never enjoyed the consistent, sustained success that many felt his talent merited. To his detractors, the explanation lay in the lengthy catalogue of excesses that built up during his career, fuelled by his sometimes unquenchable enthusiasm for alcoholic and romantic pursuits. 'It was fairly common knowledge that he would go through the annual Scarborough Festival without seeing a bed, at least of his own,' said Richard Hutton, who, like his father, played for Yorkshire and England. As Edrich's friend David Brocklehurst told me, 'He was an extraordinary man, the most exhausting I ever met. He always wanted to carry on partying or go to strange clubs in London. He would never let you get to bed. And he loved women. He had great chat-up lines and he loved singing to them, the old ballads from the forties and fifties. They were taken aback by this but it worked.' It is a view reiterated by Peter Hayter, the son of Reg: 'I did love Bill as a bloke. He was great fun. He was very often round our house, having come back with Dad and Denis and various other reprobates. He got drunk quite quickly, then stayed drunk; he did not get any better or worse. It was a nice, confused fantasy state,' Hayter recalled, adding that he sometimes met Compton and Edrich in venues like the Cricketers Club in Blandford Street near Lord's. 'After a couple of drinks he loved everyone but he especially loved women. He just kept falling in love. He had a twinkle in his eye and laughed easily. I think women loved him because he made them feel like they were the only person in the room. That is what romantic, charming men do.'

Hedonism was always an essential ingredient of his personality, as it was with his father, William Archer Edrich, who was fond of a drink and the sight of a pretty woman. Even in times of severe hardship for his family, William could often be found in the local pub. 'It does seem incredible that money could be found for that but there, immersed in conviviality, he could forget his ill-fortune for a little while,' recalled Bill's sister Ena. Bill's grandfather Harry, it might be noted, fathered no fewer than 13 children with his wife Elizabeth, four of them after he had been paralyzed in both legs by polio. Inheriting these appetites, Bill was known for his lack of restraint from his very earliest days as a top-class cricketer. His passions have often been seen in a humorous light, reinforcing his image as an endearing mischief-maker.

But there was also a darker side to his proclivities. The remorseless focus on his own self-gratification could slide into indifference towards the needs of the people around him, especially his family. Married five times, he left a trail of social wreckage with his inability to sustain a relationship or resist temptation. Harmony never lasted long within his orbit. There was a restlessness about him that made commitment impossible. His daughter Jane Palley, whom he adopted at the start of his fourth marriage, said of him:

He was just immature and difficult, the way some people are. With Bill we did have peaks and troughs all the time. He would get a new job, selling insurance or something, and he would have a new set of clients who knew who he was. It would go extremely well to start with and then he would get bored and the clients would fade away. Then we would go into a trough. Then he would find something else and we would go back up to a peak. Bill was never satisfied with life. He always left the wife for a mistress. He never married a mistress because they were not good wife material. Yet when he found a wife, he got bored and wanted a mistress. He never, ever managed peace.

Pondering the roll-call of his shattered relationships, his sister Ena wrote that 'it seemed Bill would never grow up' because he was 'incapable of staying in the mundane. Everything needed to be new and exciting.'

At his worst, Edrich could be cruel, selfish and destructive. His third marriage, to a former actress, was often tempestuous, as their son Jasper recalled. 'It was a very odd childhood. When she and my father were together, they had terrible rows, drink induced. The rows really upset me. I often cried at the time. I think that's why I got chronic depression, which was diagnosed in 2000.' Edrich's impulse towards self-sabotage badly hurt his England career, as highlighted by his omission from five Test tours after the war largely because of the distrust he provoked. But his confrontation with authority was not confined to cricket. A regular participant in the divorce courts, he was also the subject of a number of criminal prosecutions, including one for being drunk and disorderly in the West End of London at the peak of his Test fame. It is typical of the turmoil he could create that even in the usually prosaic world of life-insurance policies, which he sold from the late 1960s, he should be inadvertently caught up on the fringes of one of the biggest financial scandals of the twentieth century.

Part of the explanation for his behaviour must lie in his insecurity as the son of a struggling Norfolk farmer, whose lands were sometimes barren and whose kitchen cupboards were often empty. Conquests at the batting crease, the bar and in the bedroom became central to Edrich's self-validation as a man, even if there was an air of desperation about his eagerness to grab opportunities that came his way. As his son Justin put it, 'he spent so much of his time battling with various demons and never reached the stage where he was truly contented. Dad got his pleasure from short-term highs rather than overall fulfilment or peace.' On his mission to achieve acclaim and status, Edrich adopted a front of bravura that concealed his inner awkwardness. His sister Ena once described him as 'pretentious' and it was true that he adopted many different guises, several of which were in direct conflict with each other. At various times in his life he was: the yeoman county professional and the gifted, social-climbing amateur; the colourful rebel and the aspiring England captain; the louche metropolitan night-clubber and East Anglian squire; the family man and playboy; the possessive husband and roving lothario; the defier of convention and staunch Conservative. This was the charmer who once received a black eye from the celebrated commentator John Arlott; the stickler for the moral traditions of the game as a batsman who loved to con umpires as a bowler; the cherished icon of Lord's who alarmed the MCC in his last years with his maverick campaign to rebuild sporting links with apartheid South Africa; and the international celebrity who worked as a paint salesman and once tried to make his fortune by promoting a mobile sewage plant.

But it is precisely these contradictions that make Bill Edrich so interesting. This is a version of his story.

1

CROSSING THE ROPE
1932–1934

'He is a stocky, sturdy little chap, fields beautifully anywhere, bowls pretty fast (for one of his age very fast) and is an excellent batsman.'

Michael Falcon

The harrowing scene that greeted Geoffrey Edrich, one of Bill's two younger brothers, was to be imprinted on his mind for the rest of his life. It was the autumn of 1932 and Geoff had just arrived home from school. Only weeks earlier, the family had moved into Merrison's cottage, a picturesque, thatched building in the village of Blofield, Norfolk. But for all its quaint aesthetics, the property was much smaller than their previous home of Upton Hall, a manor house with 500 acres of farmland. The contrast in size was a graphic indicator of the drastic change in the financial circumstances of the Edrich family. On the heels of a global Great Depression, Geoff's father William had been unable to make a viable financial return from either crops or livestock at Upton. Heavily in debt to his suppliers and the leaseholder, he was declared bankrupt, a humiliation for a well-known figure in the region.

Even worse was now to follow. Having walked through the cottage, Geoff reached its gunroom where he found his father in an agitated state and holding a loaded weapon in his hand. It was obvious that, in despair at the penury into which he had plunged his family, William Edrich intended to use the gun on himself. Oblivious to his own safety, Geoff leapt forward and after a brief tussle, managed to wrest it from his father's grasp.

The immediate danger had passed, but the anguish of William Edrich remained. In the mid-1920s he and his wife Edith had been able to provide a comfortable home for their four sons, Eric, Bill, Geoff and Brian, and daughter

Ena. The trappings of their affluence included domestic help and fresh produce from the lands they farmed. It was an abundance that magnified William's joviality, the health of his children and the camaraderie of his extended family, as the eldest son Eric recalled. 'We were really well fed. Dad got his beef on Sunday. I'm not exaggerating when I say it was 20 pounds or more. Uncle George, before he got married, used to come for lunch. There were lots of relations and friends.' But all that had disappeared at the beginning of the 1930s, as crops failed and liabilities grew. After they lost their livelihoods with their departure from Upton Hall, William and Eric tried to get work as farm labourers, but even that proved impossible because so many other Norfolk farmers were strapped for cash. Given the fraught atmosphere at Merrison's cottage, William and Edith's daughter Ena had been sent away to live with relatives, but overwhelmed by homesickness she had returned, though any happiness at being back with her family was dissipated by her father's despondency. 'We were in a desperate state,' she wrote later in her memoir *Girls Don't Play Cricket*. 'My handsome, genial father was never the same again. Life had presented him with a challenge that was almost more than he could handle.' She recalled how her father now maintained 'an aggressive manner that showed itself in constant bickering with my mother, terse replies to questions and unusual hours'. The sounds of 'laughter and song' that had characterised life at Upton Hall had now gone; so had the family's animals and staff. Discord prevailed in the cottage. Even Brian, the youngest of the siblings, turned nasty, throwing rotten potatoes at Ena one day with such vigour that he gave her a pair of blackened eyes. 'He had never hurt me like this before. Our miseries showed in different ways. I would constantly complain of headaches, tummyaches, anything so that I could remain safely in bed with a book in my own little fantasy world,' Ena recorded. Jane Edrich, the widow of Brian, told me that her late husband remembered that period with anguish: 'It was incredibly tough for the family when the old man went bankrupt. They had nowhere to live but luckily someone came up with a farm cottage. They sometimes had no food and people used to leave them a sack of potatoes outside their front door. Or if there had been a pheasant shoot, they would be given some pheasants. It was very difficult for them.'

Amid all this gloom, one shining light was the phenomenal cricketing success of Bill Edrich, William and Edith's second son. By the summer of 1932, he was already a precocious junior star within Norfolk, not just as a batsman but also as a fast bowler. At the age of just 16 and still a pupil at Bracondale, a private school in Norwich, he was picked to play in early June for the county against the visiting All-India team, which had just been awarded Test status. Given the stature of the opposition, the match was a major event in the region and a crowd of over 3,000 filled Norfolk's ground at Lakenham at its start, among them a large contingent of boys from Bracondale who had been given a special break to watch the opening day. Initially the Norfolk team seemed to be galvanised by the enthusiasm of the local public and, on a lively pitch, their bowlers dismissed India for just 101. Building up an impressive pace, Edrich was among the wicket-takers, taking 1 for 11 from eight accurate overs. But the visitors' low total was soon put into perspective when Norfolk had to face their attack, led by the formidable Mohammad Nissar, one of the fastest bowlers ever produced by India. A few weeks later, as India played at Lord's in their first Test, Nissar caused a sensation when, in only his second over, he demolished the stumps of Herbert Sutcliffe, one of the all-time great openers, part of his five-wicket haul in England's first innings. At Lakenham, he was even more deadly, as the speed and bounce generated by his high, flowing action ripped through the Norfolk team. When Bill Edrich came in at Number 7, Norfolk had already lost five wickets for just 20 runs. It was a baptism of fire for the Bracondale schoolboy, as Edrich later recalled of the first ball he faced. 'I remember hanging on like grim death to my bat as Nissar approached with his long, bounding run, and the ball came from his hand and struck like lightning from the pitch.' Edrich played and missed, but with the kind of determination that would characterise his batting, he refused to wilt under pressure.

When he was eventually out for 20, Edrich was easily the top-scorer in Norfolk's dismal total of 49, Nissar taking six for 14. The Indians went on to a comfortable victory, but Edrich had given an early indication of his class and temperament, as the *Eastern Daily Press* commented in its match report: 'It was a severe examination for a boy of 16. His nerve was unshaken by the rapid fall of wickets and if anyone expected him to display timidity facing bowlers flushed with success they were probably amazed and delighted at the splendid note of aggression in his batting.' Edrich went on to play another six games for Norfolk that season. His highlights included an innings of 40 against Lincolnshire at Lakenham and a 50 against Buckinghamshire at High Wycombe, where he also took 3 for 35 in the home side's only innings. In its 1932 annual, *The Cricketer* magazine noted, 'W.J. Edrich's debut, awaited with some interest, was made in the match against All-India and the good impression he created was confirmed in his later appearances.' That favourable verdict was important, for the magazine was edited by Pelham Plum Warner, the ultimate establishment grandee and former captain of Middlesex.

Almost six years later, when he was on the verge of making the England side, Edrich told a reporter from the *News Chronicle,* 'If you want to know when I started, you might put it about 18 years ago, when I was three or four. My father was mad keen on cricket and he made all of us hold a bat as soon as we could get our hands round it.' Edrich's father William had inherited this devotion to the game from his own father Harry, a shrewd, ambitious businessman and sporting philanthropist whose charisma was undented by the disability of polio. Although there had been Edriches farming in Norfolk as far back as the eleventh century, the fruitful, domineering Harry could be regarded as the patriarch of the cricketing clan that became so well-known to the English public in the middle decades of the twentieth century through the exploits of his grandchildren Bill and his three brothers, and their cousin John, the greatest of them all. Harry had fallen in love with the game at Bracondale and before he was struck down with polio in 1903 at the age of 45, he had been a useful local cricketer. Incapacity did not lessen his enthusiasm, and he became an important patron of the Norfolk cricket scene, epitomised by his foundation of a club at Lingwood where he lived from 1900. Nor did Harry's paralysis end his habit of driving himself around Norfolk in his pony and trap to collect rent from his many properties or to deal in livestock. His only concession to his physical condition was to carry a bottle as a makeshift urinal so he would not have to haul himself to and from his vehicle, especially when he had drunk a few beers in Norwich on market day. On several occasions when he was slightly inebriated, he fell asleep and let go of the reins, but his reliable pony knew the route so well that he always brought Harry safely home.

Born in 1890, his son William Archer Edrich, also known as Bill, took the family interest in cricket to new heights. He too had attended Bracondale, which had given him a thorough understanding of the game's technical basics, though the onset of his father's disability meant William had been forced to leave the school at 14 to work on the family farm. He still had time for cricket, however, and he was good enough to play for Norfolk Club and Ground, just one tier below Minor Counties level. Like his father Harry, William was also an active promoter of new clubs wherever he set up home, and in addition he created concrete pitches on his land so that his sons could learn to bat and bowl on true, even surfaces. At one property he even established an indoor net in a barn so that their practice would not be interrupted by rain. Throughout all this nurturing, William emphasised the need as a batsman for a correct stance, strong footwork, a straight bat and a sound defence. He also inculcated his sons in the ethics of the game, particularly the requirement to walk if caught behind, without waiting for the umpire's decision. It was a principle that Bill junior upheld with vigour throughout his own playing career. 'He had a strong sense of justice and fairness. With him, if you edged it, you were out,' recalled his son Jasper.

In 1907 William Edrich met Edith Mattocks, whose own farming family had moved from Cumberland to Norfolk at the turn of the century, drawn by the more productive soil near the Fens. Both were good-looking, lively and sociable, and their shared agricultural background deepened the mutual attraction between them. Courtship led to marriage in June 1913, followed by the arrival of their five children between 1914 and 1924. Just months after Eric was born in March 1914, the First World War began, heralding carnage on a scale never before seen by mankind. Yet William had a remarkable stroke of good fortune that enabled him to avoid this cataclysm. Called up for a medical examination in advance of his enlistment in the army, he was told to his surprise that he had failed the test. William could not understand it, since thanks to his work on the farm, he enjoyed good health and an excellent diet. Having made further enquiries, he was informed that there was nothing actually wrong with him but that, in view of his father's disability, he could not be spared from the farm, since the maintenance of food supplies on the home front was becoming ever more vital against the backdrop of predatory U-boat attacks on Allied shipping in the Atlantic. While the slaughter continued on the Western Front, William was therefore able to remain with his family, build up his business and indulge in his passion for cricket.

Right in the middle of the war, on 26 March, 1916, Bill Edrich junior was born. But not for him the absent father and anxious mother that so many other children experienced in wartime, or the constraints and sense of loss that came after the Armistice. On the contrary, Edrich's upbringing appeared – at least on the surface – to be idyllic. In the first decade and a half of Bill's life, the family leased a series of imposing properties, first at Lingwood on the Burroughs estate, then at Cantley Manor and finally Upton Hall. The architecture was impressive, the food bountiful. Bill's parents both loved to entertain, and a retinue of maids, gardeners and servants enabled them to act as generous hosts. '"Come in! Come in!" my mother would cry, her hands extended, her auburn hair surrounding a face alive with warmth and vitality,' wrote Ena in her memoir. She also recalled, in another sign of her mother's elevated social connections, that at Cantley 'there was a table in the hall holding a silver tray set on its polished top for cards of visiting ladies'. The family even had a car, a rare luxury item in the 1920s.

Indeed, the impression sometimes given by accounts like Ena's is that this branch of the Edriches were almost part of the landed gentry. But others feel that this is a distorted picture of their status. The commentator Henry Blofeld, whose family also came from Norfolk, said that though Bill's father was 'a dear old boy', the Edriches were 'always regarded by my father as being slightly roguish, yeoman farmers out for a better bargain'. It was a point with which Rodney Edrich, another member of the clan and the great-grandson of the patriarchal, fecund Harry, agreed:

Henry Blofeld is right. The family was slightly roguish. Bill's father was a rogue and could not farm for toffee. If you read between the lines of Ena's account, you can see that Bill's father was a pretty hopeless farmer. He was the most delightful man and his wife Edith was one of the most lovely people you could ever wish to meet; she was just adorable. We used to call him Old Uncle Bill. He wasn't a womaniser and wasn't a drunkard, though he liked a pint. But he had very limited farming ability, I think, and went through farms like hot dinners. The interesting thing is that my great-grandfather Harry never encouraged him to buy a farm nor did he ever buy him a farm. Ena got the manorial touch and tried to put a very good gloss on this. In another age, his family might have been called a bunch of gypsies, though that would have been unfair.

Derogatory past references to the Edriches' background can sound incendiary. But it is a fact that whispered insults circulated about the family and at school, where Bill Edrich was sometimes called 'a right little tinker'. Such language can only have exacerbated his insecurity, making him even more determined to climb the social ladder. There is an interesting parallel here with two of the most distinguished names in British sport. One is that of the World Cup-winning football manager Sir Alf Ramsey, who was often mocked in his youth for his supposedly Romani heritage as the son of a Dagenham labourer. Known as 'Darkie Ramsey' among his East London contemporaries, he completely changed his voice and manner so that after the war he came across as the quintessential, suburban English gentleman. The other was Wally Hammond, who, like Ramsey, had swarthy features and was said by some hostile colleagues to be of mixed race or a Romani. He too changed his social position. The son of a professional soldier, Hammond married into wealth, mixed in sophisticated West Country circles, took a job with a motoring company and became an amateur cricketer. Interestingly, though Hammond was far more saturnine than Edrich, there was an affinity between the two, based on their social ambitions and their fondness for drink and women. As Edrich's first Test captain, Hammond's faith in him was astonishingly steadfast in the face of ferocious media criticism about favouritism. In the end his belief was rewarded.

Apart from personal sentiment, the reason why Hammond backed Edrich so strongly was because he recognised the young player's all-round skills. That talent had been on display in Bill's early childhood, encouraged by his father and strengthened by watching adults in action at local village matches and on the occasional visit to the county ground at Lakenham. Although cricket was their overwhelming interest, the four boys indulged in other energetic activities, with Bill at the forefront of most of them, such as using airguns at night to keep down the local rat population or picking fruit in their orchards. Full of adventure and curiosity, Bill was also, predictably, an energetic tree-climber, and, just as in his batsmanship, he appeared oblivious to risk or pain. But there was one incident that at first seemed alarming, as Jean Beecroft, the daughter of Eric, related: 'Dad told me that Uncle Bill fell out of a tree one day and knocked himself unconscious. In fright, Daddy ran into the house and said to his mother, "Oh Ma, Bill's fallen out of a tree and is dead." He really thought Bill had been killed. Neither of them could have been very old at the time.' But, Lazarus-like, Bill was soon running around again. 'My word, he was quite a lad,' Eric once said. The same sentiments were soon being expressed about Bill's cricket performances for local colts' sides and for Bracondale, where he became a boarder at the age of ten. The school, which had a roll of 170 pupils at this time, had been founded in 1821 for the education of 'young Norfolk gentlemen'. When Edrich enrolled, it occupied a large Victorian house that also served as the home of the headmaster Francis Bean Williams and his family. One of Bill's contemporaries, Alan Le Fèvre, recalled that 'F.B. Williams was a very impressive headmaster but he was unfortunate in that he had lupus on one side of his face which made him look rather terrifying. The poor man must have had to put up with this all his life. He was a good teacher, rather strict.' The standards of the school that Williams had run since 1912 were satisfactory but not outstanding. A report of an inspection conducted in February 1935 by the Board of Education praised the quality of much of its teaching, especially history, geography and mathematics, while the behaviour of the boys 'both in and out of the classroom made a very favourable impression'. But the Board's inspectors also found plenty to criticise at Bracondale. Sanitary facilities were said to be 'inadequate'. Written and spoken English among the pupils 'still leaves something to be desired'. There was a tendency for science lessons to be 'taken too fast at the expense of a thorough grip of the subject matter'.

Crucially, in the context of Bill's future, the inspectors recorded that 'games appear to be competently organised and satisfactorily provided for', as evidenced by the 'practice cricket pitch on the school premises'. With its emphasis on sport, Bracondale was the ideal environment for the Edrich brothers, who excelled not just at cricket but also football, tennis and athletics. 'Inter-house matches were almost private contests between the Edrich brothers,' said Le Fèvre, while another former pupil, Russell Underwood, felt 'privileged to be at the school when the Edrich brothers were there; they were all very efficient sportsmen of medium build'. Underwood admitted, however, that after his comfortable home life, he found the spartan atmosphere of Bracondale 'a bit of a shock, all lino and margarine.'

As always in Bill's life, cricket had priority. At the school, he was fortunate in having two wise, experienced figures to guide him into a deeper grasp of the game. One was the youthful sports master, Frederick Scott, who, like Bill's own father, had insisted on the installation of a concrete pitch to foster confident stroke play. The other was the 'leathery and lion-hearted' – to use Bill's vivid phrase – professional, Jack Nichols, who had appeared for Worcestershire before the First World War and was a mainstay of the Norfolk side throughout the 1920s. In addition to his role at Norfolk, for whom he was an outstanding all-rounder and occasional wicket-keeper, Nichols was employed as Bracondale's coach. 'He had a wonderful gift for imparting his knowledge to boys,' said Edrich in a 1938 interview. Through his well-judged advice, Nichols tightened Bill's batting technique and heightened the pace of his bowling, but perhaps his most lasting legacy was to hone Bill's powerful leg-side stroke play, thanks to a quirk of geography at the school. To the batsman's left on the concrete practice pitch lay a set of gooseberry bushes, treasured by the boys for the succulence of their fruit. By tradition, any pupil who hit the ball directly into these bushes had to collect it. But at the height of the summer, when the berries were at their juiciest, this was no punishment but rather an incentive to perfect the hook and pull. With his canny understanding of the juvenile mindset, Nichols encouraged such pomological aggression among his charges, though he never made it too easy for them. 'It took the absolute best of one's batting to hit him into the gooseberries; no wild swipe or cow-shot would do anything other than produce a death rattle behind the right shoulder,' recalled Edrich. Throughout his career, he attributed the strength of his leg-side technique to the bushes in F.B. Williams's garden. Moreover, his use of the term 'gooseberry' for any ball that he dispatched cleanly to the leg boundary was taken up by Denis Compton, who deployed it even in the Test arena. In his autobiography, Edrich described how, in a tense Ashes encounter, he watched from the non-striker's end as Compton cracked a delivery from Ray Lindwall through square leg: 'The ball goes bounding along the turf and as Denis Compton and I cross in our run, I hear him say, "That was a gooseberry!"'

It was Edrich's bowling rather than his batting that initially made the biggest impression at Bracondale. In June 1930, when he was only 14, he achieved his first favourable notice in the press after he took 10 for 18 in just 49 balls, four of them in consecutive deliveries, in a match against Norwich High School. 'Medium-fast, right-hand, fast off the pitch,' noted the *Eastern Daily Press*. For Bryan Stevens, a Bracondale schoolboy who played in that game and later became the cricket correspondent for the *Eastern Daily Press*, the most striking memory of this performance was the sight of his 'furious sprint to the bowling crease, the ball catapulting from the hand and Edrich himself following through at full pelt'. Later in the summer, he took 8 for 20 against Diss Secondary School, though he also showed his batting prowess in this fixture by hitting his first century for Bracondale. The following season, 1931, he majestically topped both the bowling and batting averages, with the result that he was selected for a Norfolk senior side. A mature innings of 59 in this appearance brought another burst of praise from the *Eastern Daily Press*: 'Edrich belongs to the class of all-round cricketers whom it is impossible to efface. He has a great variety of strokes, his wristwork and footwork are good, and his style is quite correct. He also hits the ball very hard.' In addition, Edrich was proving himself to be a fine footballer, with excellent ball control and an instinct for goals from his position on the left wing. In 19 games for Bracondale, he scored no fewer than 100 goals.

His stature as Norfolk's pre-eminent youthful sportsman was cemented by Edrich's appearance against All-India. 'That boy will play for England,' Nichols told his parents. But by then, a shadow had been cast over his immediate future by the collapse of his family's farming business, which at the time, in the absence of a comprehensive welfare system, threatened them with the workhouse and destitution. 'The family was very hospitable and pleasant but they didn't have a penny to bless themselves with,' Rodney Edrich told me of this straitened period. For Bill, the end of his happy spell at Bracondale looked inevitable, along with hopes of progressing into a higher class of cricket. But then, in the depth of this crisis, he and his family had a couple of strokes of luck. The first came when

Bracondale decided to waive its fees for the remainder of his time there in recognition of his extraordinary achievements for the school. The second arose when his father William was appointed the manager of some Crown land in Pocklington, Yorkshire. This was a long way from Norfolk, but financial pressures meant that the family had no choice but to move. In fact, once they had settled in, they were delighted with their new home, called Woodhouse Grange, which was much bigger than Merrison's cottage. Ena wrote in her memoir that the 200-year-old 'ivy-covered rambling' house was 'beautiful' and 'reminiscent of Jane Austen novels', with lawns that ran down to 'tall beech trees and a copse of low, flowering bushes'. But this tranquil spot was not all it seemed. There was a reason why the Crown had struggled to fill the vacancy at Woodhouse Grange. 'My father had taken over a very run-down farm,' wrote Ena, 'and the previous farmer had obviously been caught up in the depression.' Despite his attempts to clean up the land and introduce new crops, William was in financial trouble again by late 1933. What deepened the family's anxiety was the revelation from a neighbour, soon after the Edriches had moved into Woodhouse Grange, that the previous tenant farmer had committed suicide by hanging himself from one of the bannisters on the central staircase.

Still at Bracondale, Bill Edrich missed much of this new bout of drama. That summer, in further recognition of his burgeoning ability, he was a regular at Number 3 in the Norfolk XI, which competed in the Minor Counties Championship. The side was led by Michael Falcon, a superb fast bowler and a useful batsman who would almost certainly have played for England if his first-class appearances had not been restricted by his devotion to the cause of Norfolk and his commitments in business, the law and public life. During the immediate post-war period he had been the Conservative MP for East Norfolk, but he was too mild-mannered for the ruthless world of politics, losing his seat in 1923. On the cricket pitch, however, the combination of his natural authority and all-round talent made him a highly respected leader of the Norfolk XI. 'He was, of all the cricketers I have known, one of the most unselfish, courageous and inspiring,' wrote Edrich in 1947. With Falcon at the helm and Edrich on board, in 1933 Norfolk had one of its best seasons since the war as the team came near to winning the Minor Counties Championship, only to be beaten at the finish by

Lancashire Second XI. In praising Norfolk's improvement, *The Cricketer Annual* for November 1933 highlighted the performances of Edrich. With three fifties in the Championship, and a stubborn defensive innings against the pacemen of the West Indian visitors at Lakenham, the magazine wrote that he had 'fulfilled the promise of the previous year'.

His success encouraged Edrich in his ambition to become a full-time cricketer. The alternative career he contemplated was teaching, which he knew his parents would favour because of its much greater long-term financial security, a major consideration in view of their own precarious circumstances. Furthermore he was a bright pupil, who had done well in his examinations in July 1933 and could have won a university place, something that was much more rare in Britain at that time than from the 1960s onwards. In the mid-1930s, just 2.4 per cent of young men went into higher education. But his love of cricket continued to pull Edrich in the opposite direction. Anticipating his parents' negative reaction, he did not mention his enthusiasm for the idea of taking up the game professionally. He thought he might get a more positive response from his brothers, yet when he confided in them they were dismissive. 'The proposal seemed to them such a joke that I was inclined to abandon it altogether,' he wrote. But not quite. Even as he tried to concentrate on his academic studies that autumn, the siren call of the game would not be silenced. At the end of 1933, he decided to act on his own initiative, writing to Northamptonshire to ask for a trial. The choice of club was largely dictated by its position as the nearest first-class cricket county to Norfolk as well as the weakness of its playing staff, which Edrich felt might give him a better chance of progress. His next step was to tell his parents what he had done. With a deep sense of unease, he took the train to Yorkshire at the end of that term and told his father that he had requested a trial. The reception of his father was as hostile as he feared. 'He held the view that the job of a cricket professional was not a suitable one for a fairly well-educated boy who intended to make a future for himself. He pointed out to me, with truth and without exaggeration, the drawbacks of a pro's life. Finishing up at 35 or 40, just when another man is gaining recognition and big rewards,' wrote Edrich.

Throughout his life Edrich was a stubborn individual, never easily persuaded to follow an unwanted course advocated by others. That was true in the winter of 1933–34. His father's disapproval only galvanised him to step up his efforts to go into cricket. 'He was a brainy boy but he was so wrapped up in the game I doubt that he ever intended to go into teaching,' said his elder brother Eric. In fact, before the start of the new term in January 1934, Bill decided to leave Bracondale, undeterred by a non-committal answer from Northants which suggested that, if he were still interested, he should contact the club again in the spring. On a visit to Norwich to collect his belongings before making the journey back to Yorkshire, he consulted Falcon, his county captain. At first during their discussion, Falcon was reluctant to back Edrich's dream because of the uncertainties that went with professional sport. 'I can get you into the Norwich Union,' he said in reference to his role as a non-executive director of the celebrated insurance giant (which was demutualised and became Aviva in 2002). Ironically, Bill Edrich was later to work for another insurance leviathan, thereby bringing friction into the heart of the Norfolk dressing room, but at the age of 17 he was interested in cricket, not personal finance. Falcon was impressed by the boy's determination but felt that he should aspire to a stronger club. According to the aristocratic cricket historian and author Sir Home Gordon, whose accuracy was not always dependable, Falcon thought of Kent and even made an approach to the club at Canterbury. 'It is not generally known that Kent might have obtained the services of Edrich, suggested to them by Michael Falcon,' wrote Gordon in his column in *The Cricketer* on 19 June, 1937, though there is no evidence to back up this claim. Even if this were the case, Falcon soon decided that Middlesex, in the heart of London, was the best option. In one account, Edrich wrote that Falcon told him, 'Go to Lord's, that's the place to be. The eyes of those who matter will be upon you and you will enjoy it immensely.' Another advantage of Middlesex was that Edrich would come under the influence of the veteran batsman Patsy Hendren, a legend of the game now in the glowing twilight of his career. One difficulty, however, would be that even if Edrich were taken on by Middlesex, he would not be able to play for them immediately. Instead, under rules designed to strengthen the geographical integrity of clubs in the Championship, he would have to spend two years living in the county to gain the required residential qualification.

Such concerns were lost in Edrich's excitement at the latest hope of becoming a professional. Soon after Bill had returned to Woodhouse Grange to work on the family farm, Falcon wrote to Billy Findlay, the Secretary of the MCC, which at the time effectively ran all aspects of Middlesex, including the recruitment of professionals and the administration of their contracts. It was not until 1952 that Middlesex even had their own office at Lord's. Now in the MCC archives, Falcon's letter to Findlay, dated 2 February, 1934 and sent from his ancestral home of Burlingham House in Norwich, gives an insight into the high regard that the young Norfolk all-rounder inspired:

There is a lad here called Edrich (pronounced Edrige) who has been playing cricket for Norfolk for two years and now wants to take up the game professionally. He is a superior sort of boy and his people having been farming folk in a biggish way for many generations but they have been beaten by this agricultural depression which has hit Norfolk so hard. He has just left school and will be 18 this year and should make a really first-class player, having been well coached all the time he has been at school. He is a stocky, sturdy little chap, fields beautifully anywhere, bowls pretty fast (for one of his age very fast) and is an excellent batsman. I want if I can to help him get a good start and above all be with decent people. Is there any chance of his being taken on at Lord's with a view to qualifying for Middlesex? If so I would suggest he should come to Lord's to be interviewed one day. His father having had to leave his farm near here is now in Yorkshire and the boy is up there, but I am sure he could easily get to London if you required him. My own impressions are that Edrich will develop into a sort of Hendren and as such would be extremely useful either to MCC or Middlesex or both.

A month later, with no sign of action from the MCC, Falcon tried to crank up the pressure on Findlay by exaggerating Northants' interest: 'I have been asked to help this Edrich. Northamptonshire have been after him and I thought it would be far from good for a lad of this sort to go about with those fellows and that if he really intended to take the game up professionally he could do so much better for himself and be better looked after if he was attached to a more important centre than that of Northampton. Take him under your wing if you can; looked after, he will do well.'

Falcon's insistence worked. Edrich was summoned for a trial at Lord's in April 1934. But the appointment was almost to end in a personal disaster.

2

ALL-ROUNDER
1934–1937

'The thought of having Lord's as my own home pitch nearly sent me crazy; I could not sleep because of it.'

Bill Edrich

Bill Edrich always had an air of perpetual motion about him. Passivity was never part of his style. 'He was an action man and felt life was for living,' said Robin Marlar, the late Sussex captain. The post-war Australian all-rounder Colin McCool wrote, 'I have never seen any Englishman play cricket so 100 per cent as he did. When he was batting, you thought you'd need to dynamite him out. He bowled as if he was trying to blast a hole in the sightscreen.'

But this unceasing flow of energy could land him in trouble. In the spring of 1934, while he waited to hear the response from Lord's to Michael Falcon's entreaties, he refused to be idle. Instead, he dived into work on the family farm at Yorkshire, the task made all the more urgent by the shadow of mounting debts. Then to his excited relief, he was summoned for a trial at Lord's in mid-April. 'The thought of having Lord's as my own home pitch nearly sent me crazy; I could not sleep because of it,' he wrote. As he prepared for the big event, practice sessions with his brothers in the net at Woodhouse Grange acquired a new intensity. For hour after hour, he kept going over the technical advice of his former coach Jack Nichols, especially the emphasis on 'keeping the head still and getting weight into the stroke'. Edrich continued to perform his filial duties on the farm, but as his anticipation mounted about the upcoming trip to London, he understandably became distracted. This was almost to prove his undoing.

Shortly before the Lord's trial, he was out in one of the fields in the first weeks of April, trying to unyoke a large Suffolk shire horse from a cart. Unable to give his full attention to the job because his mind was on cricket, he clumsily got his right hand caught in the chain, splitting his palm from the bottom of his first finger to the root of his thumb. Bill never showed pain or self-pity, but on this occasion, having rushed to the house to seek emergency treatment, he could not conceal the extent of the wound. His mother Edith disinfected and bandaged the hand, but she was unable to perform any stitching, with the result that the wound opened up again when pressure was applied to it. Looking at the scarlet dressing, the family became apprehensive about the trial. 'I think you ought to cancel the appointment and go another time,' said Eric. But Bill, characteristically, was having none of it. 'I'm not going to let this chance slip. I shan't tell them what has happened,' he declared.

Two days later he was on the train from York to London. It was his first visit to the capital, and Edrich was about to enter a very different environment to the one he had known in his rural Norfolk upbringing. This was a time when London was still the centre of global finance and the heart of the largest empire that mankind had ever seen. On this crisp April morning, looking out of the window of his cab on the way from King's Cross to Lord's, he felt a rush of excitement that never left him. 'The smoke shot with sunshine, the size of the buildings and the hurrying crowds stirred something in me that still responds every time I journey through London's busier streets,' he wrote much later, in 1948.

Excitement was combined with nerves on his arrival at the ground, where he met the chief MCC coach George Fenner, who had played a few games for Kent in the 1920s before his appointment as a professional at Lord's. Once Edrich had changed into his whites, Fenner took him along to the nets, where Ronny Aird, the former Hampshire player and MCC Assistant Secretary, was waiting. Under Aird's watchful eye, Edrich took his guard to face Fenner's bowling, uncertain how his injured hand would react. After a few balls, his anxiety evaporated. 'My hand was stiff and awkward, but as soon as I felt the ball on the thick part of the bat, I knew I was all right,' recalled Edrich. His confidence grew when he was told to bowl at Aird. Immediately he found his rhythm and sent down a succession of quick, accurate deliveries, several of which beat Aird's outside edge. 'I think you'll do, my lad. Go along with Mr Fenner now,' said Aird.

Edrich had performed as well as he could, but what really impressed the coach was their exchange after he took the young triallist into the pavilion. So far, Edrich had managed to hide the wound to his hand, even though blood had soaked into the inside of his right batting glove during his net. Once he was in Fenner's office in the pavilion, however, his need to stem the bleeding with a handkerchief drew attention to his battered hand. Questioned by the coach, Edrich told him the full story of how his fingers had been trapped in the horse's chain on the family farm. His session in the net had probably already done enough to win him a contract, but this was the moment when Edrich clinched the deal, for Fenner now recognised that, in addition to his talent and technique, he was a young man of courageous determination.

The trip to Lord's could not have gone better. Bill's refusal to bow to caution had been rewarded. Soon after he had returned to Yorkshire, he received an offer to join the MCC groundstaff. The pay started at just £3 a week, augmented by his commission on the sale of scorecards during Test and county matches. The work of the apprentices was also physically demanding. Among their chores were: clearing pigeon dirt from Lord's seats, weeding the pathways, pulling the heavy roller over the turf and painting the woodwork at the ground. Despite his family's dire circumstances, Edrich cared little about his modest initial earnings or the tough manual labour now that he had the chance to fulfil his dream of employment as a professional cricketer. Another factor that countered any potential regret about the nature or pay of his job was the camaraderie with other members of the groundstaff, who included Jack Robertson, Syd Brown, Harry Sharp, Jack Young, all of them to become Middlesex stalwarts, and, above all, Denis Compton, with whom Edrich established an immediate rapport that was to last the rest of their lives. 'In the 50 odd years we knew each other we never once had a cross word. We exasperated each other a lot of times, but never to the point that we fell out,' recalled Compton.

The 1934 season was a pivotal one in English cricket, for it marked the first visit by the Australians since the explosive controversy of the 1932–33 Bodyline tour, which had almost severed cricketing ties and diplomatic relations between the two countries. At the heart of the row, which caused perhaps the biggest crisis in Test history, was Australia's fury at England's resort to persistent, short-pitched intimidatory bowling on the line of the batsman's body to a packed leg-side field. So deep was the anger at this method that Australia's Board of Control even sent a telegram to Lord's, accusing the visitors of 'unsportsmanlike' behaviour. But the wheels of reconciliation, already well oiled by the British National Government and the oleaginous Plum Warner, were given further momentum by the retirement of Douglas Jardine, the austere, Ashes-winning captain, and by the unavailability of Harold Larwood, his premier fast bowler, whose refusal to apologise for his tactics effectively ended his Test career. In place of Jardine, England were led by the upright, defensive Bob Wyatt of Warwickshire, who was later, as Chairman of the Selectors, to be Bill Edrich's nemesis. As the home Test skipper in the series defeat, Wyatt had no answer to the pulverising dominance of Don Bradman except at Lord's, where the Yorkshire left-arm spinner Hedley Verity took 15 wickets on a rain-affected pitch. Altogether the Australians played at Lord's four times that summer: against England, the MCC, Middlesex and the Gentlemen of England, the amateurs' representative side whose very existence was a pointer to the profound social divisions within the game. Having just embarked on his professional career, Edrich was not considered for any of these fixtures, though, as a groundstaffer, he had the opportunity to see the top players in action. Verity's performance left him both mesmerised and overwhelmed. 'His fingers curled around the seam, his arm came over high and easy and the ball, slung along just too fast for the batsmen to go and meet it, exploded from the turf,' he wrote, adding that though he was rarely given to negative introspection, the standards of accuracy and turn that Verity achieved left him to ask how a Norfolk farmer's boy could have any hopes of 'ever doing anything better than pulling the big roller and selling programmes'.

Indeed, for all his delight at his appointment, Edrich resented some of the more demeaning aspects of the hierarchical culture at Lord's. A proud, spirited young man, he loathed the streak of snobbish disdain that ran through parts of the MCC membership, as he wrote much later in 1978: 'The junior pro was recognised as the lowest of the low, almost a feudal serf, good for kicking if business was bad. It was often, "Edrich, go there" . . . "Edrich, get changed" . . . "Edrich, go home" . . . "Come here, you so-and-so . . ." Life could be miserable for the sensitive youngster.' Occasionally, Bill exacted a form of revenge when he was on duty bowling to members in the nets. Anyone who had slighted him earlier was likely to feel the force of his whippy action. 'A couple of short, sharp bumpers were normally sufficient to win some peace for a week,' said Edrich, though such hostility was unlikely to result in the usual tip given to the young pro after a net session. Yet, as he implied, the emotional scars of this treatment may have lasted into his later years. 'There was a shyness about him and that stemmed from his going to Lord's from his Norfolk background. He may have felt inadequate, and I think that feeling never really left him. It was one reason why he wanted to climb the social ladder,' his son Justin told me.

But cricket more than compensated for such awkwardness. As with Compton, who had joined Lord's a year earlier, Edrich's ability was obvious. An early progress report in May 1934 stated that, 'Edrich is a good, natural player, and a good bat, though he has a bad habit of running about with his back foot when playing forward. He is quite fast as a bowler but at present is rather uncertain with his length.' A more fulsome report followed a few weeks later in which he was described as 'a very promising player, being a good bat, a useful bowler and an excellent field'. Although he could not play for Middlesex until he had completed his two-year residential qualification, he was still available for both the MCC and Norfolk. For the latter, his new status as a professional brought a significant improvement in his standards, as *The Cricketer* commented: 'Edrich was most consistent and as he headed the bowling averages he was the most successful all-rounder of the side. In addition his fielding was a joy to watch. Bowling a little faster than last year, Edrich obtained twice as many wickets at a much cheaper rate.'

His summer was studded with highlights. In a remarkable performance during Norfolk's big victory over Lincolnshire at Lakenham, he scored 138, his first century in the Minor Counties Championship, and then took 6 for 23 in the visitors' second innings. In mid-August against Kent Second XI at the same ground, he scored 57 and then twice ripped through the batting order with 5 for 63 and an astonishing 5 for 9. Earlier that season, his glowing reputation in Norfolk had led to his first-class debut when he was picked for a combined Minor Counties XI to play Oxford University in the Parks, where he scored 55 and put on 155 with Bill Farrimond, the Lancashire wicket-keeper who played occasionally for England. Edrich also scored a 50 in his only first-class appearance for the MCC, when he made 63 in a big win over Cambridge University at Lord's.

At the end of that 1934 season, two important developments occurred in Edrich's life. The first came when his family's unhappy spell in Yorkshire came to an end after the Crown managed to sell Woodhouse Grange to a wealthy farmer. But the Edriches were not abandoned. Instead, another farm was found for them by the Crown to work as tenants, back in Norfolk at Heacham Manor near Hunstanton on the coast. This was an Elizabethan mansion with tall chimneys and a gravelled frontage that opened out on to a lawn that was easily big enough not just for a pitch, but a complete cricket field. 'Spirits were lifting. We were back on home ground. My father was bringing in a weekly wage of three pounds ten shillings and my brothers were contributing,' wrote Ena in her memoir. All the upheaval of recent years was finally over. William and Edith seemed to have found security. With their habitual gregariousness, they not only made Heacham Manor into the vibrant centre of the neighbourhood's social life, but also re-energised the local village cricket club.

The second development arose from Bill's need to increase his meagre earnings at Lord's, which covered just the summer months. Although he was provided lodgings by Lord's, he admitted that he had already acquired tastes as a 'sophisticated young townsman'. He therefore decided to seek work as a footballer, having already proved himself as a skilful outside left both at Bracondale and Norwich City reserves. The dual role of professional cricketer and footballer has long disappeared from first-class English sport, wiped out by the demands of league clubs whose seasons are longer and whose managers are more fearful about the risks of injuries to their expensively assembled staff. But in the 1930s there was nothing unusual about combining these occupations. Some of the biggest names in English cricket had followed this path, including Wally Hammond, who played for Bristol Rovers, and Les Ames, who appeared for Clapton Orient and Gillingham. The tradition of playing both sports was particularly strong at Lord's. Among the Middlesex players who had also been on the books of football league clubs were Jack Durston, Patsy Hendren, Walter Robins, Joe Hulme and Denis Compton, the Arsenal star who, like Bill, played mainly outside left. Just as in cricket, however, Compton was the more naturally talented footballer of the two. Bill Shankly, the legendary Liverpool manager who played in some wartime matches alongside Compton, was so impressed that he told him, 'throw away the cricket bat, Denis, and concentrate on football'.

Inspired by Compton's example, Edrich was also making an impression on the football pitch in the autumn of 1934. With a strong sense of self-belief, he wrote to a number of London clubs offering his services. As with his cricketing approach to Northamptonshire a year earlier, the response was courteous but non-committal. But then, by another of those strokes of luck that littered Edrich's career, Tottenham Hotspur's chief scout happened to be staying at a hotel in Heacham, Norfolk, where he ran into Bill's father. 'My lad wants something to do in the winter,' said William, which led Spurs, then in the second division, to offer Bill a trial. Edrich felt he had performed badly. 'I was nervous and somehow my passes and kicks were not as scientific as I would have liked,' he recalled. Yet he cannot have been that poor, for Spurs offered him a place in their reserves the following weekend against Brighton and Hove Albion. Everything clicked for him in this game. He scored a hat-trick, ran past defenders and hit his passes with pinpoint accuracy. The performance did not result, as he had secretly hoped, in a place on the playing staff at White Hart Lane, but he was rewarded with a contract at Northfleet United F.C., the Tottenham nursery club in the Kent League based at Stonebridge Road, near Gravesend. For the remainder of that winter, he terrorised local defences with his dribbling and shooting. On his way to 30 goals in the 1934–35 season, he put four into the net during a 9-2 thrashing of Sheppey United and scored twice in the Kent League Cup Final win over Gillingham.

This was a happy period for Edrich, who divided his time between his parents' manor house in Heacham and his lodgings in West London. Aged just 19 in 1935, he was glad his family was settled in Fenland rusticity, but he was now captivated by the attractions of cosmopolitan vibrancy. 'It was great fun living in London on my own,' he later wrote, adding that 'youth's an exciting time, or it ought to be; for me, it was.' Apart from his burgeoning success in professional sport, which fed his dreams of playing at the highest level, he also relished the appeal of the capital to satisfy his potent libido. He once listed his pursuits as 'food, drink, sport and women', and his London life provided plenty of opportunity to indulge in the latter. 'He adored women, just loved them. He was extraordinary. He used to say to me, "I tend to fall in love with a woman once a week,"' recalled his friend David Brocklehurst.

Success in the cricket arena added to his self-confidence. Still waiting to qualify for Middlesex, he scored heavily for Norfolk at the start of the 1935 season, including centuries against Hertfordshire and the touring South Africans. The latter innings brought him to the attention of the national press, the *Daily Mail* reporting that 'the South Africans were surprised at Norwich yesterday by the splendid batting of a 19-year-old local boy William Edrich. Playing for Norfolk against the tourists, Edrich hit 111 runs in two hours 40 minutes, scoring 11 boundaries.' In similar vein, the *Yorkshire Post* hailed his 'sound' contribution, 'his defence being strong and his runs being made with attractive strokes, hooking, late cutting, driving, and skilful leg-side play being special features of his innings'. At the Bracondale prize-giving less than a month later, the headmaster Francis Williams spoke of the school's pride in 'the magnificent performance' of its former pupil. Yet Edrich faded towards the end of the summer of 1935 and in fact only made two first-class appearances that year, as his batting average with Norfolk dropped to 32 compared to 47 in 1934. One minor single-innings match, however, that had major implications for the future, took place at Old Windsor in Berkshire, where Beaumont College, a Roman Catholic Jesuit school, played an MCC side led by Alec Waugh, a prolific novelist whose literary talent was exceeded by that of his younger brother Evelyn. It was Alec who coined the phrase 'the Cricketer's Bible' to describe *Wisden*, though in later life he admitted that his attempts to teach Evelyn cricket 'inculcated in him a permanent repugnance for the game'. On this occasion at Beaumont College, Alec had in his team two young enthusiasts in Compton and Edrich, who were playing together for the first time.

'What do you two do?' asked Waugh when the pair turned up, having taken a bus to the ground.

'We're bowlers,' replied Edrich.

'Right, you go 10 Compton and you 11 Edrich.'

After Beaumont had built an impressive total, the MCC innings quickly subsided, only for Compton and Edrich to put on an unbroken stand of over 60 for the last wicket that brought victory, 'much to Mr Waugh's delight', in Edrich's words. It was the first of many influential partnerships between the Middlesex pair.

Despite his erratic form in 1935, Edrich thought he had done enough to qualify for Middlesex when the next season began. But he was in for a shock when he was summoned to the office of MCC Secretary Billy Findlay, who told him that, due to an administrative error, his application from Norfolk had been received, not in April 1934 as Edrich had presumed, but in October that year. This meant that his qualifying period would not end until October 1936, so in practice he would not be able to play for Middlesex until the 1937 season. Edrich was bewildered and angry. He demanded to know how the mistake happened, then claimed he could provide proof of his residency since April 1934 either from his wage slips at Lord's or by an affidavit from his landlady in St John's Wood. But Findlay told him neither of these steps would be of any use. The only solution, he said, was for Edrich to show a sense of perspective. 'It will do you no harm in the long run to mature a bit before starting here properly,' urged Findlay.

Edrich had no alternative but to accept this advice, though he always harboured the suspicion that Norfolk had deliberately delayed sending his papers to Lord's so the club could have him for another season. But his disappointment was alleviated that winter by his advance through the ranks of Tottenham Hotspur. After impressing in the reserves, he made his first-team debut in front of 35,800 fans at White Hart Lane against Blackpool in October when he deputised for the injured outside left Willie Evans, a Welsh international. Even in muddy conditions, Edrich showed a precocious skill, assisting in two of Spurs' goals and scoring one himself with a low centre that was deflected into the net by a Blackpool defender. Extolling his 'very fine display', the *Daily Mail* described him as 'the man of the match' and 'the chief danger point of the attack' by Spurs. Despite this bright start, he was left out for the next match after Evans had recovered from his injury. Edrich returned, however, in early December for the away game against Nottingham Forest at the slippery, frost-bound City Ground. In a heavy 4-1 defeat, he was one of Tottenham's few successes and scored their only goal. 'With the solitary exception of Edrich, the forwards finished feebly,' reported the *Daily Mail*, which added that 'their shooting was very poor, although Edrich sent over the right king of centres. It was left to him to find the net.' Altogether, he played nine games during that 1935–36 season as Spurs finished in fifth place in the Second Division.

In April 1936, just as the football season was ending and the cricket season was beginning, Edrich took a step that was to become a recurring theme in his story. Throughout his life he was not only an unrestrained hedonist who revelled in physical passion, but also an incurable romantic who hankered after domestic contentment. Inevitably the two traits were in perpetual conflict, as shown in his chequered record as a husband. 'He was quite hopeless – you had to laugh – he could not resist a woman,' said his sister Ena, who used the phrase 'tragi-romantic' to describe her brother. Denis Compton recalled how he was once at a cocktail party when he eyed Bill in conversation with an attractive woman. The next morning in a match at Lord's, Denis and Bill were standing beside each other in the slips.

'I saw someone last night whom I'm going to marry,' said Bill.

'Don't be silly, Bill. You've only just met her,' replied Denis. According to Compton, however, Bill was insistent.

Just after he reached the age of 20, Edrich went down the matrimonial path for the first time, after he fell in love with another woman, a typist from Acton called Betty Hobbs, whom he described as 'the prettiest girl in London'. Through a mixture of infatuation and a quixotic sense of chivalrous honour, he proposed soon after they had started their relationship and she accepted. Her looks, accentuated by her physical fitness as a keen amateur swimmer, may have captivated Edrich, but her background was an incongruous one for Bill. For a start, his prospective father-in-law Sidney Hobbs was teetotal, not a label that was ever attached to Bill. There was an even bigger difference over politics. By inclination, Edrich was a staunch Conservative: 'a Tory through and through, and so was his family. He was a man for empire and tradition,' said Rodney Edrich. This was in stark contrast to Betty's father: a trade unionist, socialist and railway clerk from Pontypridd, one of the closely knit mining communities of south Wales. In the early 1920s, he and his wife, along with young Betty and her elder sister Marjorie, had moved from Wales to Acton, where he became a leading figure in the local Labour Party and trade-union movement, standing regularly for the local town hall and the London County Council, as well as serving on the borough's education committee. Such was the high regard for Hobbs in the party that in 1933 he was selected as the Labour candidate to fight the parliamentary seat of Westbury. An admiring profile in the local *Wiltshire Times* emphasised his strong Labour roots and commitment to the cause. 'It might almost be said that Labour principles are in Mr Hobbs's blood. His boyhood was spent in south Wales, where Keir Hardie was fighting at Merthyr Tydfil, so that he absorbed his political faith from one of the pioneers.' Failure to win the seat did not lessen Hobbs's determination to campaign for socialism, which he believed was 'the only thing to make this country a better place'.

It was Bill's youth, rather than any clash of opinion, that worried his family when he brought Betty to Norfolk to meet them. There was no denying that Betty was attractive and amiable; 'Daddy always said what a nice girl she was,' Jean Beecroft, the daughter of his elder brother Eric, told me. But in the eyes of his parents and siblings, the proposed union was premature, especially since Bill had yet to achieve any kind of professional security. According to Ena's memoir, his father told him, 'You are only twenty, time for marriage when you are fully established in your career.' Ena took the same line herself. 'Betty was a very nice person but so young, only 18 years old. In fact, my father was correct; they were both far too young.'

Despite these reservations, the marriage went ahead, another indicator of Edrich's stubbornness. With Eric acting as the best man, the ceremony was held on 5 April, 1936 at St Dunstan's Church in Acton, followed by a reception at the Hobbs's family home in Perryn Road nearby. It was a minor celebrity occasion, though, interestingly, the local press gave more prominence to Bill's reputation as a footballer than as a cricketer. 'Spurs Winger Married', proclaimed the *Acton Gazette* and *West London Post*, alongside a picture of the couple, Bill dapper in his formal morning coat, Betty in 'a becoming dress of heavy satin trimmed with pin tucks, a fine tulle veil, and halo head-dress with orange blossom'. For all his determined bravado in front of his parents, Edrich was inwardly consumed by doubts on the wedding day. Years later, he confessed to his son Justin, 'I was standing by the altar as she came down the aisle on the arm of her father, and I thought to myself, "Oh my God, what have I done?"' It was too late to pull out, but Edrich's ambiguous feelings about his marriage soon manifested itself in his reluctance to be tied by his vows.

After a brief honeymoon at Heacham, Edrich and his new bride moved into her parents' house at 127 Perryn Road. As the 1936 cricket season began, his frustrations over the administrative error about his Middlesex residential qualification drove him to a new level of batting consistency. In five first-class matches that season, he scored 440 runs at an average of 55, finishing second in the national averages behind Wally Hammond. Among his three centuries that summer was his maiden first-class ton made for the MCC against Surrey at Lord's, during which he shared a huge partnership of 296 with the veteran Patsy Hendren. It was an innings that prompted *The Times* to rhapsodise about 'the excellence of his strokes' and 'the seasoned judgement and maturity of his style'. That maturity stemmed partly from the guidance of Hendren, now aged 47 but still a force to be reckoned with at the batting crease. Lacking in self-importance but not humour, Hendren was an ideal mentor because of his rich experience and his technical understanding of batsmanship. He was a master of the hook shot, a skill that he passed on to Edrich, while he constantly emphasised the importance of decisive footwork. 'Watch my feet,' he told his young charges. Under his influence, both Compton and Edrich became adept in playing quick bowling off the back foot, which gave them fractionally more time to respond than if they had lunged forward. 'Against exceptional pace, Bill and I were on the back foot before the ball was bowled,' recalled Compton. Another vital lesson was how to exploit a bowler's rhythm, as Edrich later recalled: 'The greatest thing I learnt from Patsy was to play my shots in the direction the ball was swinging or turning, and play with the tide.' Edrich was also successful that season for Norfolk as he averaged 44.11 with the bat and 20.68 with the ball, figures that led *The Cricketer* magazine to write that, 'Norfolk have suffered a severe loss for Edrich will be qualified for Middlesex next season.' In the view of the *Daily Mail*,

Edrich was 'one of the coming men of the cricket world', whose record in the 1936 season 'promises great things'. Having explained how his potential was enhanced by his abilities as 'a fast bowler of considerable pace and stamina', the paper even argued that the England selectors should think about giving him a place on the MCC tour to Australia that winter under the captaincy of Gubby Allen, the amateur Middlesex all-rounder: 'A young man who combines an ability to bowl at a fast pace for long periods with such excellent batting is entitled to serious consideration.'

But such claims belonged to the realm of fantasy. Edrich spent much of that early winter, not on the other side of the world, but playing for Spurs. Yet just as he was becoming a regular fixture in the side, he suffered a serious injury while playing at Swansea. Chasing a long, crossfield pass, he was tackled heavily, fell awkwardly and felt an excruciating pain in his ankle. After he had been carried off the field in agony, his foot was put in splints ready for the long, difficult journey back to London, where he was seen by a specialist at a private clinic at midnight. Both the urgency of the appointment and reputation of the consultant indicated the esteem in which Edrich was held at White Hart Lane. Although he had broken no bones, the ligaments in his foot were badly torn. This entailed a long, slow recovery and he could not play again until the spring of 1937. During this lengthy period of inaction, he contemplated his future as a professional sportsman and decided that he would have to give his priority to cricket, both because that was his real passion and because, playing football at outside left, there was always the danger of a career-wrecking injury. 'It was asking too much of my limbs,' he later said. He did not tell Spurs directly of his decision, but broached the subject by asking whether, if he were selected for an overseas cricket tour, he could be released from his professional football duties. The club agreed and the curtain began to fall on Edrich's time at White Hart Lane. Over two seasons, he had made 20 appearances, offering glimpses of his potential quality as a winger. His manager at White Hart Lane, Jack Tresadern, a shrewd judge of the game who had been good enough to play for England, once said that Edrich 'could have been one of the best outside lefts in the country'.

But in any contest between cricket and football, the former would always be the winner. In a handwritten note after Bill died in April 1986, Len Hutton wrote, 'I am unable to think of anyone who loved cricket and life more than Bill Edrich.' That devotion was reinforced by his first triumphant season with Middlesex in 1937. Billy Findlay, the MCC Secretary, had been correct in his claim that the extra year spent qualifying for the club would actually improve Edrich's standard of play. At the start of the season *The Cricketer* wrote that he 'seems destined for a most successful career. He gets his nose well over the ball and is quick on his feet.' The promise was extravagantly fulfilled in the County Championship, where he scored 1,559 runs at an average of 48.71 and had a total first-class aggregate of 2,154 runs. 'My first season went like a dream,' he wrote in 1978. Denis Compton, whose birthplace of Hendon had meant that he didn't need to serve a qualifying period, was already an established star, usually batting at Number 4 or 5; but Edrich, generally batting at Number 3, began to look almost his equal with a series of powerful innings, like his epic 175 and 73 in a losing cause against Lancashire at Lord's on a crumbling pitch. The *Daily Express* reported that the '21-years-old farmer's son from Norfolk . . . impressed everybody not only with the soundness of his display but with the variety of shots he employed. His driving was as clean and well-timed as the forcing stroke off his body that brought him many runs.'

As he showed his class against all types of bowling, speculation began to mount that Edrich might be selected to play for England in the Test series against New Zealand. Although that prospect did not materialise, the improvement in his technique was noted by commentators, several of whom perceived the influence of his county captain, the innovative and inspirational Walter Robins, who also led England that summer. 'Edrich developing for England,' declared the *Daily Mail* after Edrich scored a century against Somerset at Lord's in mid-August. The paper's report went on: 'It was good to see Edrich, who reached 100 in two and a half hours and hit 13 fours altogether, making aggressive strokes in front of the wicket, thus wisely following the advice of his captain. The ability and disposition to punish bowling in front of the wicket is the one thing needful to make an England batsman of Edrich. Yesterday's sign of development was therefore very promising.'

His progress over the summer fuelled a debate as to whether he might actually be a better batsman than Compton, who had made a successful

England debut against New Zealand in 1937. In the opinion of *The Cricketer*, 'at the moment Edrich is probably the sounder of the two', but Compton 'is full of strokes, adaptable and with a touch of genius'. *Wisden* thought that Edrich was 'the more consistent and, if not so attractive to watch, the more reliable'. Middlesex was only too relieved to have two young professionals able to fill the gap left by Hendren, who finally retired at the end of the 1937 season. The club's annual report urged members to 'note the fine form of Compton and Edrich, who both batted extremely well. Both are very young and have big futures before them.' The pair were each offered two-year contracts by Lord's worth £200 per year, not a princely sum but significantly higher than average earnings, which in 1937 stood at £153 per annum across all sectors.

Further recognition of Edrich's ability came with the announcement of his selection for the MCC tour of India, led by 47-year-old Lionel, Lord Tennyson, the swashbuckling grandson of the great Victorian poet. This was not a Test trip but the calibre of the team party was high, featuring experienced campaigners such as the stylish Nottinghamshire batsman Joe Hardstaff, the Surrey fast bowler Alf Gover and the Middlesex leg-spinner Ian Peebles. Tennyson himself, a former captain of Hampshire and England, was one of the vivid characters of English cricket, with exactly the right mix of virtues and vices that appealed to Edrich. Tennyson's biographer Alan Edwards wrote that Edrich had a 'lifelong affection' for the man he called 'the Baron' because they had 'a similar outlook'. A brave soldier in the First World War and a fearless sporting leader whose most famous exploit was his batsmanship in the 1921 Test series, when he heroically attacked the Australian fast bowlers despite a broken hand, Tennyson was also a compulsive gambler, heavy drinker and habitual playboy. In his autobiography he wrote, 'a succession of lovely ladies held first place in my heart and towards them all, in turn, I was ever generous', exactly the words that Edrich might have used about his own romantic life. Tennyson's first wife, however, failed to see the generosity amid the financial disasters. A relative of the Liberal statesman Henry Asquith, Clarissa (Clare) Tennant divorced Tennyson in 1928 because of the strains caused by his recklessness. Indeed, the reason he was keen to go on the tour to India, despite his expanding girth and advancing years, was because he had just lost £40,000 and wanted to avoid his furious father.

Before he accepted the invitation to tour, Edrich requested approval from the Middlesex Committee and his football club. 'We have no objection to your accompanying Lord Tennyson's team to India during the coming winter,' the committee told him. Spurs were just as co-operative, even though the decision signalled the definite end of his days as a professional footballer. That point was recognised by the *Lynn Post*, the Norfolk local paper that had closely followed his career:

Edrich has chosen to make cricket his living in preference to football. His performances on Tottenham's left wing were full of promise, although it must be admitted that he never startled the football world with quite the same brilliance as he revealed on the cricket field. This winter there will be no football for him – the Tottenham Hotspur directors have already released him and a season's absence from the game is a good deal of ground to recover. On the other hand, cricket in India will be a valuable experience. Already his claims have been advanced, not unreasonably, for a place in the England Test match team. The selectors must realize that the future prestige of English cricket depends upon such players such as Edrich. He will return from India in time to fight for a cap against Australia.

The tour was a long one, lasting from October 1937 till February 1938, but Edrich enjoyed himself almost from the moment that the party set sail. In one of his later books, he hinted at the pleasures of female company. 'It was the first time I had been aboard a ship, the first time I had been overseas, the first time I had worn a dinner jacket, the first time I had tasted the subtle flavour of caviar. And many other firsts. Nights rolled into days. Every other passenger seemed to be a young debutante hoping to find an army officer as a husband on her arrival in India.' The taste of new, often exotic, experiences continued once the touring party had reached the Indian subcontinent. Although Tennyson and his men had to travel extensively across the vast country, this burden was alleviated by generous hospitality from their hosts. 'We were royally entertained,' wrote Edrich, who described the tour as 'wonderful'. The team were taken hunting for panthers, buck and wild pigs, shown jewellery and art collections, driven up the Khyber Pass by drivers who showed no fear of 1,000-feet drops at hairpin bends on the primitive road, honoured at receptions, and invited to a large number of banquets organised by the Rajahs and Maharajahs where, in Edrich's words, 'every variety of food appeared together with a great many varieties none of us had ever seen or heard of'. In response to this rolling culinary feast, Edrich's constitution proved stronger than those of some of his teammates, notably Alf Gover. In one of the unofficial Tests, Gover charged in to bowl his first delivery but, after the release of the ball, carried on down the pitch and then ran on to the pavilion, reaching the toilets just in time.

The political backdrop of the tour was difficult. Over the next decade, both independence and partition became realities. Already, in 1937–38, the flames of Indian nationalism were beginning to burn with a new intensity, while divisions between the Hindu and Muslim populations had grown. Even so, within the confines of the principalities and the British imperial establishment, Tennyson proved an effective diplomatic operator. During the course of making 157 speeches he spread charm and good humour, most notably with his well-worn opening line, 'when I come back as Viceroy'. He was also a successful leader on the field. His team lost just five of their 24 matches and won the unofficial five-Test series. Bill Edrich turned out to be the key figure in that triumph. He headed the batting averages with 876 runs at 46.10, including two centuries, and took 13 wickets at 24.46 with his fast bowling. More than five years after he had first encountered the paceman Mohammad Nissar as a Norfolk schoolboy playing at Lakenham, Edrich had to face him again in the unofficial Test series and proved even more resolute. In fact, it was Nissar who was on the defensive, not daring to bowl short because, in the words of Gover, 'Bill would have hooked him out of sight.' Despite their 26-year age difference, Edrich established a good rapport at the crease with Tennyson who generally batted at Number 7, reflected in the bet that they had in an early match against Sind in Karachi when they had both reached 92 in stifling heat. Alarmed at the sweat pouring off his 17-stone skipper whom he described as 'a melting man mountain', Edrich asked Tennyson if he thought he could actually survive to make the remaining eight runs for his century. According to Edrich's account in his 1948 autobiography, Tennyson turned with a broad grin and said, 'I'll bet I reach my hundred before you do, my boy.'

'A pound on it, sir?' asked Edrich. He later wrote, 'We shook hands and he won the pound all right! He looked wet through and done for, but he cracked up 18 more before being caught and bowled.' Edrich himself remained unbeaten on 140. 'I never enjoyed a game more,' he subsequently wrote.

At the end of the tour, *The Cricketer* wrote that he had been 'a great success as a No. 1 batsman, a magnificent outfield and a useful change bowler'. He now looked a certainty for the full England Test team. But his elevation would soon cast a dark shadow over his reputation.

3

TESTING TIMES
1938-1939

'Lads like Denis Compton and Bill Edrich were born to cricket greatness.'

Middlesex Advertiser, June 1938

Don Bradman was renowned for his ruthlessness. It was a trait that helped to make him both the most prolific batsman ever to have played the game and an enormously successful captain of Australia, though some felt he went too far in his eagerness to crush the opposition. The Yorkshire all-rounder Norman Yardley, who first played representative cricket overseas on Tennyson's 1937–38 tour of India and cemented a close bond with Bill Edrich then, said that Bradman 'let his relentless determination to win sometimes run away with him'.

Yet on the Australians' 1938 tour of England, his first overseas Ashes trip as skipper, Bradman indulged in an extraordinary act of sentimentality purely to boost a young batsman who seemed destined to play for England throughout the summer. The player was none other than Bill Edrich, and with Bradman's help he was about to write himself into the record books.

Fresh from his success in India, Edrich had made an electric start to the new season. In his very first match, for the MCC against Yorkshire, he scored a century, followed by another for the MCC against Surrey. His opening game for Middlesex brought 63 and 20 not out against Warwickshire, two innings that were soon dwarfed by his 182 and 71 against Gloucestershire, which led to a Middlesex victory by three wickets. Known for his sound defence, Edrich seemed to have added a new element of aggression to his technique. As the *Daily Telegraph* noted, 'He was a batsman who takes the initiative out of the bowlers' hands and into his own. He was constantly reproaching those who had been critical of his ability to really attack.' Over the first three weeks of the season, he had made 736 runs. Media interest now soared in his deeds at the batting crease, for he was within touching distance of the cherished milestone of scoring 1,000 first-class runs before the end of May. In the long history of English cricket, only five batsmen had reached the landmark: the Victorian titan W.G. Grace in 1895; the Surrey opener Tom Hayward in 1900; the Gloucestershire all-rounder Wally Hammond in 1927; Charlie Hallows of Lancashire in 1928; and Bradman himself in 1930. With his characteristic dominance, Bradman performed the feat again in the summer of 1938, reaching the target with four days to spare, which may have explained his munificence towards Edrich.

With three matches to go before the end of May, Edrich still needed 264 runs to join the elite. When he scored an epic double-century at Lord's against Nottinghamshire, whose attack was led by the deadly pace duo of Harold Larwood and Bill Voce, the achievement seemed almost inevitable. After his majestic 245, which contained 38 boundaries, just 19 more runs were required from five potential innings. 'I felt certain I could do it,' he recalled. The window of opportunity narrowed slightly when Nottinghamshire were beaten by an innings, which denied him the chance of a second knock in that match, then shrunk more dramatically when he was out first ball in Middlesex's only innings in their victory against Worcestershire. That left Bill still needing 19 from the county's final match of May, which was against the Australians. After weeks of mastery, he was now plagued by misfortune, as heavy rain fell at Lord's, washing out the first day and much of the second. Given the loss of time, it seemed that Edrich's hopes would rest entirely on a single innings. After the weather relented, Bradman won the toss and batted, only to see the Australians skittled out in damp conditions for just 132. But when Middlesex began their innings in the gathering evening gloom, their batsmen struggled against the pace of Ernie McCormick and the quick leg-spin of Bill O'Reilly. Once he was out in the middle, Edrich was just as perplexed as his teammates, especially by O'Reilly whose bounce and variations made him a handful to play. From his earliest years in Norfolk, Edrich had been coached to read a spinner from the hand, but he found this impossible with the tall Australian bowler because of his pace. So troubled was Edrich that he decided that, instead of trying to decipher the turn through the air, he would attempt to play him off the pitch, but that made his task no easier. Added to the awkwardness of facing O'Reilly was the pressure of expectations, which meant that the more Edrich concentrated, the more anxious he became. After he had scored just nine runs, the ordeal was over when he missed a googly from O'Reilly and was bowled. 'I walked in with bent head, feeling that I had as good as lost my chance,' he wrote. The final day opened with Middlesex still batting amid forecasts of unsettled, occasionally damp weather. A tame draw seemed a certainty when the home side were finally dismissed with just two and a half hours' play remaining and a lead of 56. The Australians' task was obvious: wipe out the deficit, then bat to the close. It was a goal that the visitors looked like they would accomplish easily. Steadied by a typically assured innings from Bradman, they were 58 runs ahead with just half an hour to go.

Disappointment gnawed at Edrich. Every passing minute represented another blow to his dream.

At that moment Bradman, supposedly iron-willed and with a reputation for ruthlessness, made his warm-hearted gesture. Having reached 30 not out and with the match heading towards an inevitable draw, he suddenly declared, giving Edrich exactly 12 minutes to make the necessary ten remaining runs for the 1,000 before the end of May. Downcast for most of the afternoon, Edrich immediately underwent a transformation in his mood, now he had this unexpected eleventh-hour chance of glory. 'Bradman's action gave me the confidence to knock up the runs, for I felt I just could not let him down,' he wrote. But as Edrich walked out to bat, the Australian captain warned him, 'We're not going to give these to you, Bill, you've got to get 'em. It did not take the young Middlesex player long to do so. In just five minutes, he raced to double figures, reaching the target with a cut down to third man. Bradman was the first to congratulate Edrich, who grinned broadly in relief and gratitude. Soon afterwards, when stumps were drawn, a large part of the crowd rushed on to the field to cheer Edrich and shake him by the hand. In the *Daily Express*, William Pollock described Bradman's declaration as a 'present' that brought 'a happy ending to cricket in May', while the *Daily Mail* pointed out that all the other record-holders, from Grace to Bradman, had been 'mature cricketers at the height of their prime when they achieved the feat', whereas Edrich was 'playing in his second season of first-class cricket'. Uniquely among this select group, Edrich had scored all his runs at one ground, namely Lord's, the 'Home of Cricket'.

His achievement, reinforced the following week by an innings of 80 in a representative trial match, helped to secure his place in the England team for the First Test against Australia at Trent Bridge in early June. In the build-up to his debut, the media's fascination with Edrich continued. In an interview with *The People* he talked about his farming background, the influence of Michael Falcon at Norfolk, his coach Jack Nichols at Bracondale and Patsy Hendren at Middlesex, and his devotion to cricket above football. They were 'both glorious games, but I think I like the summer pastime the best because it is more difficult and there is more to learn'. Edrich also described how he had trained himself to keep on playing 'each ball strictly on its merits' and 'to allow more time for my strokes. This is one of the secrets of Don Bradman, in my opinion,' he said, though he stressed that he was not trying to bracket himself with the great Australian. Modesty slid into a sense of awkwardness during an interview with the *News Chronicle*: 'I don't think that there's anything particular about my batting. It's pretty ordinary. No stunts. I just hope I can pick up the right ball and hit it.' He then turned reluctantly to his domestic life: 'I am only 22 and I have been married two years. I got married when I qualified for Middlesex.' At this point, the *News Chronicle* correspondent recorded, 'he fell silent, faintly embarrassed at having said so much about himself'.

The weight of expectations on Edrich was enormous as the Trent Bridge Test in Nottingham approached. Perhaps the closest historic parallel is the case of Graeme Hick, the Zimbabwean-born middle-order batsman who piled up runs in domineering style from the late 1980s into 1991 as he waited to qualify to play for England by residence. Such was his youthful supremacy against county bowling attacks that he was hailed as a new, almost freakish, phenomenon. In 1988, three years before he made his Test debut, Hick became the first domestic cricketer since Edrich exactly half a century earlier to score 1,000 runs before the end of May. Yet his first appearances in the Test arena, against the lethal pace of the West Indies and Pakistan, brought a succession of low scores amid disillusion from the public and the axe from the selectors. Hick never fulfilled his promise during a decade in and out of the Test team, averaging just 31.32.

Promise was what Edrich seemed to offer in abundance in 1938. 'Edrich may well be the Arthur Shrewsbury of this century,' wrote the well-connected historian Sir Home Gordon, comparing him to the supreme professional batsman of the Victorian age. 'Lads like Denis Compton and Bill Edrich were born to cricket greatness,' declared the *Middlesex Advertiser*, the local paper for Lord's. Edrich himself wrote that, on receiving the news of his selection for the start of the Ashes series, he was excited rather than anxious: 'After my run of big scores, I felt this was going to be my happiest summer.' But there was one dark cloud on the horizon. His struggles in Middlesex's first innings of the recent game against the Australians indicated a potential vulnerability that could be exploited by the visitors, especially O'Reilly and McCormick.

On the first morning at Nottingham, however, the Australian attack had to toil as Len Hutton and Gloucestershire's Charlie Barnett put on 169 for the first wicket by lunch. Even when their opening stand of 219 was finally broken in the afternoon, the runs continued to flow, with Compton making his first Ashes hundred and Eddie Paynter a double-century. The total reached 658 for 8 before Wally Hammond, leading his country for the first time, declared. During the winter, Hammond had abandoned his professional contract to become an amateur, taking on a job as a director of Marsham Tyres. Through this appointment, he had made himself eligible for the England captaincy, which by custom had to be held by an amateur. It was a move that delighted the Chairman of Selectors, Plum Warner, who was both a strong supporter of Hammond and a defender of cricket's hierarchical traditions. The elevation as the England captain was a personal triumph for the status-conscious Hammond, but, despite his majesty as a batsman, his aloof, reserved and temperamental personality meant that he was neither a natural leader nor popular with his teams. 'His mood could change with the wind,' wrote William Ferguson, the much-loved international scorer and tour organiser. When Warner told the Gloucestershire amateur Basil Allen that Hammond was 'a wonderful chap', Allen responded, 'To be honest, Plum, I think he's an absolute shit.' Yet one player with whom Hammond struck up a rapport was Bill Edrich. 'Wally was mad about Bill,' said Jim Swanton, the doyen of cricket correspondents. The bond between them may have seemed incongruous, given that Edrich was far more gregarious, affable and open than the new Test captain. But they had much in common. Both came from modest provincial backgrounds. Both were socially ambitious and sexually libidinous. Both were heavy drinkers. Both adored motor cars, which made Hammond highly suitable for his appointment at Marsham. Edrich knew so much about them that many years after the 1938 Ashes series, during the 1954–55 tour of Australia, he surprised the England management by fixing their broken-down vehicle at the roadside.

Sustained by a deep belief in Edrich's natural talent, Hammond became both a mentor and protector. But his faith was sorely tested over the coming months, as Edrich changed in the public's estimation from being an admired hopeful to a figure of ridicule. In that first mammoth England innings at Trent Bridge, he made just five before he was bowled by a quicker ball from O'Reilly. Batting at Number 3, Edrich put the blame on the long wait he had to endure while Hutton and Barnett were compiling their massive partnership. 'When my turn came at last, I was screwed up a bit too tight,' he wrote. During the Test, John Thompson of the *Daily Mirror* visited Norfolk and, despite this setback, found widespread confidence in the local hero. 'Every other resident seems related to Bill,' he wrote, adding that Bill's grandmother still thought he was 'the best cricketer in England', though Bill's own father seemed subdued. 'The boy didn't do so well,' he told Thompson.

His son's failure had little impact on the result, as Australia were guided to the safety of a draw by Stan McCabe's spectacular innings of 232, one of the great counter-attacking performances in Ashes history. The second Test at Lord's also ended in a draw, despite Hammond making 240, probably his greatest ever innings. Edrich was out twice cheaply for a total of just 10 runs, both times to misdirected hook shots from fast bowler McCormick. On the first occasion, the ball crashed into the stumps; on the second, it flew into the hands of square leg. Now the whispers began against Edrich's inclusion in the England side, reinforced by accusations of favouritism by the Lord's establishment towards one of their own. There was no dispute that Warner was one of Edrich's staunchest supporters, unmoved by the chorus of disapproval that rang out from the press and public. As the long-serving Middlesex professional Harry Lee said of Warner, 'When he has made up his mind that a man is worth backing, he will back him through thick and thin.'

The criticism increased dramatically in volume after England's defeat at Headingley in the Fourth Test, the Third Test at Old Trafford in Manchester having been washed out without a ball being bowled. Once more, Edrich was dismissed in both innings for low scores; bowled by a vicious googly from O'Reilly in the first innings for 12 and stumped off left-arm spinner Leslie Fleetwood-Smith for 28 in the second. Thompson of the *Daily Mirror*, this time inside the ground, noticed Edrich sitting in the pavilion, 'white-faced and grim-looking after he had failed yet again'. Edrich was now viewed as a privileged passenger, who was keeping better batsmen out of the side. Questions were asked about both his technique and temperament at the highest level. Len Hutton, perhaps the most technically gifted player of his era, wrote that Edrich was inclined to move across the crease as O'Reilly delivered the ball, so 'consequently he went across the line of the ball and did not last long'. Bob Wyatt thought the problem was that 'Edrich did not keep his head still'. Edrich's deficiencies were also picked up by Bill Bowes, the Yorkshire pace bowler, who played in the 1938 series and noted his habit of 'placing his left leg directly in the line of the flight of the ball, with the result that the bat must be moved around his left leg in order to make a stroke. The principles of a straight bat and a pendulum swing are therefore impracticable.' In Bowes's view, Edrich was an easy target for the 'special guile' of O'Reilly. 'We used to say that O'Reilly would pay the England selectors to pick Edrich.'

His omission for the final Test at The Oval looked inevitable. After Headingley, the former England medium-pacer Maurice Tate predicted in *Reynolds Newpaper* that 'Young Edrich will be out. We can take that as read. Sir Plum Warner and company have done splendidly in giving Edrich every possible chance and I salute them. You cannot judge a promising young 'un in Tests on the basis of one or two appearances. Edrich did not live up to expectations though I hope he will not be ignored completely. The Middlesex player is a grand cricketer.' But Tate was wrong. Much to the outrage of the public, Edrich kept his place, while Barnett, the brilliant centurion of Trent Bridge, was dropped. Tellingly perhaps, Hammond's admiration for Edrich was matched by his loathing for Barnett, who reciprocated the feeling, partly out of his disgust at the skipper's adulterous personal life. But Hammond argued for Edrich's retention, not on the basis of any personal affinity, but on the grounds of Edrich's all-round skills and promise for the future, as he explained in his 1949 book *Cricket My World*: 'A brilliant beginning had become a handicap . . . They said he had not got Test-match psychology, whatever that may be! They said he was kept in the England side through favouritism at Lord's and Neville Cardus, as nearly as infallible as any cricket writer has ever been, was one who thought he ought to be dropped. Edrich himself was very badly upset by the violence of the attacks on him and his play – which naturally became more streaky and wretched than ever.' Hammond remained insistent. 'I never believed in a selection policy of nervous alterations. There had been too much of that in the past and England had paid dearly for it. Bill's fielding was always superb, perhaps the best we had and he was always a worthwhile bowler and he improved. I knew that it was a matter of time alone before a very great batsman would emerge from his shell.'

He did not emerge at The Oval when England enjoyed a glut of runs on a featherbed pitch. The team's total of 903 for 7 was a record, as was Len Hutton's individual score of 364, which eclipsed Bradman's 334 made at Leeds in 1930 as the highest score in Ashes Tests. But Edrich was a bystander in this orgy of accumulation. Even on an easy track, he managed to fail yet again, falling lbw to O'Reilly for just 12. 'Local Boy Makes Bad', proclaimed the *Sunday Pictorial* in its headline above a passage that read: 'We imagine that if Edrich of Middlesex had a nightmare, it would consist of a massed group of the scoreboards which have registered his batting in this year's Test matches.' In four Test matches, he made just 67 runs at an average of 11.16. Nor did his bowling inflict much damage, despite Hammond's praise for his all-round skills. Only four Australian wickets fell to his pace, each one costing 34.75 runs. Edrich could not but help ponder his disastrous series, a process that dragged him further into the mire of despondency. 'I had been a hopeless and complete failure. There was not one ray of hope or vestige of excuse,' he wrote later, recounting how he was assailed by 'a wild chorus of accusations. No Test match temperament. Poor style. Risky shots. Bad footwork. Over-confidence. Weakness against slow bowling. Weakness against fast bowling. Tendency to use pads instead of bat. And so on and so forth. It was like attending one's own inquest.'

One of the features of the 1938 season was that Edrich's dire international form did not translate into the first-class arena, which further fed the theory that he had a psychological problem at the highest level. In fact, in a total of 30 matches, he scored 2,378 runs at an average of 52.85, with six centuries. Nor did he allow his miserable Test run to undermine the physical bravery for which he became so well-known in the cricket world. Opening the batting with Hutton for the Players late on the first day in the annual fixture at Lord's against the Gentlemen in mid-July, he was confronted by gloomy conditions, a lively pitch and the extreme pace of the Essex amateur Ken Farnes. A thoughtful, well-read schoolmaster by profession, Farnes was a mercurial cricketer whose bowling speed could be a barometer of his temper: the greater his discontent, the quicker the delivery. On this occasion, he was in a foul temper after being dropped from the England team. His first ball rose steeply from just short of a length outside the off stump, flying past Edrich's head. The second was on the same length but this time closer to the line of the leg stump. As the ball reared straight towards his eyes, Edrich instinctively lifted his hands to shield his face. But Farnes's speed was too swift for him. The ball clipped one of Edrich's gloves before striking his head, from where it looped up to the gully and was caught by Jack Stephenson. By the time the fielder had grasped the ball, Edrich had collapsed at the crease. But his state of unconsciousness did not last long. He was soon on his feet again, telling everyone that he was ready for the next delivery, at which point the umpire told him he was out. After he had trudged off, he was replaced by the nightwatchman Fred Price, who was heard to mutter as he left the dressing room, 'I have a wife and children to think about.' Price, perhaps unsurprisingly, did not survive the over.

Hammond, who was captain of the Gentlemen for the first time, later told Edrich that Farnes's over was 'the quickest he had ever seen'. Hutton too, watching from the non-striker's end, felt it was 'the most ferocious bowling' he had witnessed, adding 'I find it impossible to think Bodyline could have been more frightening and intimidating.' Despite the severity of the blow to the head, which prevented him from fielding, Edrich batted resolutely in the Players' second innings in a losing cause. His innings of 78 was described by the *Daily Telegraph* as a 'superb effort' that was 'proof of his courage and determination as well as his skill. He had spent the previous day in bed, nursing his wounds, and his success gave the greatest satisfaction.'

After the vicissitudes of the 1938 summer, Edrich was relieved to go up in September to his native Norfolk, where he led an Edrich family XI against Michael Falcon's Norfolk XI in a match to raise funds for the Blofield recreation ground. Alongside Bill were his father, his brothers, Eric and Geoff, who were now firmly established in the Norfolk team, and Brian, who was still at school, plus three cousins and three uncles. It was the start of a long, much-cherished series that featured the Edriches' own side against visiting charity and celebrity teams, often in front of large crowds and even broadcasters drawn by the peculiarity of the fixture, which had been conceived by the local vicar, Canon Hugh Shillito. He recognised that the lustre of Bill's name, allied to the size of the Edrich cricketing clan, would arouse local and even national media interest. So it proved. The BBC sent one of their star correspondents, the former Royal Navy officer Thomas Woodrooffe, to broadcast a half-hour commentary from the match. There was a slight risk about including Woodrooffe in an event with Bill Edrich at its centre, for the previous year the correspondent had caused a major controversy when he was meant to commentate at length for BBC Radio on the Coronation Review at Spithead. Unfortunately, Woodrooffe had met some naval friends for drinks before his stint behind the microphone. By the time he began his commentary, he was hopelessly inebriated. Listeners were bewildered by his incoherence, illustrated by Woodrooffe's slurred repetition of the phrase 'the Fleet's lit up'. After just a few minutes, he had to be taken off the air, the BBC later apologising for how he had become 'tired and emotional', a euphemism that became part of the lexicon of journalism to describe intoxication.

But trouble of a different sort occurred in 1938. Woodrooffe was due to start commentating at half-past three, and the BBC hoped that, as the star attraction, Bill would be batting at that point. Indeed, to accommodate the corporation's schedule, Falcon deliberately closed the Norfolk innings early, enabling Bill and his father to open the innings just before the broadcast began. Unfortunately, in another example of the bad luck that plagued him after May, Edrich edged the first ball straight into the hands of slip, and he had to return to the pavilion before Woodrooffe had even taken up his position. As it turned out, this new failure hardly mattered, as rain soon arrived and led to the abandonment of the match. A few weeks later, Woodrooffe had a much bigger assignment, covering the return of the Prime Minister Neville Chamberlain from the Munich conference with Hitler.

Edrich was always close to his family, who took tremendous pride in his rise to Test stardom, as his sister Ena recalled: 'The years 1938 and 1939 seemed to go in a whirl at Bill's emerging success that overwhelmed all else. My father bought a portable wireless set particularly so that we could turn to the cricket.' On the surface, Bill's own marriage to Betty seemed to be happy; his closeness to his in-laws was shown when he was the best man at the wedding of Betty's sister Marjorie to electrical engineer Joshua Parsons in April 1937. Bill and Betty also had a less cramped existence, since they now had 127 Perryn Road in Acton to themselves, after her parents moved to Bournemouth to take over a private hotel. But the couple's apparent harmony was about to be tested to the limit, following Edrich's selection for his first full England tour.

Given his record against Australia, there was widespread puzzlement and dismay at his inclusion in the team party led by Hammond to South Africa. Even the loyal Ena admitted that the decision was 'a surprise'. Within the MCC, the concern was not just about his lack of Test runs, but also his fondness for partying. In fact, on his return from the Tennyson tour to India earlier in the year, he had been warned 'in future to be more restrained in your reported Bohemian jollities'. Tennyson himself, no moraliser, thought that Edrich had 'overdone the Bacchanalian rites' on the India tour. Yet Hammond and Warner were again adamant about his selection, the captain emphasising Edrich was useful at all the 'bits and pieces' of the game. The same point was made by Warner in his role as editor of *The Cricketer*: 'Generally speaking he is a very sound batsman with a partiality for the on side. But there are other strings to his bow for he is a brilliant field in any position and a most useful and enthusiastic fast bowler who bowls with tremendous energy.'

For all his obvious abilities, however, Edrich seemed unable to break the pattern of the summer. After a productive beginning in the provincial matches, including a century against Griqualand West and 98 against Natal, the stench of failure returned with renewed pungency at Test level. In the first, drawn match of the series at Johannesburg, he made 0 and 10, prompting the *Daily Worker*'s sports correspondent George Sinfield, a Communist and former boxer, to write that 'Hammond has now gone the length of tolerance. This young Middlesex player is an enigma: brilliant in club games, moderate in the extreme for Test stuff.' In the *Daily Express*, William Pollock said, 'Poor young Bill Edrich. He just cannot get going as an England opener in the Tests. A great many fine judges, including Don Bradman, believe that Edrich is an exceptionally gifted batsman but his repeated failures must be disheartening to him. Perhaps he would do better if he was lower in the batting order.' That is exactly what happened in the next game at Cape Town, which again ended in a draw, but the drop down the order did nothing for Edrich, who was bowled by Norman Gordon for a duck in his only innings. The next two Tests saw England go 1-0 up in the series, but Edrich contributed little, making just six runs the only time he batted. Hammond's faith in Edrich was beginning to look like dogma. 'Bill really ought not to have been in the side after the first three Tests,' said Jim Swanton. Before the Fourth Test, Geoffrey Simpson wrote in the *Daily Mail*:

We know that it is not lack of ability that causes his downfalls. It's his temperament that beats him and Edrich alone can conquer it. No cricketer can expect more opportunities than he has been given. People in Lancashire and Yorkshire write me to say that 'Edrich is persevered with because he's Middlesex.' That is the feeling in many places so Edrich owes it to the authorities at St John's Wood, as well as to himself, to put up a show this time. I am sure the selectors champion his cause for no other reason than their belief in Edrich. England has a star of uncommon brilliance; but if he doesn't shine now he will have to go.

But the distinguished sports commentator Howard Marshall doubted that the problem was psychological. 'He just has had no luck at all and the odd thing is that to meet him, you would imagine that he has the ideal temperament for the big occasion. Perhaps he has and depressing though his Test match record is, he remains a very fine player and his day must surely come,' wrote Marshall in the *Bystander*.

Edrich later wrote that he worried 'whether or not I had passed the summit of a short and unsuccessful career and would be one of the fairly numerous players who start brilliantly and then fade out'. The Irish journalist Bryan Egan, writing in the *Dublin Evening Herald* in 1987, recalled running into Edrich at a Middlesex party in the early 1950s when he was an established international player. Egan suggested to Edrich that 'he must have reached the stage when anything and everything seemed possible'. Edrich laughed and said, 'Whenever I start thinking like that, I remember the bad days. There was a time when I genuinely began to wonder if I would ever make a big Test score. I had almost given up hope.' His plight became so desperate that, at one point, he even took the drastic step of cutting down on his consumption of alcohol and tobacco. But he could never be a puritan. One of the antidotes to his despair was the solace of female company, and his odyssey across the sun-kissed land of South Africa, far from the domesticity of life with Betty in Acton, offered him plenty of chances for liaisons. What made his romantic episodes so striking was his openness about them. At one official function, he turned up with a well-endowed woman called Roxy, whom he described as his 'masseuse' and whom the *Rand Daily Mail* called his 'bosom friend'. With a note of mild but amused disapproval, Swanton said that this was 'not an entirely isolated fall from grace'. There was no sense of any disapproval from Hammond, who was conducting his own affair with Sybil Ness-Harvey, once dubbed 'the most beautiful woman in South Africa' and later to be his second wife after his divorce from Dorothy Lister.

Hammond's sympathetic admiration was undimmed even as the Fifth and final Test approached at Durban in March 1939, where gossip about Edrich's extra-marital gymnastics was common currency. At the city's only nightclub, the band leader mocked Bill's personal life as he indulged in some light-hearted wordplay about members of the England team. 'He Edrich his wife, but didn't bring her to Durban', went one rather feeble line. According to a later account given by Edrich to the Norfolk and Essex batsman Graham Saville, Hammond felt some pleasurable relaxation would take Bill's mind off his troubles: 'Bill told us how, before the Fifth Test, he was called to Hammond's room. He was expecting Hammond to say, "Well Bill, you've had enough chances, I'm leaving you out." Instead, Hammond told him to go down to Durban early and forget about cricket. So he did as he was instructed and arrived in the city a few days before the Test. "I did have rather a nice girlfriend there. We spent the time together, enjoying ourselves. We lived on sex and oysters."'

Again, there was no attempt to hide the relationship, as Jim Swanton noted during the Test itself: 'One of the singularly pretty girls in which Durban abounded used to pick him up and take him for a swim while in the evening one could always make do with oysters at Umshlonga Rocks. There was no shortage of amusement and hospitality.'

The Fifth Test was to mark a crucial turning point in Edrich's career, but it did not start any more promisingly for him than his previous internationals. With the visitors still 1-0 up in the series, the governing bodies of South Africa and England had agreed that the match would be played to a finish, regardless of how long it took. But far from producing decisive cricket, this 'timeless' format was a recipe for extreme caution, made worse by a rock-hard, flat pitch at Kingsmead. Batting first at a sedate pace, South Africa took almost three days to compile 530, their highest Test score; in the nine wicketless overs he bowled, Edrich showed even less capacity for penetration than his colleagues. In response, England had limped to 169 when the fourth wicket fell, bringing Edrich to the crease. Having stuck his neck out so far, Hammond felt an immense sense of responsibility as the Middlesex player began his innings, as he vividly described it: 'I sat watching him from the pavilion, wishing like mad for a whisky and soda to brace myself. It was a moment of real crisis for me. I had put Edrich into the team for that Test right against his form and advice. He had been no good in the previous Tests in South Africa and I believed in him. I sat there glaring across the sunny grass, past the white figures of the fieldsmen who closed in significantly. I saw Bill take his guard nervously and tentatively touch a bail.'

Edrich had made just a single when he had to face another over from the brisk medium-pacer Arthur 'Chud' Langton, South Africa's best bowler. Hammond continued his account: 'The ball came down. Bill thrust at it nervously and hit up a little schoolboy catch which was taken easily. There was a sharp clatter of clapping. With a sinking heart I felt I had lost my gamble.'

Edrich's 1 was the lowest score as England reached 316 on the fifth morning. Even though South Africa had a lead of 214, their captain Alan Melville did not enforce the follow-on, but batted a second time, with the aim of exhausting the opposition. When his side was finally all out for 481 towards the end of the sixth day, England had a target of 696 to win, far beyond anything that had ever been achieved in the fourth innings of a Test match. That evening, sensing he had nothing to lose, Edrich decided to cut himself loose from the ascetic regime he had adopted early in the tour. Worse than ineffective, it seemed to be counter-productive because it deepened his nervousness. He signalled his freedom from the shackles of alcoholic restraint by attending a party hosted by Tuppy Owen-Smith, the former South African all-rounder with whom he had played at Middlesex, at the Athlone Gardens nightclub, just a rickshaw ride away from the England hotel. He did not finally make it to bed until the early hours of the morning, and he was said to still be smiling broadly when he was woken up by some England teammates the next day.

In the Kingsmead pavilion, as Hutton and his fellow Yorkshireman Paul Gibb opened for England, Hammond boldly decided on one last throw of the dice for Edrich. Instead of shielding him, he moved him up the order to Number 3 with an injunction to be aggressive. 'Don't be afraid of them, Bill. If you can see them, hit them right from the start,' Hammond told him. Then the skipper added, 'If you can get a couple of hundred, we might stand a chance.' More unorthodox support came from the England and Worcestershire fast bowler Reg Perks, playing his only Test of the series, who handed Edrich a tiny white elephant and said, 'Here Bill, put this in your pocket. It will bring you luck.' The charm, along with Hammond's words, appeared to inspire Edrich, who went in just before lunch at the fall of Hutton's wicket and almost immediately hit two fours. The interval seemed temporarily to jolt his confidence at the start of the afternoon session. 'For two or three overs he was nervous and erratic,' recalled Hammond, 'but then he suddenly got going again.' Showing more positive intent than any previous English batsman, he made the fastest 50 of the match, then consolidated in assured style as he moved towards his first Test century and the South African bowling attack tired. The milestone was reached after Edrich had been batting for just over three hours and, according to *Wisden*, was greeted by 'a rather remarkable scene when high up on the balcony shouts of triumph came from his colleagues'. The experience was deeply moving for Edrich, as he remembered in a 1947 interview: 'I shall never forget that moment. The South African crowd had taken a kindly interest in my bad luck. Now they cheered me and went on cheering. All the South African team gathered round to give me a pat on the back.' In the *Daily Express*, William Pollock wrote that 'nothing has been more cheering in this grand England fight than the last-ditch century of Bill Edrich'. It was 'no exaggeration to say that his whole future hung on success or failure today and the gods decided it was time they smiled on him'. The *Daily Mail*'s Geoffrey Simpson claimed to be 'genuinely pleased that Edrich had come off at last', but felt that he had been 'a lucky young man. His case is the most remarkable in Test cricket. No other young batsman had been chosen for a ninth consecutive Test after failing in eight matches.'

When bad light ended play prematurely, Edrich was still there on 107, while England's total of 253 for 1 held out the prospect that Hammond's team could pull off a sensational win. The gloom gave way to a series of downpours on the eighth day and second Saturday of this draining marathon, so no play was possible. As the match dragged on, a new element of potential urgency entered the equation, for the England party was booked to take the express train from Durban on the following Tuesday night to Cape Town, ready to board the *Athlone Castle* so they would be back in England for the start of the cricket season. The 'Timeless Test' might not be timeless after all. On Day Nine, a Monday, Edrich progressed serenely to a double-century, having batted for six and a half hours and hit 23 fours, 'a brilliant innings' in the words of Hammond. When he returned to the England dressing room at tea, the team manager Jack Holmes was waiting for him with a glass of champagne. 'I hear you train on the stuff,' said Holmes as he handed the glass to Edrich, who quickly drank it and then had another. Changing his sodden socks, he admitted that he was 'thoroughly fagged', a point confirmed soon after the resumption when he played a tired shot to Langton and was caught at short leg for 219.

His epic innings had brought England to within touching distance of an unbelievable win. But this was far more than just a monumental, record-breaking innings. It was an act of redemption that wiped Edrich's slate clean, repaid the faith of Hammond and the selectors, ended months of humiliation, silenced his critics and offered new hope for the future. 'The crowd loved him for that last-minute comeback and he got one of the biggest ovations of the tour,' said Hutton. Edrich's Middlesex teammate Denis Compton, who had not been able to make the tour because of his commitment to Arsenal, sent him a telegram of congratulations on 'a great performance'. Another Middlesex legend, Patsy Hendren, said he was 'very glad young Bill Edrich got those runs. I knew he would some time – he is good enough.' The Lancastrian Eddie Paynter called it 'the most amazing innings of the tour', accomplished 'with style and authority and seasoned with a fair measure of guts'. The display of valour was the key for Plum Warner: 'When one realises the rough seas he had encountered for so long, his coming into his own again was a rare tribute to his courage.' At the height of his fame after the war, Edrich singled out his 219 at Durban as his 'greatest moment'.

Unfortunately, after his personal triumph, the match ended on a slightly farcical note. Just 42 runs short of the target with five wickets left, England had to give up their quest when rain started to fall so heavily that there was no chance of a restart before the visitors had to leave for their boat train. It was an anticlimactic end to cricket's longest match and the last ever 'Timeless Test', which had involved 43 hours and 16 minutes of playing time, 1,981 runs and 5,447 deliveries. Neither worn-out players nor weary spectators had any appetite for this version of the sport, especially when it failed in its central purpose of achieving a clear result. In his diary of the tour, Ken Farnes wrote: 'As day followed day and we trooped in and out of the pavilion, the whole performance became somewhat ludicrous.' Hammond, a winning captain on his first overseas tour, sounded the death knell in a verdict with which most of the public and the cricket world agreed: 'I don't think Timeless Tests are in the best interests of the game and I sincerely hope that the last one has been played.'

Nothing could put a dampener on Bill Edrich's relief and happiness. He celebrated in style on the long, overnight rail journey from Durban to Cape Town, and later, when asked whether it was true that he had drunk champagne throughout the trip, he replied with a twinkle, 'Undoubtedly – and I can't possibly remember.' The revelries continued on the voyage home aboard the *Athlone Castle*. Even a raging storm at sea could not deter him from holding an early 23rd birthday party, during which he noticed that Hammond had 'for company a well-upholstered young American lady who was wearing a low-cut dress and a diamond tiara and was telling him how much she wanted him to bowl a maiden over. I think we'd earned our night out because it wasn't as if any of us got rich from the tour. When everything was added up I got about £200 in the bank for five months' work.' Edrich further reflected that he had 'a great time' on the ship. 'At least everyone told me I did. Somebody stuck a Red Indian headdress on my bonce and when I woke up that's all I was wearing. Luckily we were crossing the Equator later that day and we greeted it in fancy dress.' His sense of euphoria was enhanced by the large number of prospective brides who were travelling to England in search of romance or marriage, as Swanton again noted: 'Bill Edrich was a lively young fellow at the time and I daresay he added to his winter's score, as it were.'

But soon it was back to the realities of his own home life and England under the shadow of a looming war. On the very day that the England team travelled by train into Cape Town, Hitler's armies marched into Prague, making a mockery of the Munich agreement and conflict in Europe an inevitability.

4

THE SHADOW OF WAR
1939–1941

'A bon viveur who would have been in his element in the more riotous days of Hollywood.'

Trevor Bailey

The warm glow of success in the final Test inevitably coloured Edrich's memories of the 1938–39 trip to South Africa. 'I never remember a tour I liked better,' he later wrote. Away from the cricket, the team were taken down diamond and gold mines, watched Zulu war dances, went salmon fishing on a boat, undertook hare hunting at night, viewed exotic wildlife, and visited historic sites and natural wonders. They also met the great statesman Jan Christian Smuts, the former Boer leader who was soon to be a key figure in Winston Churchill's wartime government, though his prescience in early 1939 was far from infallible, according to Edrich's account. 'He talked about cricket while we were much more anxious to ask him about the political situation. In the end one of us did manage to ask him if he thought Hitler meant business in Europe. The General's face clouded and he told us there would be no war, as the German economy could not stand the strain.' Even at the time, Edrich was deeply unconvinced by this assessment.

Such sombre thoughts could not detract from his enjoyment of South Africa. 'Doubts and fears were overridden by daily pleasures,' wrote Edrich. His never-ending mission for entertainment during the tour was noted by South African bowler Norman Gordon, who in 2011 became the first male Test cricketer to reach the age of 100: 'I actually went out socially with Bill a few times. It is fair to say he was a bit wild but he was also a very nice chap and modest too.' But for Bill's young wife Betty, life was much tougher and more austere. While her husband galivanted through the Veldt and champagne-filled nightclubs, she was left to cope on her own at Perryn Road in Acton. Altogether he was away from home for more than five months, having been in India for even longer during the previous winter. Betty's exasperation at these drawn-out absences led her to publicly express her concern that her husband was 'burning himself out' by playing cricket all the year round. Her solution would be for him 'to go back to Spurs' in the winter months, while in the immediate term she tried to lessen her loneliness with visits to her parents in Bournemouth and to her in-laws at Heacham in Norfolk.

In fact, she had just come from Bournemouth and was about to leave for Norfolk in mid-March 1939 when the reports came through of her husband's phenomenal innings at Durban. At her Acton home, she told journalists that she was 'thrilled by the news. I have met a number of local friends during my brief visit and have been congratulated on all sides.' She then further explained, 'I have just received a letter from my husband. It was posted last Monday after the match had started. It came by air mail. It seems funny to have read a letter about the beginning of the match that came all the way from South Africa and the match not yet over! In it, he said something about his luck "being out" and I'm glad it's changed.' Betty's yearning for normality was also clear in her comment that she was 'looking forward to his return' at the end of March, 'when they will settle down in Acton until his next call'. Her sense that Bill had exhausted himself was taken up by her local paper, the *Acton Gazette*, which reported that in other letters home to Betty, Bill 'had attributed the fact that he is not quite up to his usual form to physical fatigue. Last winter he was playing for England in India, and he has had to overcome the effects of travel and change of climate.'

Bill's return, however, was not the cue for a renewal of wedded contentment. Just the opposite was true. His liaisons in South Africa, especially his last relationship in Durban, had eroded his belief in the future of his marriage to Betty and he told her so frankly. In later legal proceedings, Betty said that from 1938 'there was trouble because of her husband's association with other women and because of an admission he made after his return from a cricketing tour of South Africa'. The disintegration of their union could not be concealed from

Edrich's parents, and when Bill went up to Norfolk, he was open about his feelings, as Ena noted in her private memoir. 'He told my mother and father that he had met "someone" in Africa, and wanted a divorce from Betty. My mother and father prevailed upon him to be sensible, and finally a reconciliation was effected. Their relationship changed, however, as all was changing all around.'

The awkward truce was partly achieved because Betty decided to forgive him, but Bill had no intention of changing his ways. If anything, his South African adventure had only whetted his appetite for new dalliances with an ever larger cast of female characters. In a later tour diary, the England fast bowler Frank Tyson generously ascribed the high failure rate of Edrich's marriages to 'his frequent absences abroad', but that was only a small part of the story. The deeper reason was Edrich's voracious appetite for amorous coupling, unbounded by restrictions of morality or logistics. His expectation of conquest became a self-reinforcing cycle, where his burgeoning confidence enhanced his appeal. According to the journalist Norman Giller, who knew him well, 'He had a force of personality, charisma and a twinkle in the eye that made any woman in his company melt. He was hardly tall, dark and handsome in the Compton mould, but he had a magnetism that could not be manufactured.'

According to the Middlesex wicket-keeper John Murray, as quoted in Christopher Sandford's 2019 biography, Bill was 'not exactly a monk before the war. Compton always swore that they once found Bill sleeping it off with a blonde round the back of the groundsman's hut before play began in 1938 or 1939. He still had his dinner jacket on, or at least they were using it as a blanket, although he had managed to lose his false teeth.' Another wicket-keeper, Hopper Levett of Kent, admitted that during the 1939 season he was 'quite struck by the amount Bill put away each night' at the bar of the Parrott Hall, where Middlesex stayed when they played at Canterbury, 'let alone what happened upstairs'.

His courtship technique could be brisk, stimulated by his determination to get to the heart of the action. 'He didn't even take off his cricket boots,' recalled one participant in a hurried tryst. In his superb book about the 1939 cricket season, Sandford recounted how, on one occasion, Edrich went to dinner with some Middlesex colleagues in a West End restaurant and 'emerged later than night with two statuesque lady companions, both taller than he was, one on either arm'. On another occasion that summer, some of the Middlesex team were driving down the A23 to a match at Hove. Sitting at the wheel of his own car, Edrich 'saw a pretty girl in the next lane, and waved at her. The girl waved back. Without a word, Edrich then pulled over and so did the girl. He calmly got in her car and that was the last that any of his county colleagues saw of him until a few minutes before the start of play the following morning, when, after a quick cigarette and a cup of coffee, he went out and scored 161.' Peter Willows, a resident of Hove who later became a councillor there, recalled how Edrich sometimes worked in league with Compton to entice women they had noticed at the Sussex ground. 'I used to go fagging for Bill Edrich and Denis Compton, getting cigarettes or passing little notes to the ladies who attended the matches.'

Like Edrich's own romantic life, there was a frenetic air to the 1939 season. The threat of the impending cataclysm lent a surreal edge to the cricket, the innocent frivolity of sport standing in graphic contrast to the grim preparations for total war, now made all the more terrifying by the new menace of mass aerial bombardment against cities. In his 1948 autobiography, Edrich wrote that, in this feverish atmosphere, cricketers 'went about our matches in the spirit of trying to get each one concluded before the outbreak'. Despite the darkening backdrop, it was a season that held out the promise of more success for Edrich, who felt he had learnt from his Durban double-century how to overcome his nerves, be more aggressive at the start of an innings and show a willingness to take the initiative.

After a barren opening few weeks of the new season, he began to display solid if not scintillating form, hitting seven centuries for Middlesex in the County Championship and achieving an overall first-class aggregate of 2,186 runs at an average of 49.68. As *The Cricketer* pointed out, in every season since he had qualified for Middlesex, Edrich 'has scored 2,000 runs, a feat which few, if any, former England cricketers have achieved'. Particularly noteworthy was a hundred he hit at Lord's on a soft pitch against a Lancashire attack that contained fast bowler Dick Pollard, leg-spinner Len Wilkinson and slow left-armer Len Hopwood, all of whom played for England. In keeping with his new, more defiant approach, Edrich refused to be intimidated by the opposition, conditions or scoreboard pressures. Having reached 90, he 'positively tore along to the century mark; nor would I ease up then, but hit hard at everything I dared till I reached 125'. Far less effective was his fast bowling, which fell away badly; his haul of just 15 wickets cost 51.28 runs each. The Somerset and England batsman Arthur Wellard, a renowned hitter of sixes, felt that Edrich's theatrics had more of an impact than the quality of his deliveries: 'He was a little slinger whose preferred style was to hurl the ball down as fast as he could.' He then followed through halfway down the pitch, 'muttering all the way and if you came out of your crease to play him, you were always likely to meet the little bugger head-on'.

Nor was Edrich's exuberant off-field behaviour universally popular with his colleagues. During a visit to play Wellard's Somerset side at Frome, he drank himself unconscious in the early evening, and then had to be wheeled in a barrow to the Austin Seven motor car that belonged to the Middlesex player Laurie Gray, so he could be taken back to London in advance of his county's fixture against Yorkshire the next day. Once in the car, which also contained the Middlesex spin bowlers Jim Sims and Ian Peebles, he awoke from his somnolent state and began to run through some of his operatic favourites, forcing Sims into a desperate measure: 'It was a bloody long drive home,' Sims recalled, 'and I had to shove a handkerchief in his gob when he started singing arias from *Madame Butterfly*.' Years later Trevor Bailey, the England all-rounder, described Edrich as 'a bon viveur who would have been in his element in the more riotous days of Hollywood'; he always 'considered that a good party should never end before dawn', and one of the methods he deployed to prevent any break-up was by singing. 'His memory for lyrics was considerably more impressive than his vocal powers. The Edrich voice was an off-beat husky whisper,' said Bailey. Cricket folklore holds that these late nights did not undermine his performance. As his Middlesex teammate Denis Compton put it, 'Bill would be the last to say that he ever acquired the habit of going to bed very early but his greatness as a cricketer was never affected.' But that was not entirely true. After his sozzled trip back from Frome, Edrich was out for 1 and 9 against Yorkshire, falling both times to Bill Bowes. Similarly, playing for the MCC against the visiting West Indians at Lord's in May, his only innings had been a reckless one of just 17; he later confessed that he was suffering from a bad hangover and his fear of vomiting on the pitch had compelled him to hit out wildly rather than play himself in.

Reports of Edrich's indiscipline did not help to ensure his inclusion in the England team that summer in the three-match Test series against the West Indies. Crucially the make-up of the selection committee had altered significantly, and not to Edrich's advantage. Now aged 65, the former chairman Plum Warner, his greatest defender at Lord's, had resigned and been replaced as a selector by the Sussex captain Flight Lieutenant Jack Holmes, nicknamed 'Sherlock'. Holmes had been the manager of the recent South African tour and had therefore witnessed Edrich's poor form and peccadilloes at close hand. The new chairman was the reticent, unsentimental Percy 'Peter' Perrin, a successful businessman who had enjoyed a long career as an amateur with Essex and was often described as the greatest batsman who never played for England. Despite these changes, Edrich might have expected to stay in the England team, given that he had finally come good in Durban after being persevered with for so long. But his early performances for Middlesex had been erratic and the new committee was keen to experiment with other promising batsmen such as Harold Gimblett, Arthur Fagg, Walter Keeton and Norman Oldfield. Before the First Test in June, *The Daily Worker* maintained that 'Edrich has been surprisingly off-form this season' and 'simply could not be picked'. Even when the runs began to flow, he was still omitted from the team, much to his indignation. 'I was attempting to prove to the Selectors, who were blind, deaf and dumb as far as I was concerned, that I still had cricket in me,' he said. The sense of injustice drove him to new heights of productivity, with the result that in his last 15 innings of the season, he scored 979 runs at an average of almost 70. In the *Sunday Express*, the chief sportswriter Laddie Lucas, later an RAF hero and politician, voiced his bewilderment at the selectors' stance. 'I was never an ardent supporter of Edrich as an England bat, but to see the fellow justify himself and then, in the next match be passed over makes one wonder if there is any logic left in the world. I wonder what Sir Pelham Warner would have had to say were he still Chairman of the Selection Committee,' wrote Lucas. Warner confined himself to a mild rebuke in the pages of *The Cricketer*: 'It is a unique experience for a cricketer to play an innings of 219 in a Test match and then not be chosen for any one of the series immediately after so outstanding an effort,' though he was more critical of the selectors in his 1943 book *Cricket Between Two Wars*, where he argued that Edrich's omission was 'not logical' and he 'should have been given another chance'.

Yet this row paled into insignificance as the drumbeat of war grew ever louder. In the capital it was impossible to ignore the indicators of the coming titanic struggle. Trenches were dug in the parks, sandbags placed round buildings, gas masks distributed to the citizenry, pillboxes erected in the streets and barrage balloons sent into the skies. Bill's native Norfolk bristled with anti-aircraft batteries, searchlights and radar pylons. Cricket was directly affected by the crisis, despite the assertion of Neville Cardus that the game was 'a haven of peace in an unruly world'. During the Lord's Test, Wally Hammond made an appeal over the public address system for men to enlist in the armed forces, while plans were made for the RAF to take over the ground as a recruiting and training centre. But even as the last faint hopes of peace vanished with the signing of the Nazi-Soviet pact and the escalation of Hitler's threats to Poland, the counties continued with their fixtures. This produced the incongruous juxtaposition on 30 August of spectators in the Long Room at Lord's applauding a century by Bill Edrich for Middlesex against Warwickshire at the very moment when maintenance staff were removing historic paintings and a bust of W.G. Grace to safety.

The hour of destiny had almost arrived. On 3 September, following Hitler's invasion of Poland, Prime Minister Neville Chamberlain made his fateful broadcast to announce that 'Britain is at war with Germany'. In Norfolk, Bill's brothers Eric and Geoff were engaged in a match with a local wandering side at the country estate of Captain Michael Trubshaw, a successful but eccentric actor who ran his own cricket team and was a close friend of the Hollywood star David Niven. Shortly before play began, a servant brought out a portable radio to the field so both sides could hear the Prime Minister's address. Having come along as a spectator to watch her brothers and relatives, Ena, still just 14, was moved by the scene, as she wrote in her memoir: 'An air of excitement, even rightness of purpose, surrounded all those young men that day.' Geoff had been increasingly productive with Norfolk all season, scoring

614 runs at an average of 47, and he had made a deep impression on Giles Baring, the amateur Hampshire pace bowler and a well-connected member of the famous banking family. Like his county captain Lord Tennyson, Baring was reckless with money, overly fond of alcohol and an enthusiastic romancer of women. But respect for his judgement was such that when he recommended Geoff Edrich to the Hampshire Committee, the county immediately offered him a contract for the 1940 season. Unfortunately, the intervention of the war meant that the offer could not be taken up and Geoff was soon enrolled in the 5th Battalion of the Royal Norfolk Regiment. Yet this was not the last time that Giles Baring was to have an influence on the cricketing prospects of an Edrich family member. After the war, he played a far bigger part in an unexpected change of course in Bill's Middlesex and England career. Of Bill's other two brothers, Eric was in a reserved occupation as an agricultural worker on his parents' estate and Brian was too young to be called up, though he too planned to work on the family farm now that he had left school.

At Lord's, Bill listened to Chamberlain's broadcast with some of his colleagues. He knew it signalled the abrupt end of the season. The West Indians' tour had already been abandoned, the first time that had happened in Test cricket, and the visitors had sailed from Greenock on the Clyde on 26 August. Now the remaining first-class fixtures were cancelled, including those at the champagne-soaked Scarborough Festival, one of Edrich's favourite events of the year. England's planned tour of India that winter, under the captaincy of Jack Holmes, was also cancelled, though that did not affect Edrich, who had not been selected for the team that had been named on 2 August. Some stars, like Hammond, had opted out of the Indian tour, but Edrich had not been given a choice. His was not a special case. Despite a schedule that included three full Tests, Holmes's side was wholly unrepresentative. Not one member of the England XI that appeared in the final Test against the West Indies at The Oval was included. In fact, Bob Wyatt was the only member of the side to have substantial Test experience, and even he had not played for England since 1937. Believing that the energies of the stars had to be preserved for the top series, the Lord's establishment did not send any full-strength sides to the subcontinent until the 1970s. The reluctance to pick the best was all the greater in August

1939 because England were due to undertake an Ashes tour in 1940–41, for which all resources would have to be mobilised.

In a contemplative mood after hearing the Prime Minister's address, Edrich walked out of the Grace Gates at the main entrance to the ground and began to stroll towards Baker Street underground station. Suddenly an air-raid siren sounded, as he later recounted: 'There was a horde of people rushing past me and wholesale panic as many of them poured down into the station . . . Men and women fought for seats on trains. All the platforms were jammed. A minute or two later a guard managed to climb up onto some steps and shouted out that it had been a false alarm. People broke out into loud applause. The guard jumped down and, as I walked past I heard a man in a dark suit mutter, "Bloody fools! If they only knew what they're cheering."'

Having left Baker Street, Edrich soon found himself on the still-crowded streets alongside an attractive woman. The tension and urgency generated by the advent of war led to a frisson of excitement between them. In a later account, he said they were aching 'to make love but were unable to afford a hotel room'. But neither financial impecuniousness nor the invasion of Poland was going to deter Bill from consummation. They therefore improvised. 'There were fireworks up against a tree in Regent's Park,' he revealed.

As a man of action and a patriot, Edrich was keen to be the frontline of military service, and he swiftly volunteered for the RAF. But this was the peak of the 'Phoney War' when British officialdom seemed gripped by inertia, so the wheels of recruitment turned with agonising slowness. In the long weeks after his application, he heard nothing. Determined to make himself useful, he went with Betty to stay at Heacham Manor, where he joined Eric and Brian in working on the family farm. But Bill not only wanted to fill his time; he also needed money, for without an England tour his income had shrunk. His financial anxiety shone through a letter that he sent from Norfolk on 20 October to Jimmy Cannon, his friend and a Lord's administrator: 'I have been up here since the middle of September, doing a bit on the farm and waiting for something to happen. However, as it does not look as if I will be called up yet, I am thinking of returning to town shortly and try and find myself a job. When shall we be getting the Middlesex bonus? And how much have I to come? I should very much appreciate a line from you about this and would also be interested to hear what is happening at Lord's.'

Progress of sorts appeared to have been made with the RAF in the following weeks, after he had applied directly for flying duties and undergone a physical examination, the precursor to assessment at the RAF recruitment centre for aircrews in Uxbridge. In mid-November he wrote again to Cannon:

I have now applied for entry to the RAF in the air crew section. I passed my initial medical and am waiting for instructions to go to Uxbridge for the final entry test. This may happen any day now but I don't expect that I shall actually start training until after Christmas. With this coming off, perhaps you could send my bonus here at the earliest possible date as I have several things to attend to before I can properly depart. In the meantime, I am putting in a bit of work on the farm and believe me it is not as easy going as cricket and shove ha'penny. Hoping you will oblige at the earliest possible moment.

Farming was not the only occupation that Edrich took up that autumn. In an intriguing twist, he fulfilled Betty's wish by returning to professional football – but not with Spurs, even though the club still had him on its retained list. As early as August, when he had learnt that he would not be touring with England in India, he decided to resume his role as an outside left. Consequently, he opened negotiations with Spurs, but, in another sign of his money troubles, he was unhappy with the terms that White Hart Lane offered him, partly because he was given no assurances about playing in the first team. Instead of trying his luck with another big club, he agreed a contract with Chelmsford City of the Southern League, then managed by Harry Warren, a former centre-half who was a competent but uninspiring lower-tier boss. Despite his limited record, Warren pulled off 'a notable capture', in the words of the *Essex Chronicle*. According to the well-informed weekend football paper from South Shields, 'Spurs did not want to lose Edrich. He is a forceful outside left.' But the key, reported the paper, was that Chelmsford offered him a guaranteed wage of £8 a week, then the maximum allowed by the Football League, and greater flexibility over his working hours: 'One of the reasons why he decided to sign for the Southern League side is that the club offered to allow him two or three days a week to attend to the affairs of a business in which he is interested.'

Throughout his adult life, Edrich was always seeking the great commercial project that would make him a fortune. The catalogue of initiatives that featured in this quest ranged from theft-proof security bags and instructional films to life insurance and poultry rearing. But in this period, his attention was focused on the development, sale and installation of concrete cricket pitches, which he viewed as being essential to the improvement of youngsters' batting techniques, because they could learn to play their strokes with confidence on even surfaces, whereas many state-school and local club grounds were of poor quality. Edrich's involvement with this enterprise came through his friendship with Eddie Ward, a cricket-mad entrepreneur from Acton, who also ran a private indoor coaching school in Chiswick. The arrival of war stopped Ward's firm from expanding, but both men felt there was a potentially lucrative market to be tapped once peace returned.

It was richly ironic that Edrich's debut for Chelmsford City was against Spurs at home on 23 September, 1939. In a captivating performance that lived up to Harry Warren's expectations, he helped the Essex club to a 4-2 victory with a number of aggressive runs down the wing and ferocious long-range shots, the most remarkable of which secured Chelmsford's fourth goal. The *Essex Chronicle* was ecstatic: 'The experiment of wartime football at Chelmsford is providing first-class play. The City's 4-2 win over Tottenham Hotspur was one of the best games ever seen on the ground. City excelled throughout and Spurs were well beaten. The chief interest, as far as Chelmsford were concerned, was on Edrich, the Middlesex and England cricketer, who made his first appearance for the club at outside left. He gave a grand display, although he had not played serious football for almost two years.'

Despite this fine start, Edrich's subsequent appearances were sporadic, due to a bout of ill-health and the difficulty of organising teams and fixtures during the wartime emergency.

More importantly, there was finally some movement on his hopes of flying. Having made enquiries, he learnt that the RAF was not taking aircrew entrants directly because the flying schools were overloaded, which explained the block on his application; but the way round this obstacle was to enter the service through a less popular branch and then remuster for flying duties. That is exactly what he did. In the New Year, 1940, he applied for the Physical Training Branch, and was at once accepted on to a course at Uxbridge, where the instructor in charge was none other than his Middlesex captain Walter Robins. It was just the stroke of luck Edrich needed. Robins ensured that his remustering to aircrew as a radio operator went through smoothly. Shortly before this, in an interview at Heacham with the *Daily Mirror* in February 1940, Edrich expressed his relief that his wait seemed to be over:

> With a gun slung under his arm, wearing typical country 'clobber' over a Middlesex sweater, Edrich is busy nowadays ridding his father's Norfolk farm of wood pigeons. 'It's just like old times,' William says. Soon after the war began he tried to join the Royal Air Force – and he's been trying ever since. 'At last it looks as though I've succeeded. I wanted to get in as a member of an air crew, but they told me I'd probably have to wait six months or more for a vacancy. That didn't suit me so I tried to join as a radio operator. That was more successful and I hope to be off in a fortnight or so.'

Once accepted for aircrew instruction, there followed a lengthy spell with the Initial Training Wing that took him first to Hastings on the Sussex coast, and then, when that resort was threatened by the Luftwaffe's bombs, to Torquay, which Edrich enjoyed much more, not least because a number of top-class cricketers were based in the town, among them Wally Hammond and Les Ames. The drudgery of training was therefore relieved by 'some exciting and entertaining cricket matches', made all the more appealing by the delight that ordinary club players took in dismissing a star or clobbering his bowling. 'I saw famous players more irreverently handled at Torquay than I have ever seen them at Lord's, Old Trafford or the Sydney Oval,' wrote Edrich. His own stature within the sport had been enhanced by the 1940 edition of *Wisden*, which named him as one of its Five Cricketers of the Year, partly in recognition of his Durban double-century, partly for his feat of scoring 2,000 runs in each of his first three seasons for Middlesex. *Wisden's* profile of him made the inevitable comparison with Denis Compton:

> It is fair to say that Compton has the greater range of strokes and is rather better balanced on his feet than his frequent partner who sometimes looks slightly awkward when playing back. One of Edrich's strong points is the way in which he hits fast bowlers back past themselves to the screen, either on the ground or in the air. His hook is now under firmer control than it was, he has a profitable cut and a most effective chop through the slips. Of somewhat short stature, he is nevertheless very strong, especially in the forearms. He generally gets at the bowling as quickly as he can and only very rarely is he not interesting to watch. His out-cricket adds to his value, for he is a useful fastish change bowler with a slinging action and is one of the best fieldsmen. He originally worked in the deep but last year was nearly always close to the wicket.

At the end of the summer of 1940, as the Battle of Britain reached its climax over southern England, Edrich was sent to a Flying Training School in Derby. By now he had switched to the role of bomber pilot rather than radio operator, and was immersed in the basics of aeronautics, though some skills he initially struggled to master. Squadron Leader George Watson, who later in the war helped to sink the mighty German battleship the *Tirpitz*, recalled seeing Edrich during his training course in 1940. 'His instructor told me, "He's all right, but he can't land properly." I said I'd teach him, and before long he had passed out as a Leading Aircraftman.' Once again Edrich's duties did not stop him playing cricket, and at a match between his unit and the local Repton public school, he encountered a 13-year-old pupil called Donald Carr, who made a deep impression on him. 'Here was a young cricketer of brilliant promise,' he thought, a judgement that was largely proved correct since Carr went on to play for England in 1951–52 and served as captain in one Test match against India. He also led Derbyshire successfully for seven seasons from 1955.

Once Edrich's Derby course was completed, he was commissioned as an RAF officer, then sent for operational training at RAF Upwood in Cambridgeshire.

The plane he was learning to fly was the twin-engined Bristol Blenheim bomber, which had been a pioneer when it first went into RAF service in 1937, with its all-metal stressed skin construction, variable pitch propellers, retractable undercarriage and powered dorsal gun turret. Yet the technology of military aviation was advancing so quickly that by the time Erich reached Derby the bomber was becoming obsolescent and was highly vulnerable to the latest German fighters, naval guns and anti-aircraft defences. Nevertheless, given the intense pressures on the RAF, Bomber Command had no alternative but to use the plane on its vital missions, which included attacks on German shipping and targets within the Reich.

The Blenheim typically carried a crew of three, made up of a pilot, navigator and wireless operator/air gunner. During Edrich's spell at Upwood, the two men he teamed up with were Lancastrian Ernie Hope, a wireless operator, and Londoner Vic Phipps, a navigator. On 21 May, 1941 the trio received instructions that they were to report to Bomber Command's 107 squadron based at Great Massingham in Bill's native Norfolk. A few weeks earlier, this order would have taken Bill near to the family home in Heacham, which lay just 26 miles north of Great Massingham, but actually, in yet another of those moves that could make the lives of tenant farmers so insecure, the owner of the Norfolk farm had decided to sell it. After some years of stability, the decision came as a blow. Fortunately, Bill's father was offered the management of a small farm on an estate in Buckinghamshire and the family made the move shortly before Bill and his two colleagues reported to Great Massingham. Built in 1940 as part of the RAF's rapid expansion programme, the station was a satellite of the nearby RAF West Raynham. Together they were both controlled by No. 2 Group of Bomber Command as part of the strategic air offensive against Germany, which had so far had little impact on the capacity of Hitler's war machine.

On his arrival at RAF Great Massingham, Edrich experienced a shudder of insecurity, just as he had done at Lord's when he was first on the groundstaff there. The sense of being an outsider, a legacy of being a Norfolk farmer's son, was strong in him. His first visit to the officers' mess reinforced those feelings. He later wrote, 'As I walked into the spacious hall, I could hear the sound of voices and the chink of glasses and for a moment I hesitated. Up to this moment I had been a pupil, the lowest of the low but with many hands ready to guide me. Now I was a Blenheim pilot, about to take part in the war. Would I measure up to it? What would the other fellows be like? Had I got what it takes?'

5

COMBAT OPERATIONS 1941–1945

'He must have had a powerful guardian angel.'

Squadron Leader R.S. Pritchard

Winston Churchill was in a sombre mood when he arrived at RAF West Raynham, the parent station of Great Massingham. In this first week of June 1941 the war was going badly. Crete had just fallen to the Nazis, the British army was in retreat in North Africa and shipping losses were mounting in the Atlantic due to the deadly packs of German U-boats. That troubled backdrop made the Prime Minister's visit all the more important as a morale booster. Its significance was revealed in the impressive line-up of aircraft and the full turnout of personnel, including Bill Edrich, that the RAF had organised at the base. One of Edrich's comrades, Flying Officer Lawrence Ewels, thought the Prime Minister 'looked very pale and tired'. Another member of 107 Squadron, Kenneth Wolstenholme, who went on to become a famous football commentator, struggled to hear Churchill's speech as it was being delivered in a packed hangar: 'The acoustics were dreadful. When he did speak, I was surprised how quiet he was, having heard this strong, resonant voice on the radio.'

In Edrich's own account, 'Churchill, wearing a light grey suit and carrying an unlighted cigar, mounted a set of servicing steps and addressed us.' His message was clear: the operations of No. 2 Group were vital for the fightback against Germany. They not only represented a form of direct retaliation for the German bombing of British cities, which had so far killed 43,000 civilians in the last year alone, but they also put the Nazis on the defensive. 'Germany must be forced to move her fighters westwards. Our purpose will be to relieve pressure on other fronts and to ease the stranglehold on our lifelines. I am relying on you,' he said, while he also lavished praise on the air crews for their bravery. With a typically Churchillian historical flourish he declared that 'the Charge of the Light Brigade is eclipsed in brightness by these almost daily deeds'.

Edrich was about to find out if he could live up to this tribute. He had always shown courage on the cricket field. Now he would have to display the same virtue in the fight for his nation's survival. An official Bomber Command paper about the anti-shipping offensive carried out by Blenheim squadrons like 107 in the summer of 1941 emphasised that 'the work is hazardous and calls for special qualities of determination'. After months of training and frustratingly long delays, Edrich, Phipps and Hope would experience the reality of those words as they finally went into action against the enemy. Previous histories of Edrich's war universally state that his first operational sortie took place on 7 June, the very next day after Churchill's visit to West Raynham. But the operational log book for 107 Squadron, now held at the National Archives in Kew, shows that in fact his crew was part of a 12-strong formation sent to bomb the airfield of Haamstede in the occupied Netherlands on 4 June. The leader of this group was the 107 Squadron commander Lawrence Petley, known as 'Petters', a thoughtful, reserved leader but also one whose resolution came to be doubted by his chiefs. Indeed, that very first attack was aborted. As the log book recorded, Edrich, Petley and four other bomber crews 'were forced to abandon their task and the others were not able to locate the primary target'.

Three days later, Edrich took part in a more successful mission when he was ordered, along with eight other Blenheim crews under the leadership of Peter Simmons, to make an attack on a large convoy that was sailing from Hamburg to Rotterdam. Preparing for take-off, with Phipps sitting next to him and Ernie Hope behind, Edrich began to roll forward at Simmons's signal. 'I was apprehensive, yet in a curious way I was also exhilarated,' he recalled. Quickly the Blenheim gathered momentum as it sped across the grass and then leapt into the sky. Flying close to Simmons's plane, Edrich took his Blenheim to a low level to avoid enemy radar once he had left the English coast. As he raced at under 100 feet above the water, he endured a moment of deep anxiety when his plane ran into thick cloud and he lost Simmons. Fearful that he was about to crash into the sea, he thought of abandoning the sortie. But eventually, to his relief, the cloud thinned and he caught sight of Simmons once more. Minutes later, Vic Phipps called out, 'There they are!' The convoy was just two miles ahead, dominated by a pair of large merchant vessels. At once, Simmons went on the attack against the larger of the two ships, climbing to 250 feet before he released his bombs, one of which scored a direct hit. Edrich could not afford to be a spectator at the scene. By now the Germans were unleashing a ferocious barrage at the Blenheims, much of it from a flak ship embedded in the convoy. Undaunted by his inexperience or the sight of the tracer fire heading towards his plane, Edrich carried on towards his target, the smaller of the merchantmen. At close range and from a height of 300 feet, he pressed his own gun button to direct a stream of bullets at the Germans manning the onboard anti-aircraft defences, then ordered Phipps to release the Blenheim's four 250-pound bombs. As the bombs plummeted towards the ship, a new danger suddenly emerged. 'I held on until I was sure they were gone. The deck of the merchant ship filled my windscreen. I felt certain we must hit her.' With astonishing coolness for a novice, he avoided calamity. 'I pulled back viciously on the stick and, with a prayer of thankfulness, we zoomed upwards, just in time to clear the masts.' The crew looked down on the stricken ship, which was starting to belch black smoke, before Edrich turned to port and took the Blenheim back down to a low level at the start of the return to Great Massingham. On landing safely at his base, he found that on his Blenheim 'a lot of the rudder had been shot away', but it was a rugged type that could take a lot of punishment. Edrich's comrade Bernard Marshall thought 'the Blenheim was a very fine aircraft. It could take an awful beating, but it did not carry a sufficient bombload, only 2000 pounds.'

Bill, too, had proved himself in combat. After that performance, there could be little doubt that he had the temperament and capability to be a bomber pilot. On all his missions, he always wore his England cricket sweater as a lucky mascot, but it was fearlessness as much as fortune that was the key to his survival. During the remainder of the month, he undertook nine more missions, with mixed success. A sweep over Calais on 14 June failed to detect any enemy shipping, while on a raid to Zeebrugge on 15 June he was, according to the squadron log book, 'unable to locate the primary target' and was 'hit by light flak'. Germany's invasion of the Soviet Union on 22 June (Operation Barbarossa) led Churchill to demand an intensification of aerial activity in Western Europe as a means of forcing Hitler to shift military resources from the Eastern Front. A favoured tactic was called 'Circuses', where RAF bombers, heavily escorted by fighters, mounted assaults on targets in occupied Europe to draw up German planes. At first, Edrich found these 'Circuses' less concerning than anti-shipping operations, but he reassessed that view after he was twice hit by flak.

A much bolder attempt to distract Germany and support the Soviet Union was made on 28 June, when ten crews from 107 Squadron, alongside another ten from 105 Squadron led by the Australian Hughie Edwards, were dispatched to Bremen, the Third Reich's second-largest port. It was a raid that, if completed, would require the Blenheims to fly over German territory for 150 miles, a scale of daylight penetration that had rarely been attempted before by Bomber Command. Lawrence Petley was again the leader, and this time his second-in-command was Edrich, an illustration of the confidence that the cricketer had already inspired barely a fortnight into his operational tour. As it turned out, Edrich had to take charge when the Blenheims were preparing for take-off at 4.30 in the morning and one of Petley's engines would not start. In an urgent message, Petley told him to lead the planes of 107 Squadron, meet up as planned with Hughie Edwards's 105 Squadron, and then head across the North Sea to the target. Petley explained that if he could resolve his engine trouble or find another plane, he would catch up with the formation. That is exactly what he did, and just after the Blenheims left the coast, Petley arrived at their head. But, on the approach to Bremen after more than two hours in the air, Petley began to feel that the risks of carrying on were too great. There was little cloud cover. The formation had lost its shape. Flak ships had opened fire, robbing the RAF of the element of surprise and ensuring that hordes of German fighters would soon arrive. Once he had decided that the attack would be a suicide mission, Petley abandoned the raid and led his planes back to Norfolk. There he was subjected to a brutal harangue on the telephone from the Commander of No. 2 Group, Air Vice Marshal Donald Stevenson, known as 'the Butcher' because of his willingness to tolerate extremely high casualty rates among the Blenheim crews on their low-level raids. His style of command, said pilot Dickie Leven, amounted to 'a gross misuse of air crews'. In his account, Edrich reflected on the nature of leadership: 'All eyes were watching "Petters" as he took the receiver. We saw his face blanche and tauten with anger and humiliation as he listened to the voice that we ourselves could not hear. In the silent ops room we were watching our leader be accused of cowardice and we knew that in Stevenson's mind we were all tainted with it. Watching "Petters" and remembering how nearly the leadership had fallen to me I wondered again what I would have done.'

But there was no question mark over Edrich's valour, which he demonstrated again on the next sortie, an attack on 30 June against the heavily defended fighter base on the German island of Sylt. This dangerous mission, which was to be led not by Petley but by the New Zealander Zeke Murray, was to act as a decoy for a raid by four-engined Halifax heavy bombers against Kiel. Edrich was in the leading vic – a formation of three aircraft flying in a V-shaped pattern – and the unit of Blenheims had to fly the whole way across the North Sea to the target, a distance of 360 miles. 'The long crossing at low altitude demanded intense concentration. Several times I felt my back stiffen up but it was impossible to relax,' Edrich recalled in his memoir. Soon after they had reached the island, the German guns opened up. 'Never have I seen such an inferno of firepower as was directed at us for the next few minutes. We not only had to fly through this hail of metal. We had to fly through plumes of water too. I shut my mind to everything and concentrated on Zeke's port-wing tip to my right. In close formation, we might present a better target, but I knew the heavier guns would have difficulty in ranging on us at low level.' Such protection was limited. By the time Edrich began his bombing run, the Germans had shot down two of the seven Blenheims that had arrived over the island and put another out of action. Even in this mayhem, the four operable bombers carried on with their task. Although Edrich struggled to see the detail of the target in the fog of combat, he still managed to drop his bombs on one of the buildings on the airfield before racing his plane out to sea. Once they were 100 miles from Sylt he thought the quartet of planes had escaped, but then they encountered the fighter defences on the island of Terschelling. Soon four Messerschmitt 109s were in pursuit of the Blenheim formation. With one of the German planes close on his tail and with its machine guns blazing, Ernie Hope opened up from the dorsal turret. 'We sniffed the rank stench of cordite. Ahead of me I could see the water bubbling and foaming as the bullets from the 109 churned the sea,' he wrote. The four Blenheims suffered repeated hits and their guns had soon jammed or run out of ammunition. Badly mauled, they appeared to be sitting ducks.

Destruction and death looked inevitable. But then the hand of fate made a dramatic intervention. Worried about their limited supply of petrol, which was always a problem with the Me 109, three of the German fighters turned back to Terschelling. One remained and 'was coming in for the kill'. Approaching from the port rear, it drew closer and closer. Yet to Edrich's astonishment, the pilot did not open fire. 'As he overtook us, he banked above me and I looked straight up into his face. His look of exasperation was unmistakable. He too had run out of ammunition. With a shrug of the shoulders, he turned away and headed south.' In another version, which he gave to his friend David Brocklehurst, Edrich said that the Messerschmitt pilot circled his plane twice and then for a moment they had been flying alongside each other. They exchanged waves before the German gave Edrich the thumbs up and flew home. In Edrich's view, the Luftwaffe pilot was convinced that the Blenheim was so badly damaged that it did not stand a chance of reaching England – and if it did, the crew deserved to survive for their fortitude. Edrich made it, along with the three other bomber crews that had escaped the fighter planes. At the Great Massingham airfield, they were talking animatedly about the trip when, to their astonishment, a fifth plane. which they thought had been lost over Sylt, came staggering in to land, its pilot having managed to drag the wrecked Blenheim across the North Sea aided by mental willpower, physical strength and a leather belt that strapped up the aileron controls. Edrich later wrote that the pilot, Dickie Leven, received 'an immediate decoration', though this is contradicted by Leven's own memoir: 'I was informed that I had been recommended for the VC but this was not awarded and I was not given a decoration.'

Leven was, however, awarded the Distinguished Flying Medal (DFM) at the end of 1941 for his heroics in combat, followed by the Distinguished Flying Cross (DFC) in 1944. His mix of innovation and resolve was characteristic of Blenheim squadrons in the face of daunting odds. An official report by the RAF Inspector General on 30 June declared that these air crews 'have been doing remarkably good and successful work from a very low altitude. The greatest credit is due to the crews for the determination and boldness with which their attacks have been pressed home and to the Command for their enterprising initiative.' But Air Vice Marshal Stevenson, the Commander of No. 2 Group, felt that, for all the men's bravery, the Blenheim was not a suitable aircraft for the low-level anti-shipping role and he asked instead for a unit of Hawker Hurricanes, fitted out as dive bombers. 'Low-level attack with Blenheims against armed ships is definitely unsatisfactory and wasteful,' Stevenson wrote to the Air Staff, though no change was made that summer.

The whole experience had been a draining one for Edrich. One airman told him, 'We thought you'd had it, sir.' Another said he 'looked like a ghost'. Eager for a change and some rest, Edrich took the leave he was due and spent a week in the Wye Valley, not with his wife Betty, but with a female companion that he had met at Great Massingham. At the end of his break, he returned to his base. Immediately his sense of reinvigoration evaporated as he learnt that much of 107 Squadron had been wiped out in a further raid on Bremen. But the fight had to continue. On 10 July, flying in support of 21 Squadron, he took part in an attack on the French port of Cherbourg, dropping his bomb successfully on a large dockside warehouse. In an account for the *Sunday Express* in 1974, he recalled the French delight at the appearance of the RAF overhead: 'I distinctly saw French civilians waving handkerchiefs at us from the fields and gardens. I also saw a German gun crew running to their gun and I shouted to Ernie Hope, my rear gunner, to let them have it. I didn't see the result, but we weren't fired at.' In recognition of his sterling contribution, Edrich was now promoted to the rank of Flight Lieutenant, but as he wrote laconically, 'Senior rank conferred no benefits of invulnerability. We lost six commanders in one week. We became almost inured to the almost daily recital of casualties.' In fact, on 12 July, the new squadron commander of 107, Arthur Booth, was killed in an anti-shipping operation off Holland. Apart from cargo ships, Bomber Command also wanted to attack innocent-looking 'spotter' vessels, which were used by the Germans to provide radio and radar warnings of enemy movements. According to the log book, during this sortie, 'Edrich attacked a 160-foot sail boat believed to be a reporting vessel but the bombs overshot by 10 yards.' His aim was more accurate a week later, on 19 July, when he 'scored a hit' on an 80-ton sailing vessel off the Hook of Holland.

Towards the end of July, Edrich was sent for a brief spell to Manston in Kent to support operations in the English Channel, aimed at deterring German vessels from sailing through the Strait of Dover. Despite waiting in readiness for several days, he was never sent into action, though he enjoyed one raucous party in the evening there, which was made livelier by the presence of some American RAF volunteers and the extroverted, aristocratic West Raynham commander, Paddy Bandon, whose official title was the Earl of Bandon. 'He was always tremendous fun,' wrote Bill, for whom conviviality was a survival mechanism. 'Even in our worst moments, morale remained high, and I'm quite sure that the frequent high-spirited parties which were a feature of squadron life did a lot to maintain it,' he wrote in the *Sunday Express*. But some of the more exuberant gatherings carried physical risks. One night Bill ended up at the bottom of a massed, collapsed scrum between two squadrons and he ended up with a neck injury that was to plague him for much of his cricketing career. Other occasions were more genteel. About eight miles from Great Massingham was the Crown Hotel in Fakenham, the main attraction of which for Bill and his comrades were the proprietors' three glamorous daughters, nicknamed 'The Crown Jewels'. To the sound of gramophone records, Bill and his friends would dance with the girls, and 'when it got past closing time, the police turned a blind eye'.

But there was a moment of more serious business to attend to at the Manston party. Paddy Bandon drew Edrich to one side to tell him in confidence that he had been promoted to Squadron Leader and was to be posted to 21 Squadron based at nearby Watton as the commander of A Flight. 'I had gone from Pilot Officer to Squadron Leader in 19 days,' wrote Edrich. But he was not overawed by his new role. 'For my own part, I felt fully capable of carrying out the duties of a Flight Commander in 2 Group. I liked the responsibility and even enjoyed it.' His first fortnight in charge was occupied in rebuilding his new squadron, which had been severely battered in the previous weeks. As he recalled, 'there were new crews to train and new tactics to learn. A half-sunken ship in the Wash provided us with a practice target, and I took my crews out on low-level formation flying daily, gradually whipping them into shape. Careering round East Anglia at tree-top height was a thrilling experience and the crews soon began to enjoy it.' The practice became more focused when he was briefed about his next mission, which was to be by far his most important and ambitious yet. In line with the RAF's strategy of giving support to the Soviet Union by forcing Germany to defend vital parts of its infrastructure at home, the Air Staff had decided to mount a daring, low-level daylight raid on the Ruhr valley near Cologne against two large power stations that housed Europe's largest steam generators and supplied 20 per cent of the power in this huge industrial region. The attack was audacious in conception and massive in scale. It would involve 72 bombers, mainly Blenheims, and 314 fighter planes, and would be supported by a major Circus operation against St Omer on the French coast.

In preparation for this enormous task, all anti-shipping strikes were suspended, while the air crews held dummy runs over St Neots power station in Cambridgeshire. So realistic and intense was this specialised training that no fewer than seven Blenheims were lost or damaged in the run-up to the raid. The attack was to be made by two waves of bombers: the larger group of 36 had the station at Knapsack as their target; the smaller group of 18, whose number included Edrich, was to hit the plant at Quadrath. Divided into three boxes of six planes each, this formation was to be led by 21 Squadron's chief, Wing Commander Owen 'Daddy' Kercher, whose luxuriant handlebar moustache fulfilled the classic image of the wartime RAF officer. Although Bill, usually warm-hearted to others, said that 'I never got very close to Kercher', other airmen described their leader as 'quiet, decisive, considerate and absolutely calm'. On the morning of the raid, 12 August, the atmosphere among the crews was tense. In a revealing memoir, Charles Patterson, who called himself, unfairly, 'a fundamental coward', recalled how he was weighed down by the recognition that 'statistically the chances of survival were negligible. The only thing to do was to say to myself that I'm not coming back and live with it.' Patterson rose at six, had breakfast and then went out to the dispersal area. 'It was the only time I remember seeing some of my crew grey and shaking. Seeing the others so frightened bolstered me a bit.'

At 8 o'clock the raiders took to the sky from Watton, joining up with the other bombers and fighter escorts over the Suffolk coast. 'I had never seen so many aircraft flying together, stretching as far as the eye could see. It was exhilarating,' recalled Sergeant Jim Langston of 21 Squadron. Because of their limited range, the fighters could not accompany the bombers all the way to the target. Once Kercher's planes were over Germany, they were on their own. Yet as they approached the target, there was no sign of action from any German fighter defences. Complete surprise appeared to have been achieved by flying at low level. Soon the chimneys of the two power stations could be seen in the distance, with the magnificent medieval twin towers of Cologne Cathedral behind them. Edrich left this memory of going into action against the Quadrath plant: 'With four 250-pound, 11-second delay bombs each, we had to clear the target in fairly quick time. My box was going in last. At St Neots, we had got everyone across the target in less than three seconds. Could we manage it now? The tall chimneys of the power station stood out ominously, forcing us up to 400 feet and more. The three sections were stepped up slightly from front to rear. There was some light flak coming up from the target area but otherwise we were unopposed.'

Keeping in tight formation, Edrich dropped the bombs successfully and as he flew away he could see the core of the power station in flames. Without incident, his Blenheim sped over Germany, but trouble began when he came near the Belgian coast. Over the Schelt estuary, he first ran into a thunderstorm, followed by an encounter with a huge flock of wading birds, then heavy flak from coastal batteries and finally an attack by Messerschmitt 109s. With his plane damaged, Edrich managed to reach his base, as did Patterson, who wrote that reaching the English coast was 'the greatest moment of elation I ever experienced in my life'. Others were not so lucky. Of the 54 bombers that took part in the Cologne raid, 12 did not return, while 25 crewmen lost their lives. It was a rate of attrition that would have wiped out the whole of No. 2 Group in a fortnight. Nor were the results as spectacular as hoped, despite the wreckage that Bomber Command researchers estimated would reduce the output of electricity by at least 10 per cent. Photo reconnaissance showed that the turbine sheds in the power stations, which were key targets, had not been hit.

Nevertheless, the attack was a political and propaganda triumph which, after months of retreat, showed that Britain was willing to challenge the previously impregnable Nazi war machine. In a post-war interview Sir Ivor Broom, who had served in 107 Squadron, described the operation as 'one of the most memorable raids of the war and the first deep penetration by a major force into Germany in daylight. We lost 25 men but we gained a lot of publicity.' Recognition of the achievement also came in decorations. Three of the commanders were awarded the Distinguished Service Order, and the leaders of the boxes of six, including Bill Edrich, received the Distinguished Flying Cross. His citation read: 'This officer had the difficult task of bringing his formation in to attack the main power station immediately after the leading box had attacked. This needed fine judgement as it was imperative that the target should be bombed from as low an altitude as possible. He had to delay his attack in order to avoid his formation being destroyed by explosions from the delay-action bombs of the previous boxes. This required coolness and courage.' The document concluded, 'by carrying out his orders with the greatest exactitude, he must be given credit for a large part of the success of the attack'.

Towards the end of his life, Denis Compton said, 'I cannot believe that a braver man than W.J. walked on to a cricket field. He showed his courage time and again during his wartime bombing missions when he continually cheated death.' The award of the DFC to Edrich was not only tangible proof of that heroism, it also refuted the idea that his temperament was too soft for Test cricket. The *Daily Mirror* pointed out that during his run of poor international form before the war, his detractors sneered that 'he was jumpy and nervy and too easily put off his strokes'. Now Edrich, declared the paper on 13 September 1941 soon after his DFC had been announced, had 'persevered to make liars of them all . . . Squadron Leader Edrich has proved his critics wrong.' His growing authority as an airman was also noted by Frank Butler of the *Daily Express* when he visited Watton in late August on the day that Edrich led an anti-shipping strike: 'I turned to see a young, squat airman plodding towards us. He appeared weighed down by his big boots and Mae West (life jacket) and the parachute that he carried under his arm. But there was something familiar about the determined, business-like stride which obviously meant trouble for somebody.' The public enhancement of his reputation was matched by the respect he had already won among his fellow airmen. Sir Ivor Broom maintained that 'Bill's dynamic and cheerful leadership imparted tremendous confidence in those that followed him.' His gunner Ernie Hope later said that 'Bill was a great man' and 'I shall always feel I can thank him for the fact I am still alive.' After Edrich had led one anti-shipping mission in 1941, the Canadian pilot Frankie Orme told him, 'Billy Boy, we'd follow you anywhere,' a comment that Bill always treasured.

After Cologne, Edrich undertook five more missions with 21 Squadron in August. One was an assault on the German airfield at St Omer on the northern French coast, when he managed to hit the target despite heavy flak. Another, on 26 August, was a low-level attack on a convoy heading for Rotterdam. It was the type of operation that was Bill's personal favourite, since he 'loved the low flying and there was a strong element of the hunt in the way we had to seek out our prey'. On this occasion, Edrich selected a flak ship and opened up with his guns as he went into a dive: 'I pressed the bomb release button four times in rapid succession and then pulled up. There was no flak on the run-in but as we pulled away the tracer overtook us, racing past us like a blizzard. A mile or so away I did a half turn to starboard, and as I looked back, I saw that the ship was already going down, bow first and stern up.'

The next mission was due to be a strike on Rotterdam harbour, and Edrich was surprised when he received orders not to fly on this raid. His place as leader, he learnt, was to be taken by Dick Shuttleworth, a pilot he liked but regarded as too inexperienced for such a risky sortie. Edrich appealed to the station authorities, who were sympathetic to his argument, but No. 2 Group was adamant that Shuttleworth must lead. All Edrich's worst fears were realised. Of the six Blenheims that took off from Watton for Rotterdam, just two returned, one of them badly shot up. Among the dead was Shuttleworth and, in a tragic turn, Edrich had the duty of conveying this news to his widow, who happened to be staying at a hotel at Watton. It was, wrote Bill, 'one of the saddest nights of my life', though 'Dick's wife was very brave.'

The next day, Edrich was given the reason why he had been held back from the Rotterdam raid. He had been posted to No. 2 Group headquarters and his tour of operations was over. Although at the time he regretted his removal from the front line, he came to recognise that he needed a rest, having been flying under tremendous pressure for almost the whole summer. Despite all the excitement, controversy and acclaim he experienced in the years to come, these months in the middle of 1941 were to form the most dramatic period of his life. 'I experienced the highs and depths of emotions – supreme elation, like the effects of good wine, and profound remorse at losing so many fine friends.' Above all, he had survived, partly due to his own valiant skills, but also due to luck. 'He must have had a powerful guardian angel,' wrote Squadron Leader R.S. Pritchard, another Great Massingham veteran, in his private wartime memoir, where he also confessed that Edrich 'was one of my idols' because of his deeds on the cricket pitch for Middlesex.

Now posted to a staff job, Edrich had more time for cricket. Even at Great Massingham he had enjoyed the occasional match for local villages or scratch sides, but freed from his combat duty, he was able to play at a more serious level, especially for the RAF and representative sides. In contrast to the First World War, when top-class cricket had been banned, Churchill's government, in keeping with the Prime Minister's generous, expansive character, allowed major sports to continue, because they were seen as a way of boosting public morale. Indeed, the day after the announcement of his DFC award, Edrich turned out for the Air Force against the Army at Lord's, in front of a crowd of over 10,000. It was a highly moving occasion, recalled his friend Bryan Stevens from Norfolk: 'The crowd rose to Bill when he came out to bat. He was cheered all the way to the wicket.' But his innings turned out to be brief, as Edrich recalled: 'I had just got off the mark and then unleashed a towering shot towards the pavilion. A certain Army sergeant sprinted 30 yards to take a blinding catch. It was of course Denis Compton. "Sorry, W.J.," he said to me later as we broke open the bubbly in celebration of my award. "It's all right," I told him, "that's cricket.'"

During the winter, he also played football to a decent level, turning out not just for Chelmsford City but also for Bournemouth and Lincoln City. But he did not have complete freedom over his schedule. In 1943 he was one of eight RAF officers to be sent to the Army Staff College at Camberley for a course that usually took two years but was crammed into 16 weeks. The challenge of the curriculum precluded any chance of cricket, even on Saturdays. His disappointment was conveyed in a letter of 3 August, 1943 to Geoffrey Moore, the Secretary of the Buccaneers Cricket Club, who had invited him to play in one of their games. 'I am on a course here till the end of September and they won't even give me time off to play for the RAF or England so I am sure you will appreciate my position.' It was the much the same in the early summer of 1944, when he was working in the RAF Group Operations Room and the intensive planning for D-Day meant that he had little time for cricket, though once the invasion was underway he managed to turn out for the RAF more regularly, participating in two tough games against the Royal Australian Air Force, where the all-rounder Keith Miller, another bomber pilot, emerged as a dashing young talent. But in wartime even cricket could be dangerous, as Edrich discovered when playing for the RAF against the Army at Lord's soon after D-Day in 1944. The former England captain Bob Wyatt, an RAF station administrator, was about to bowl to Middlesex's Jack Robertson, then serving in the Duke of Wellington's regiment, when a German V-1 flying bomb, known as a Doodlebug, was heard overhead. Suddenly the engine stopped, a sure sign that the missile was about to come to earth. The players threw themselves onto the grass but the V-1 just missed the ground and instead detonated in a nearby residential street, though the force was sufficient to shatter the windows in the pavilion. While emergency crews rushed to the scene of the explosion with sirens blaring, the cricketers resumed their match with remarkable calmness. Having risen to his feet, Wyatt ran in again, apparently unperturbed by the incident. Equally unperturbed was the batsman Jack Robertson, who proceeded to hook the delivery for six into the grandstand, much to the admiration of his Middlesex colleague Edrich, who felt the episode encapsulated the British wartime stiff upper lip. 'If Hitler had seen them, it would have broken his heart,' he said.

Occasionally, Edrich was able to combine cricket with other pleasures, even when he was still on operations. In fact, there was one match near Great Massingham in 1941 that spawned a host of legends and, through florid retelling, came to be seen as the distilled essence of Bill's vibrant character. Although the details and personnel vary, the main ingredients of this tale are the same. They feature a high-octane, dangerous mission in the morning, a friendly game of cricket in the afternoon, a well-lubricated dinner in the evening, and an assignation with a young local woman at night. Perhaps the definitive version came from Bill himself, given when he was on the Middlesex Committee after he retired as a player. During a rain break in a match at Lord's, he was having a drink with several other committee members and one of them asked, 'What was the best day of your life?' Bill looked thoughtful, puffed on his pipe and said:

It was during the war. I was with the RAF and we had been briefed to look for a German ship in the North Sea that had been damaged and was limping back to port. We took off before it was light, and we flew in corridors, up and down, covering as much sea as possible. Suddenly we saw smoke ahead so we flew down to take a look. The ship's guns started firing at us but, as I drew near, I got the ship perfectly in my sights, and pressed the bomb release button. We saw the most horrific explosion. The ship was engulfed in flames and smoke, and started to sink and men were getting in the lifeboats. We claimed that as a kill, flew back to base and were really chuffed.

This could be a more colourful account of Edrich's first successful combat mission on 7 June, when he sank a 5,000-ton merchant vessel. His story continued:

The crew and I went to the mess where we treated ourselves to a bottle of champagne. Then in the afternoon, I took part in a needle match between our village and the neighbouring one. It was one of those days when I could do no wrong. Everything I did worked. I batted well, got a few wickets and I caught the decisive catch that ended their innings and we won by five runs. Off the pitch we were all great friends so we went down to the pub. After a while, the local vicar came up to me and said, 'Bill, would you like to come and have dinner with us?'

'That's very kind, I'd love to.'
'Very good, the Vicarage is only a short distance away.'
So I went there in my car.

As Edrich recalled, there were a large number of guests at the Vicarage:

We were seated at a long table and there was a very attractive girl whom I had been told was the Vicar's daughter. Unfortunately she was seated several places away on the opposite side of the table. We just kept smiling at each other but we couldn't talk. As the party broke up, I thanked the Vicar and went out with him to my car, only to find that it wouldn't start. The Vicar said, 'Oh Bill, that's bad luck. Why don't you leave your car here overnight and stay? There is plenty of room.' So I went back inside with the Vicar and was shown to a lovely room. I was just about to get into bed when I looked at my watch. The time was ten to twelve. I said to myself, 'This has been a terrific day.' But it was not over. There was a knock on the door, and when I answered it, in came the Vicar's daughter.

Edrich looked at the other members of the Committee and said, 'Now *that* was a great day.' A short while later, Denis Compton was asked by the same members if Bill's story was really true. He replied, 'There is one thing that's not true. It wasn't true that the car wouldn't start. Bill never even tried the ignition.'

The combination of the liberated wartime mood and feminine allure meant that Edrich was often in his element. His fellow 107 Squadron member Anthony Richardson, a successful author and poet whose work was sometimes compared to that of Rupert Brooke, conveyed the erotically charged atmosphere at the station as members of the RAF and WAAF sought to relax from the strains of conflict. The opening of his poem 'Mess Dance' went as follows:

Frankie is here and he's brought both his 'popsies',
And George and Joe and Bill and all the rest,
Some of the WAAF have got a special permit
And show themselves uncommonly well-dressed.

Another quartet of lines read:

Rustle of skirt and silk, rustle of footsteps,
Rhythm of foot and form that glide, out, in –
Hot up the saxophones, wake up the drummer,
Bring out your crooners, then, stir up the din!

David Brocklehurst told me that his friend Bill was remarkably free of moral doubts about his ardour. 'He never felt any guilt about his affairs. He loved all women.' The war reinforced his determination to live every day as if it were his last, recalled Brocklehurst: 'When I asked him why, he explained about the incident coming back over the North Sea, where the Messerschmitt had drawn up alongside his damaged plane. Bill said, "The German could see me struggling to keep the plane in the air. He gave me the thumbs up, implying that if I made it home to Blighty I deserved to live."'

To many of his relatives and friends, his almost obsessive quest for gratification stemmed from his time in the RAF when he had repeatedly been forced to look at death in the face while on active duty. His younger son Justin explained to me how complex his father's feeling were. 'I am certain his moral compass was largely dictated by his war experience. I think he found it very difficult to be regarded as a war hero when so many of his mates did not come home. It is called survivor's guilt and as a Squadron Leader he felt some responsibility for these losses. After the war, his life was very hedonistic. There was a bit of George Best about him. He was much loved and popular, but he could be incredibly irresponsible.' Another, more distant relative, Rodney Edrich, described him as 'an immensely lovable rogue, too open and charming for his own good. It was no wonder he was a party animal. During the war he never knew if he was going to be alive the next day or not. I think his philandering today would be classified as post-traumatic stress. It was forgivable because he had a bloody awful time.'

But his outlook put an impossible strain on his marriage to Betty, who herself joined the WAAF in October 1941, rising to the rank of section officer. Their relationship had already frayed badly before the war, and the last straw came when Bill began a relationship with another WAAF, a married officer called Marion Fish. In September 1943 Betty began divorce proceedings, as reported by the *Acton Gazette*:

Section Officer Betty Edrich petitioned for a decree nisi against her husband Squadron Leader William John Edrich on the ground of his adultery with a woman named Marion Fish. The suit was undefended . . . She first met the woman named at a dinner with her husband in a hotel in London. She noticed that their relationship was 'more than friendly' and later, in reply to a letter from her she received a hotel bill. As a result of inquiries she now charged adultery at an hotel at Nottingham in April this year. It was stated that the respondent had been co-respondent in a petition by Mr Fish in July this year. After evidence from the hotel, the judge granted a decree nisi with costs.

In his 1948 autobiography, Edrich glosses over his first marriage to Betty, but admits he was involved with Marion as early as 1942, when he took her to a cricket match at Lord's. On that occasion he was captaining the RAF against the Army and he settled her into a good seat for the start of play. But he noticed, to his concern, that she had disappeared from her place in the mid-afternoon and only came back shortly before stumps. When he caught up with her, he asked her what had happened. According to his account, 'She calmly replied that she had become so bored with the game that she had gone off and ridden round London on top of a bus by way of change.' It was hardly the best augury for an enduring romance, given how cricket dominated Bill's life.

Marion Fish was later described as a 'surprise choice' for Bill. She was born in April 1914 in Blackburn, the daughter of works manager Albert Forster, and had a precocious talent for music. When she was just 18 she had married a commercial traveller from nearby Darwen called Edward Fish, who previously had been a clerk and had served in the Royal Flying Corps during the First World War. They settled in Wilmslow, Marion becoming a housewife, but the advent of the Second World War had fired her higher ambitions, both on the domestic front and in her career. Following both her own and Bill's divorces, they married at Brentford registry office in February 1944. A glimpse into her character can be found in the memoir of the distinguished RAF pilot Ronnie Waite, who for a time was on the same base as her: 'The lively conversation over coffee was enhanced by the WAAF officers who shared the mess, the most senior of whom was Squadron Officer Edrich. She carried her responsibilities and rank with unobtrusive authority. Her husband was the famous cricketer Bill Edrich. Commentaries on important matches were frequently broadcast on the radio and she accepted good-naturedly the ribbing every time Edrich's name was mentioned.'

His second marriage was one of the many consequences of the war for Bill, as was his desire 'to live with the throttle full-out', to use Denis Compton's vivid phrase. Another was his fondness for speed, as expressed by his driving. His England teammate Trevor Bailey said, 'I always felt he needed a 36-hour day and a trip by car with him at the wheel was not for the nervous.' Edrich's son Jasper told me that 'he loved cars. He used to tear around the lanes in Suffolk, it was amazing. He loved speed and getting into tight corners, though I would not give him too much credit as a driver. He relied more on luck than judgement.' The war also played a big part in breaking down social barriers and rigid hierarchies, which suited Edrich's upwardly mobile streak. His acceptance into the higher ranks of the RAF as Squadron Leader can only have fed his wish to make the same journey in the cricket world. Less than three years into the war, during a match between the RAF and the Army in July 1942, the *Reveille* newspaper picked up on the potential change in the structure of the sport that would occur once peace arrived. 'Democracy will be forced on the MCC after the war by the topsy-turvy nature of professionals' status. In this match we saw a man who used to come out of the pros' gate, Bill Edrich, captaining the RAF as Squadron Leader,' a development that suggested 'there should be no visible dividing line between amateurs and pros after the war'. Even in *Wisden*, often seen as a mouthpiece for traditionalism, Raymond Robertson-Glasgow, the iconoclastic Scottish cricket writer and former Somerset bowler, said in the 1943 edition that 'the hour is ripe, indeed over-ripe, for the sweeping away of anachronisms and the exploding of humbug. I would welcome the total deletion of all distinctions between professionals and amateurs in first-class cricket.'

Yet for all the excitable speculation about the future, there is little doubt that the war left Edrich with deep psychological scars, which could manifest themselves in his slightly manic behaviour, his flirtation with alcoholism, his extreme restlessness and habit of sabotaging his own interests. 'Bill had a massive self-destruct button,' the commentator Henry Blofeld told me. It is impossible to be certain whether Edrich suffered from some kind of breakdown during the war, because the Ministry of Defence has refused to release his unredacted war record, even to his own family. Yet there are hints that this is exactly what happened. On 7 January, 1943 he was admitted to the RAF hospital in Ely. Although the reason was not given, there is no mention of any aircraft accident involving him and he undertook no combat operations after 1941. Moreover, he himself wrote that in 1943 he was sent to the Army Staff College in Camberley after he was declared 'unfit for operational flying duties'. Further evidence for the belief that he was battling inner demons came from his own revelations about the frightening dreams he experienced in 1941, when he had premonitions of which comrades would live and which would die. In almost every case, the morbid warnings turned out to be true. Perhaps even more disturbing was the episode when he climbed into his Blenheim bomber at the start of a mission, and glanced over at another pilot strapped into his plane. Edrich recalled, 'For a split second the man's face was a skull, and then it changed back again and he took off. He did not make it.' Bill's own sister Ena detected something was wrong with him when he came to stay at the family home in Buckinghamshire towards the end of his operational tour. She writes in her memoir that 'It was strange to see Bill, usually so ebullient, now quiet and introverted. He would sit for hours on a deckchair on the lawn doing nothing, seemingly in a daze, only going fishing with Dad at the lakes.' One day Ena, whom Bill always called Dinah, suggested that they go swimming together. 'I shall be swimming soon enough, Dinah,' he replied.

But that was one prediction that was not fulfilled. 'To be alive, to be able to see, to walk, to have food, drink, sport, women – it's all a miracle,' he said of his feelings at the end of the war.

6

VICTORY
1945–1947

'Bill just stood there and took it. He was unflinching. He scored
16 runs and it was one of the greatest innings I ever saw. It was worth
200 on any other wicket.'

Keith Miller

In his 1948 autobiography, Edrich described how the war had matured him. 'My own character had developed a lot faster than it might have done if I had had only peacetime cricket to cope with.' That new maturity was demonstrated in the Victory Test series between England and Australia, which was arranged after the end of the war in Europe to satisfy the public yearning for a swift return of first-class cricket. Acting with commendable speed, the authorities were able to utilise the enormous pool of talent within the Australian armed forces in Britain. Although the five matches had only unofficial Test status, they were keenly fought and attracted huge public interest. More than 70,000 people turned up for the first game at Lord's in mid-May 1945 as the euphoria from VE Day (8 May) still lingered in the capital.

In the absence of Don Bradman, who had been discharged from the Australian Army on medical grounds, Lindsay Hassett led the visitors, while Wally Hammond, a physical instructor during the war, continued to lead England, much to Edrich's satisfaction. 'We could not have had a better man to knit us together after the almost cricketless years,' he wrote. The series ended 2-2, and Edrich played a central role in this achievement of parity, topping the England batting averages and making five scores of over 40. After Edrich had secured a draw in the fourth match with a fighting innings of 73 not out, Denis

Compton, who was still serving in India, wrote to Plum Warner, 'I have had my ears very close to the radio during the progress of each match and I must say that I became frequently most excited. I am so glad Bill Edrich is playing so well. His two innings in the last Test must have been grand to watch.' *The Cricketer* thought that in the series 'Edrich played better than we have seen him for some time. He is a strong stroke player who is fond of the straight drive. He used to move his head before deciding on his stroke but we think he has overcome this fault.'

After the end of the series against the Australians, England played a single match against a Dominions XI, in which he hit 78 in the first innings. Inspired by this performance, *The Cricketer* now declared that 'Edrich is on the verge of greatness in his batting. His off-driving and forcing strokes through the covers with the weight on the back foot was particularly good.' Beyond the actual playing arena, Edrich's essential charm and decency were captured in one incident during the third Victory Test when the newly selected 18-year-old batsman Donald Carr turned up in his military uniform. It was five years since he had met Edrich, back in 1940 when he was a pupil at Repton where his father was the school bursar. Edrich had been learning to fly at a training school in Derby, and Carr, a natural leader and precocious organiser, had at the age of just 13 arranged for a Repton team to take on a local RAF side. According to Carr's account in Mark Rowe's 2010 book *The Victory Tests* about their second meeting in 1945: 'Bill came up to me and said, "We've met before, haven't we?" I was absolutely amazed that he recognised me from the age of 13 and he said, "Come and stretch next to me down here." And he put me at my ease and could not have been nicer. I was always grateful to him for the rest of my cricketing career. He was a very nice chap.'

Bill Edrich was still in the services during that summer and was not formally demobilised until the end of the year. In November 1945 he was actually offered a permanent commission in the RAF and later admitted that at first he was 'inclined to accept it' before deciding to stick with cricket. All three of his brothers had also survived the conflict and like him were involved in professional cricket. His older brother Eric, having been in a reserved occupation as a farm worker, had been taken on by Lancashire as a wicket-keeper/batsman after several successful years with Norfolk. At Old Trafford, Eric joined his younger brother Geoff, a solid batsman whose wartime experience had been harrowing. Taken prisoner by the Japanese after the fall of Singapore in February 1942, he spent three years in brutish captivity, which included a long spell of forced labour building the infamous Burma railway. 'We did not know what day it was. So many boys had cholera, dysentery, fever,' Geoff later recalled. Less agonising had been the service of the youngest brother Brian. Because of his reserved occupation as a farm worker, his call-up to the RAF had been deferred until March 1942. Unlike Bill, he did not see combat against the Luftwaffe. Instead, Brian flew first in India and then carried out air-sea rescue work in Ceylon. An off-spinner and all-rounder, he had signed for Kent in 1939, but did not make his first-class debut for the county until after the war. Ena also undertook military service, enlisting in the WAAF in 1943. Based in an operations room in Norfolk, she had a highly sensitive, responsible position as a tracker of enemy night-bombers.

Britain in the first year of peace after the war was a spartan land, symbolised by the strict rationing of consumer goods and the devastated urban landscape of a number of cities. 'I was always hungry and I had to renew a lot of cricket gear so the coupon situation grew difficult,' recalled Edrich. Some kind of normality returned to cricket in 1946, with the recommencement of the County Championship and the visit of the Indian touring side. After his acclaimed performances in the Victory Tests, Edrich harboured understandable hopes that he would be back in the England team for the first time since his Durban triumph of 1939, but in a summer of damp weather his form in May and June was poor, though he dramatically improved in the next two months. What depressed him even more than his batting problems was the continued decline in the effectiveness of his bowling, which lacked both penetration and accuracy. But a crucial change occurred when he visited Swansea for Middlesex's game against Glamorgan. There he had a long talk about the art of bowling with the canny Glamorgan seamer Austin Matthews, who deserved more than the single England cap he won against New Zealand back in 1937. A cricket coach by profession, employed in that role at Stowe School and then Cambridge University, Matthews was eager to help. Through demonstration and instruction, he showed Edrich how to change his grip and body action so he could extract more movement from a fuller length. Edrich became a man transformed. From being a batsman who bowled occasionally, he dramatically became an all-rounder. In 1939 he had taken just 15 wickets at a cost of 51 runs each. Now in 1946, he took 73 wickets at 19. It was his bowling rather than his batting that won him a recall to the home side for the Third and final Test at The Oval. The match was spoiled by rain, which meant that England did not have the chance to bat at all, but at least Edrich had a decent return as a bowler, taking 4 for 68 from 19 overs.

England were due to tour Australia under Hammond that winter and Edrich was desperately keen to go, not only because an overseas Ashes trip was the ultimate contest for an ambitious English player, but also because he wanted to wipe the slate clean after his nightmare performances against the Australians, and especially the devastating leg-spin of Bill O'Reilly, in 1938. Plum Warner, writing in *The Cricketer*, was a strong advocate for including Edrich, partly as a result of 'the marked advance in his bowling'. On his batsmanship, Warner continued, 'we hope we shall hear no more suggestions about his temperament. A squadron leader and bomber pilot who gains the DFC is not likely to be put off his game, even in a Test match, because of his so-called temperament.' The *Daily Worker*, seeking to break down cricket's traditional hierarchies, urged that Edrich should even be made the first professional vice-captain of a touring party because of the leadership qualities he had demonstrated in the war. Yet for much of the summer, it appeared he would not even be selected in the Ashes party. When the first 12 names were announced in July, his was not among them. In the first week of August, two more names were revealed. Again, his was not among them. Then on 12 August, just three weeks before the team was due to sail from Tilbury in Essex, the final trio was declared: the Surrey batsman Laurie Fishlock, the veteran Sussex all-rounder Jim Langridge – and Bill Edrich. It was not a universally popular decision, and there was some indignation at the exclusion of the brilliant Somerset batsman Harold Gimblett and the stylish Northamptonshire opener Dennis Brookes. In the *Daily Express*, Harold Dale wrote that the selection committee 'will be told, not without reason, that Bill Edrich has had his chance – a whole series of chances – and came off only in one timeless farce in South Africa'. But Dale argued that 'the selectors did not choose Edrich; he chose himself. His form these last weeks has been undeniable and with a new action he has reappeared as a more than useful bowler.' In fact, Edrich had timed his spurt of runs to perfection, making hundreds against Essex and Gloucestershire in late July, followed by a big double-century at Northampton in the first week of August. That season, despite his poor start, Edrich averaged 54.34 in the County Championship.

Edrich was thrilled at his inclusion, but was aggrieved that the lateness of the decision left him insufficient time to prepare everything for the long trip, especially sorting out all his cricket gear, civilian clothes and formal suits. The unlikely image of Edrich as a domestic fusspot, anguishing over his choice of clothes, found its way into some pre-tour publicity; one paper carried a picture of Bill and Marion trying to close his trunk. 'Packing was a strenuous job for W.J. Edrich and his wife Marion,' read the caption. In addition to his usual wardrobe, Bill brought 'ten pairs of flannels, 20 cricket shirts, several pairs of cricket boots and a big stock of white socks', read the commentary. In fact, at this time, Edrich was occasionally promoted as an example of domestic tranquillity, for example in one profile by *The People*: 'Bill lives quietly at Stanmore with his wife, who calls him William, and his Scottie dog Andrew. He likes a mug of beer and smokes 20 cigarettes a day.'

But the picture of wedded bliss hardly matched the reality. On 31 August, 1946 the *Stirling Castle* left Southampton on its 24-day journey to Fremantle in Western Australia, stopping on the way only at Port Said in Egypt on Friday 13 September. As well as Hammond's 17-strong England party, there were more than 200 British war brides on board, en route to join their husbands-to-be in Australia, representing a potential treasure chest of lust for Edrich to savour, as he later confided to his friend and *Guardian* columnist Frank Keating. In an article produced a decade after Bill's death, Keating wrote: 'At his 70th birthday just before he died in 1986, that twinkling carouser Bill Edrich told me what jinks had been enjoyed at the stop-off that Friday 13th in 1946. The tale is unprintable but it was lucky for some all right. To be sure, with a string of last flings by the bevy of British fiancées, so was the whole voyage if the incorrigible Edrich can be believed.'

Denis Compton decided that Bill's excitement during the trip was ripe for exploitation, as Edrich later admitted to his friend, as quoted in Norman Giller's 1997 biography of Compton: 'Denis told me that there was a certain lady who had expressed a keen interest in me. When I moved in on her and asked her for a dance, I found that, one, she could not speak a word of English and, two, her husband was at least nine feet tall. That was a typical piece of Compo winding up. He was a lovable rascal.'

Because it was still designated a troopship, the *Stirling Castle* was not meant to carry alcohol, but that was no barrier to the likes of Hammond and Edrich. In his masterful biography of the England skipper, David Foot wrote that 'occasionally Hammond invited the players to his quarters for "a tonic water". Wally had made provisions and retrieved from the depths of his personal luggage a welcome, potent accessory to tonic water.' But Compton worried that even Hammond might shudder at the excesses in which Edrich indulged:

> I recall that when sailing on the *Stirling Castle* on the 1946–47 Ashes tour Bill got very drunk one night and I had to try to get him to his cabin without skipper Wally Hammond seeing that he had overindulged. Mind you, Wally could do his share of elbow-bending but as captain he could claim that it was all part of his social duty. I was holding W.J. up against his cabin door when an elderly couple pushed past us on their way to their cabin. Goodness knows what they thought we were up to but I heard the wife say, 'Quite disgraceful. Surely they could wait until they get into their cabin!'

Once the England party arrived in Australia, the business of cricket soon began to expose the team's weaknesses, including the advanced age of many of its players, limited bowling and poor leadership under Hammond. For the great Gloucestershire all-rounder, it was a tour too far. Consumed by his envy of Bradman and hit by his loss of batting form in the Tests, he grew increasingly morose. Hammond's detachment from his team was epitomised by his insistence on travelling everywhere in his own loaned car rather than by train with his players. One journalist described him as 'a ghost of a cricketer, and ghosts seldom come back to life'. England's problems were compounded by the overwhelming superiority of the Australians in every department – a team that incorporated five of the best batsmen in the world – Don Bradman, Arthur

Morris, Sid Barnes, Lindsay Hassett and Keith Miller – and the two fastest bowlers, Miller and Ray Lindwall.

Yet amid this gloom for England, Edrich shone out like a beacon, impressing his opponents and the public with his tenacity and skill. The tour was a crucial turning point for him, as he finally fulfilled his promise on the biggest stage. He was the last to have been named in the team but he emerged as the first among its performers. Triumphing in the most hostile of sporting environments, he banished the concerns that he was too mentally fragile for Test cricket. In his book about the 1946–47 series, the Australian sports reporter Clif Cary wrote that Edrich 'developed into the complete cricketer of the MCC party. He found his true form at a time when England was in dire need of someone to give fight and determination to the batting.' In *Wisden*, the Almanack's editor Norman Preston called him 'the best batsman in the side', praised his willingness 'to assail the opposition with his pace bowling', and said that 'it seems almost unbelievable that he was nearly left at home'.

Before the Test series began, Edrich had already received a boost when the selectors named him, despite his comparative inexperience, as England's senior professional, a post which meant that he served on the tour selection committee. The move was both a vote of confidence in him and an expression of faith in his judgement. But it was in the First Test at Brisbane that Edrich provided the display that made his reputation on this tour. The opening session of the match, played in sweltering heat on a perfect pitch, was notable for one of the most controversial incidents in the whole of Ashes history. Before the series began, there had been doubts as to whether Bradman would return, given that he had been in poor health during the long wartime suspension of international cricket. The Australian public and most of the cricket world were relieved at the announcement that he would play, but when his side batted first after he had won the toss, he looked a shadow of his former self on coming in at the fall of the first wicket. As Bradman took guard, Edrich was surprised 'to see how nervous and taut he looked. His face twitched, he was full of gestures, flicking at his sleeves, rubbing his chin, moving his shoulders.' He scratched around, played and missed, failed to move his feet and was almost caught off a botched hook. Then, when he was on 28, he received a full away-swinger from Bill Voce. Sensing the chance to break the shackles, he lashed at the ball, which flew straight to Jack Ikin at second slip. It looked like a straightforward catch. But to Edrich's amazement and that of the rest of the England team, Bradman stood his ground, as if it had been a bump ball. In bewilderment, Ikin appealed, only for the umpire to say 'Not out'. At the end of the over, Hammond passed Bradman and said, 'That's a fine bloody way to start the series.' For the remainder of his life, Edrich was convinced that Bradman had not played in the proper spirit of the game, as his son Justin told me: 'Dad did not talk much about his own career but I do remember him saying to me that Bradman cheated in the First Test and was blatantly out.'

Revitalised by his escape, Bradman started to play in his pre-war, imperious manner, mercilessly demolishing the England attack and reaching 187 before he was bowled by Edrich. Australia went on to make 645, but Edrich was convinced that if the umpire's decision had gone England's way, the course of the match, the series and Bradman's career would have been very different. The fall of Bradman for 28 would have put Australia on 70 for 3 and, argued Edrich, England 'might very well have bundled the rest of them indoors by the end of that first day', paving the way to victory and a lead in the series. At the same time, he felt that Bradman, shaken by his descent into ordinariness, would have dropped out of Test cricket. It was a view strongly disputed by the Australian all-rounder Colin McCool, who wrote, 'I know Bradman pretty well and I can't think that he would have pulled up his swag and cleared off on the strength of one failure.'

England's misfortune continued. After they began their response under grey, thunderous skies, they had limped to 117 for 5 when Brisbane was engulfed by a ferocious storm that deluged the ground with water, sent down hailstones the size of cricket balls and ripped roofs off some of the stands. Remarkably, the next morning, the ground was fit for play, a tribute to the effect of the tropical Queensland sun and the excellent drainage on the Brisbane ground. Even so Edrich, eight not out overnight, went out to inspect the pitch and felt that it looked 'terrible', a verdict confirmed in the first over of fast bowler Keith Miller. His very first ball leapt up at the England opener Cyril Washbrook, knocked off his cap and grazed his forehead. Three of Miller's other balls in the opening over struck Edrich on the body. That set the pattern for the remainder of Edrich's heroic innings as he battled on the gluepot for almost two hours. Although he made just

16, his performance was a masterclass in how to survive when the ball was rearing and deviating. He explained that he had to improvise a new technique, where the aim was to avoid playing the ball. 'Strokes were at the last moment checked, wrists dropped or thrown up, and the edge of the bat kept out of the way of trouble,' he recalled. All the while, his body had to take a pummelling as he repeatedly allowed the ball to hit him rather than risk playing a shot. It says much about both his pain threshold and his adventurous nature that part of him actually relished the contest. 'I became so engrossed in it that I forgot the spectators and almost everything else.'

Despite Australia's dominance in the Test, Bradman became exasperated by Edrich's stubbornness at the crease and urged Miller to bowl faster at him. Miller later recalled, as quoted in Malcolm Knox's 2013 book *Bradman's War*, that Bradman said: '"When you play Test cricket you don't give England an inch. Play it tough all the way." Those were his words. I thought to myself, a war has just passed, a lot of Test cricketers and near Test ones have been killed and here we are just after the war, everybody happy to be alive and we have to grind them into the dust. So I thought, bugger me, if this is Test cricket, you can stick it up your jumper. Don kept up this incessant will to win but it just wasn't my way of playing Test cricket.'

But Miller was full of admiration for his fellow air-force pilot as quoted in Tim Quelch's 2012 book *Bent Arms and Dodgy Wickets*: 'Bill just stood there and took it. He was unflinching. He scored 16 runs and it was one of the greatest innings I ever saw. It was worth 200 on any other wicket.'

Others were equally full of praise. Miller's colleague Colin McCool said it was 'the finest piece of sticky wicket batting I have ever seen. He batted for a couple of hours like no other batsman of my time.' The former Test star Alan Kippax thought it was 'one of the best knocks I had ever witnessed and worth a century'. Clif Cary estimated that Edrich suffered 'more than 40 body blows' but throughout 'showed a nonchalant contempt for danger and seemed content to be battered black and blue rather than lose his wicket'. The doyen of English cricket writers Neville Cardus called it an 'innings of quite tormented obstinacy', which showed that 'he does not understand the meaning of a compromise with overpowering odds'. Edrich's resolute stance was eventually ended when McCool caught him off the bowling of Miller, and England subsided to a massive defeat, having failed to reach 200 in either innings. In his second knock, Edrich fell lbw for 7 to the unconventional slow-medium pace of Ernie Toshack, the left-armer whose command of spin and movement on a damp pitch had an echo in the deadliness of England's Derek Underwood a generation later.

Australia prevailed again by an innings in the Second Test at Sydney, but not before Edrich had given one of the greatest all-round performances of his life. What made his contribution all the more extraordinary is that the night before the start of the match, he had met his former RAF comrade Ernie Hope from Bomber Command, and the pair's lubricated reminiscences had carried on past daybreak. When Denis Compton, who was sharing a room with Edrich at the team's Sydney hotel, awoke the next morning, he was surprised to see that Bill's bed was neatly undisturbed. In one of his accounts, Compton explained:

> I rumpled his bedclothes to make it look as if he had spent the night there because I knew skipper Wally Hammond had a habit of dropping in unannounced. Sure enough, Wally arrived a few minutes later to talk about the game.
>
> 'Where's Bill?' he asked.
>
> 'Oh, uh, didn't you see him on your way here?' I said, trying desperately to think of a cover story. 'He's gone for an early morning jog. It is part of his match-day fitness programme.'

Hammond seemed to accept the explanation and, after reminding Compton that the coach would leave the hotel for the ground at ten o'clock, he walked out of the room. Minutes later, Edrich turned up still in his dinner jacket, his eyes bloodshot and his head throbbing from a hangover. 'I'm afraid the bottle got the better of us,' he said, after he had told Compton of his night on the town with Hope. Once Edrich was undressed, Compton pushed him under a cold shower, then managed to get him ready just in time to catch the team coach. As luck would have it, Hammond won the toss and decided to bat in perfect conditions on a smooth pitch in bright sunshine. Almost immediately, Edrich was out in the middle, following the dismissal of Cyril Washbrook. Compton could hardly bear to watch. 'I wondered whether he would find his way out to the middle. For about 15 minutes he was awful, but eventually he got sight of the ball and he then played one of the best innings I have ever seen.' In his own 1948 autobiography, Edrich, unsurprisingly, gave no hint of this escapade. Instead, he wrote, 'I felt so fit, saw everything in such clear detail about the field.' He went on to make 71, falling lbw to a leg-break from McCool. Back in the dressing room, the wicket-keeper Godfrey Evans congratulated him on his 'magnificent innings', then asked him, 'Tell me, what did you get out for? You were playing so well.' Edrich replied, 'I think I'd sobered up by then, Godders.'

Edrich's powerful display could not stop England sliding towards a disappointing total of 255, to which Australia in response made 659 for 8 declared. But that gargantuan total – dominated by a record-breaking partnership of 405 by Bradman and Sid Barnes, both of them scoring exactly 234 – represented a recovery from 159 for 4, Edrich taking three early wickets in a fiery spell. Hammond, always an admirer of Edrich's all-round talent, said that at his post-war peak, he was 'one of the fastest bowlers, for a few overs, who had ever taken a cricket ball in hand'. Bill Woodfull, the former Australian captain, was struck by the effort that Edrich put into his spells: 'We have rarely seen a bowler with so little desire to spare himself.' His indefatigability with the ball was all the more impressive given his heavy responsibilities with the bat. When England batted again, their only hope of avoiding defeat was to play for a draw. Once more Edrich led the way as he scored 119, his first century against Australia, only to be bowled by McCool. In the *Daily Mail* the former Australian leg-spinner Clarrie Grimmett reported that 'in each innings, he batted brilliantly, no matter what the conditions. He was the model batsman, taking not the slightest risk, yet quick to deal out punishment to any loose balls he received.' None of the other England players could attain the same standard. A second, successive innings defeat followed.

England fared better in the Third Test at Melbourne at the opening of the New Year, 1947. They restricted Australia to 365, Edrich again taking three wickets despite having been hit smack on the knee by a ferocious pull from Barnes when he was fielding at short leg. England then drew almost level with their own total of 351, in which Edrich again made the top score, though the manner of his departure led to an explosive row. He had reached 89 when a delivery from Lindwall appeared to go from the inside edge on to his pads.

According to Hammond, the snick could be heard all the way back to the pavilion. Edrich was therefore astonished to see the umpire's finger raised when Lindwall appealed. Back in the dressing room, Edrich was more upset than Compton ever saw him at a cricket match. Lindwall, however, insisted that the decision was correct. 'I saw no deviation in the ball after it pitched and heard no click,' he said. Hammond went on to mount a formal protest about the standards of umpiring in the series.

England batted strongly to secure a draw at Melbourne, as they did at Adelaide in the Fourth Test, where Edrich scored 17 and 46. The result meant that the series was lost, and Australia confirmed their supremacy with a win by six wickets in the final Test at Sydney. In defeat, Edrich again performed solidly, with 60 in the first innings and 24 in the second, figures that put him at the top of England's Test aggregate for the series, ahead of giants like Compton, Hutton, Hammond and Washbrook. No longer the object of debate and derision, he had become the undoubted star of the team. Bradman himself wrote that Edrich was 'the most difficult England batsman to dismiss', while in an effusive profile for the *Daily Express*, Bill O'Reilly – Bill's tormentor in 1938 – called him 'the Cricketer of the Year', adding that 'his sterling courage and determination and his matchless temperament for the critical occasion have made him the idol of the Australian crowds and an ornament of the game'. Hutton had an insight into the attitude of Australian fans when he received an anonymous letter from a military veteran who had been sitting on Sydney's famous Hill on the day that Edrich made his century. This veteran relayed how one spectator nearby had commented, 'Say, mates, ain't that Edrich a determined lookin' bloke. No wonder Fritz couldn't get no further than the English Channel.'

The praise was just as loud from the English side. Brian Sellers, the former Yorkshire captain who uneasily combined the roles of England selector and newspaper pundit, told the MCC that 'Edrich is the outstanding man of the team' and 'streets ahead of the rest of them'. On his return to England, Hammond, whose captaincy was publicly criticised by Sellers in the middle of the tour, described Edrich as 'a great-hearted cricketer, a grand enthusiast and one of those players who had succeeded against all difficulties. If the critics had had their way, he would have been taken out of cricket a long time ago and we should have lost an excellent player.' For Plum Warner's *Cricketer* magazine, his efforts 'when his side was in trouble earned him the title of "Lionheart"'.

Yet in the context of England's future, perhaps the most significant feature of the final Test was Hammond's withdrawal from the captaincy on the grounds of poor health caused by fibrositis and back trouble. He handed over the reins to his vice-captain, the young Yorkshire and Cambridge University all-rounder Norman Yardley, who had performed surprisingly well in the series as both a spirited batsman and useful medium-pacer, effective enough to dismiss the great Bradman three times. In placing his field, handling his attack and communicating with his players, Yardley was also perceived to have done an efficient job, with the result that he was now viewed as Hammond's natural successor. Even so, there were severe reservations about Yardley, whose undemonstrative, even gentle, personality did not exude a natural authority. Jim Swanton, a passionate defender of amateur status, wished there was 'a little more punch or bite in his make-up'. In addition, many felt that Yardley was not genuinely Test class and so his place in the England XI could not be guaranteed.

But there was an intriguing potential alternative. During the 1946–47 tour, the name of Bill Edrich began to be associated with the England captaincy. His deeds had not only cemented his Test place, but had also indicated his leadership qualities, which had already been highlighted by his war record. One of the prime advocates of his cause was the *News Chronicle* journalist Crawford White, who was both a close friend and an outspoken supporter. In an article in mid-April 1947, White described the 3-0 drubbing in Australia as 'one of the best things that ever happened in English cricket', because it had 'smashed all the complacency in the game' and could enable Edrich 'to lead England next year against Australia'. The same theme was taken up by A.A. Thomas, the cricket correspondent of the *Daily Worker*: 'Yardley has no qualifications as a Test player. I can name at least a dozen batsmen better than him. What about Edrich? Writing in the *Daily Worker* three years ago, I said that if England ever wanted to pick the best captain to succeed Hammond, they must go to the professional ranks and to Middlesex for him. Edrich is the man.'

But there was a fundamental flaw with that argument. Edrich might have led the RAF in the exigencies of wartime, but the Lord's establishment was not about to abandon the hallowed custom of always having an amateur Test captain in peacetime. The unpaid status of the national Test leader was a central part of English cricket's unwritten constitution. If this keystone were removed, the whole edifice might crumble. 'Pray God that no professional should ever captain England,' the Yorkshire grandee Lord Hawke had said in 1925 amid speculation that the Surrey master Jack Hobbs might be appointed to the post. Hawke's nightmare had still not been realised more than 20 years later. Even in county cricket, professional captains were rare.

Edrich and his backers, however, saw a simple way round this obstacle. Following the example of Hammond in 1938, Edrich too could become an amateur by taking a commercial position. Apart from his hope of attaining the England captaincy, one of the appealing aspects for Edrich of switching status was the possibility that he might achieve greater financial security by earning his living outside the game. After all, it was hardly as if his salary with Lord's was generous. According to MCC's minutes for 1946, his basic payment under his three-year contract as a member of the groundstaff, excluding match appearance fees and bonuses, was just £225 per year. Even that was £72 less than the sum he had initially understood he would receive when he first raised the subject of his earnings with the club after the war. 'He played in days when pay was really pitiful,' recalled Denis Compton. On another level, amateur status would be tangible proof of Edrich's elevation up the social hierarchy from his roots as a farmer's son from Norfolk to a new rank as a figure of substance in the cricket establishment. Consciousness about his status, which his sister Ena said could make him 'irritating on occasions and somewhat pretentious', was part of his nature. As soon as he first moved to London in the 1930s, he had been keen to present himself as a fashionable young blade about town, while his accent became more refined through his involvement with Lord's and his commission in the RAF. It was telling that when Edrich first captained the RAF at Lord's during the war, he had lunch with those two grandees, Plum Warner and Gubby Allen, his arrival at the pavilion in officer's uniform having caused 'a bit of a flutter among the MCC ties', in the words of the *Daily Mail*. Drawn to aristocrats like Lord Tennyson, Edrich had an unlikely friendship with the great conductor Sir John Barbirolli, even acting as Master of Ceremonies at Sir John's 50th birthday celebration in December 1949.

The war had also reduced Edrich's sense of inferiority, partly because of his outstanding record and partly through mixing with officers from more privileged backgrounds than his own. That new sense of confidence in his own worth was highlighted in an incident during the tour of Australia when he was invited for drinks at the country home of Tom Ramsay, whose family had made a fortune from Kiwi boot polish. Ramsay started to explain that the company's factory in Rouen, France, had been devastated during the war. Edrich rose to his feet and said, 'I think I had better go. As an RAF squadron leader, I planned the raid that polished off your factory.'

It was through an aristocratic connection that the idea of Edrich's amateur status became a reality in 1947. The architect of the move was Giles Baring, a member of the Baring banking family whose father Guy had been the Tory MP for Winchester from 1906 until his death in 1916, during his service on the Western Front with the Coldstream Guards. One of Giles's grandfathers was Lord Ashburton, who had a strong connection with Norfolk as the MP for Thetford and Lord Lieutenant of the county before he succeeded to the family title. Giles himself went to Gresham's school in Holt before he won a place at Cambridge, where he proved himself to be a superb fast bowler. He went on to become a regular in the Hampshire XI under Lord Tennyson, though he never quite lived up to his early promise because of a car accident. Baring and Edrich were not only frequent opponents in county games, but also played alongside each other for the MCC.

Cricket, Tennyson and Norfolk helped to forge the link between Baring and Edrich, but what really made their relationship fascinating was the similarity in their characters, as Baring's grandson, Alexander Ward, told me. 'I was extremely fond of him. He was tremendous fun but he was a child right to the end of his life, a good-time guy. I would not have said he was a heavy drinker but he certainly loved his drink and was very much a ladies' man. Like his four brothers he was extremely good-looking and never short of female company.' Just as with Bill, Baring's tangled love life led to chaos, controversy and court appearances, including a difficult arrest when he was described by the police as 'staggering drunk', and a sensational divorce case when he was ordered to pay £2,000 in damages to the husband of his mistress. It was a sum that crippled him. This was not the first time that Baring had been on the wrong end of a judicial intervention. In 1944 he was fined for drink-driving after he crashed into a bollard in Chelsea, while in January 1959 he temporarily lost his licence after he was seen by police in Hampshire struggling to drive and park his vehicle. When questioned by an officer in his intoxicated state, he became abusive and used obscene language.

Edrich was embroiled in his own string of similar court cases during the same period, and it cannot be said that Baring's influence was ultimately beneficial to his career. But back in the winter of 1946–47, Edrich was enticed by the prospect of a dramatic change. At the time, Baring had a range of commercial interests, including cement production and imports from West Africa. But his most important enterprise was the chairmanship of Latham, Brown and Company, a paint and varnish manufacturer established in 1871 in Mitcham, south London. The firm had grown steadily, bolstered by new products like fire-resistant materials and the expansion of new light industries and construction, prompting Baring to boast that its output embodied 'the cream of British workmanship'. The company's prosperity was evident both by the size of its works at Mitcham and also by its headquarters at Walpole Street in Chelsea, where Baring had his office, a London home, and a chauffeur paid for by the company. He now wanted to add the lustre of Edrich's name to the Latham ledger, so he and his fellow directors proposed that Bill should become a sales director. Edrich provisionally accepted the position, but said he would have to discuss terms on his return from Australia before he formally agreed.

In Edrich's mind, the prize of the England captaincy could soon be within his reach. He later denied that this had been his primary motivation for the switch to amateur status, absurdly claiming instead that his real purpose was to improve the lot of professionals. 'One reason I took the plunge was that I thought I would have a better chance of presenting the case of the professional to the powers that be,' he wrote in 1958. But such an argument carried little conviction, as his fellow cricketers and family recognised. Trevor Bailey, the Essex and

Central Press/Getty Images

Barratts / Alamy Stock Photo

Edrich in 1937 when greatness seemed to beckon… But the start of his international career the following year was traumatic.

Edrich in action for Spurs against Reading, May 1937. His manager at White Hart Lane said that he 'could have been one of the best outside lefts in the country.'

Edrich leaping forward to drive, June 1938. His wonderful form at the start of that season brought him past the milestone of 1,000 runs in May.

s&g / Alamy Stock Photo

Edrich arriving at Lord's with his first wife Betty. His infatuation with women fated their marriage from the start.

The Edrich clan was sufficiently large and talented enough to have its own team. Here, Bill, as captain of the family side, tosses up with Michael Falcon, the Norfolk skipper at a charity match in September 1938.

Edrich opening with Len Hutton in South Africa on the 1938–39 tour. After a long run of failures, Edrich came good in the final Test.

Mirrorpix via Getty Images

Reg Speller

As Edrich's first England captain, Wally Hammond showed tremendous faith in the young Middlesex player. The pair also shared enthusiasms for drink, cars and women.

Edrich as an RAF recruit, 1940. He turned out to be one of the bravest leaders in Bomber Command.

s&g / Alamy Stock Photo

A match between the RAF and the Army at Lord's in 1944 is interrupted by the descent of a V-1 bomb near the ground. Edrich is among the players throwing themselves on the turf.

Edrich with his second wife Marion, who served as an officer in the WAAF. Their relationship did not survive long after the war.

Edrich sends down one of his fast deliveries at Brisbane during the 1946–47 Ashes tour. 'He bowled as if he was trying to blast a hole in the sightscreen,' said the Australian all-rounder Colin McCool.

Edrich walking out to bat with Denis Compton. The extraordinary feats of the 'Middlesex Twins' in the summer of 1947 captivated the British public and temporarily banished the mood of post-war austerity.

Edrich's form in 1947 was irresistible. Here he hits a six on his way to 189 against South Africa at Lord's.

Edrich cuts late down to third man against New Zealand at the Oval in 1949.

Lord's 1950. On the way to a historic defeat by the West Indies, Edrich is caught by keeper Clyde Walcott off the unorthodox spinner Sonny Ramadin. 'It's like someone throwing a handful of confetti at you,' he said on Ramadin's unfathomable deliveries.

Edrich's nemesis, Bob Wyatt. As Chairman of the England selectors, he was appalled at Edrich's disciplinary record.

Edrich plays the hook, one of his favourite shots, on the way to England's famous Ashes victory at the Oval in 1953. His teammate Trevor Bailey described Edrich's hooking as 'one of the most exhilarating sights I ever witnessed on a cricket ground.'

Edrich pulls off a brilliant, one-handed catch to dismiss Alan Davidson off the bowling of Jim Laker at the Oval in 1953.

After 19 years, England finally win the Ashes. Edrich and Compton fight their way back to the pavilion through a delirious crowd.

Edrich and his teammates Reg Simpson and Denis Compton backstage at an Adelaide theatre with some glamorous showgirls during the Ashes tour of 1954–55. Jessy, Edrich's third wife and herself a former actress, was not pleased when the pictures appeared in the English press.

Edrich bowled by a long-hop from Bill Johnston just 12 short of his century in Brisbane, December 1954. It was his last significant innings for England.

Edrich, now captain of Middlesex, in action against Surrey at the Oval in 1956.

Edrich and his former England teammate Godfrey Evans demonstrate a new type of anti-theft device in 1959, part of a doomed business venture. Other initiatives from Edrich included concrete pitches, a plastic cricket ball and a mobile sewage plant.

Three great cricketing sons of Norfolk: Edrich on the balcony of Lord's in 1970 with Peter Parfitt (left) and Clive Radley (right), who both played for Middlesex and England. Edrich was a crucial influence in their early careers.

Still going strong at the age of 54, Edrich top scores in the Gillette Cup tie in April 1970 against Middlesex, though his runs were not enough for victory.

Just a year before his death, Bill embarks on another evening of revelries with Denis Compton and Keith Miller, with the more austere Len Hutton briefly joining them. 'They made cricket such fun,' said Ray Lindwall of the Middlesex Twins.

England all-rounder, believed that 'as a result of the war, Bill had moved into the officer class from which came the average amateur at that time. He felt he was right for the job – and went that way.' Edrich's son Justin explicitly said that his father 'became an amateur because he wanted to be England captain', a view shared by Ena who wrote in her memoir that 'for Bill, the last of the great nationalists, who considered himself to be the luckiest of men playing for England, to captain England would represent the Holy Grail of cricket'.

It was during the Fourth Test at Adelaide in early 1947 that news began to spread of Edrich's bold step. On 6 February, Harold Dale of the *Daily Express* sent a cable that clearly relied on information provided by Edrich himself. It read: 'W.J. Edrich will almost certainly play for Middlesex as an amateur next season. Negotiations are in progress for Edrich to take up a business appointment. Edrich would thus become eligible for the captaincy of England with the unavoidable sequel that Yardley's succession is less of a foregone conclusion.' The urgent need to settle the talks before the start of the 1947 season was highlighted in a letter of 3 March from the MCC Secretary Colonel R.S. Rait Kerr to the tour manager Rupert Howard about the travel arrangements for the journey back to England: 'It has been suggested that Edrich has some business matters to discuss and it might be helpful to be on an early plane.' His wish was accommodated, and a deal with Baring was quickly struck. On 22 April, Edrich wrote to Rait Kerr from his home in Stanmore:

> It is with regret that I have to report to you that I will not be signing my contract for engagement as a member of the MCC groundstaff for the 1947 season. I have been offered an engagement with Messrs Latham, Brown and Co. which is so attractive that I feel bound to accept the offer. One of the terms of my engagement, however, is that I shall be able to play cricket as an amateur for a number of years to come. I would like to take this opportunity to place on record my appreciation of the kindness and consideration that have always been extended to me by you and all at Lord's.

Rait Kerr replied swiftly, 'We are naturally very sorry indeed that the time has come for you to cease to be a member of our groundstaff but it is splendid news that you have got an appointment which will enable you to continue to play as an amateur for the years to come.' In recognition of his 12 years on the staff, the MCC Committee voted 'to pay W.J. Edrich the sum of £200 as a personal testimonial'. The MCC were also generously accommodating about his use of the pavilion dressing room, practice areas and car park. 'I have much pleasure in sending you the enclosed pass which I think will give you all the facilities you want,' Rait Kerr wrote to Edrich on 6 May, 1947.

Two days after Edrich had written to the MCC, his decision was made public. In the vanguard of correspondents breaking the news was his friend Crawford White of the *News Chronicle*, who boasted of his insider sources: 'W.J. Edrich is not re-signing for Middlesex as a professional but will continue to assist the county regularly as an amateur. He has accepted a business appointment with a group of companies, the chairman of which is A.E.G. Baring, the former Hampshire cricketer. My recent hint, not without some knowledge of the player's intentions, that Edrich might be our next captain against Australia is thus carried an important step forward.'

In the wake of the announcement, Harold Dale of the *Express* felt that 'there is a strong body of opinion at cricket's headquarters that favours Edrich' for the England captaincy, a view shared by the wily former England bowler Fred Root, now a respected pundit, who wrote, 'Edrich in my opinion will be England's future captain.' For Jim Swanton, the best aspect of the news was that it appeared to buttress the amateur tradition:

> Cricket generally has been at its best when the amateur element has been strong, for those who play the game without being responsible to it for their livelihoods normally bring a slightly lighter spirit, blending well with the sounder technique of the professional . . . Everyone should be pleased in these days of fewer amateurs to find their ranks augmented by a distinguished player such as Edrich. His cricket has always had about it something of the free Norfolk breezes and we can hope for many years' enjoyment from him with England as well as Middlesex.

But Yardley was not deposed for the 1947 series against South Africa. The paint company did not turn out to be the route either to the Test captaincy or personal wealth, though Edrich claimed to 'have no regrets' about the move. Looking back, he wrote in 1958 that the job had enabled him 'to build my career while still playing cricket', unlike many sportsmen who made no preparations for their retirement. He could certainly be useful to Latham Brown. When, in January 1954, he appeared on the BBC TV show *What's My Line*, in which a panel of celebrities had to work out the occupations of certain invited guests, none of them guessed that he was a paint salesman, but Latham Brown's sales went up 300 per cent. Edrich's position at Lord's was highly attractive to the sociable Baring, who relished the access to the ground's hospitality that his closeness to Edrich provided. 'A request from Mr A.E.G. Baring for the hire of a Clock Tower Box on the occasion of the Middlesex v the South Africans match was agreed subject to the box being used for the entertainment of his personal friends,' read an entry in the minutes of the MCC Finance and General Purposes Committee for 18 August, 1951.

Yet Edrich's decision meant that he lost the chance of a benefit, which might easily have brought in over £10,000, given that, of his professional England contemporaries, Cyril Washbrook made £14,000, Denis Compton £12,200 and Len Hutton £9,700. In his memoirs, the novelist Frederic Raphael recorded an encounter he had in the late 1950s onboard a ferry travelling to Gibraltar, when he fell into a conversation about cricket with another passenger, a Mr True, a furniture salesman from Knightsbridge.

'I know Bill Edrich,' said True. 'Met him in business. Reckon he lost £10,000 by turning amateur. Only did it because he thought he'd get to captain England. My guess is that he hasn't made above £10,000 in his job. I would have coughed up for his benefit. Can't help liking old Edrich.'

'Drinks, doesn't he?' interjected Raphael.

'Not only drinks, old boy. That's why they daren't take him on tours. Every time they did, his wife divorced him. Some people have all the luck.'

One of the key problems for Edrich was that Latham Brown went into decline under Baring's erratic leadership. Edrich said that he found him 'an understanding and charming chairman of the company'. In truth, however, Baring was better at socialising than running a profitable company. According to his grandson Alexander Ward in an interview he gave me, 'In the fifties, he was part of the glamorous set around Princess Margaret, who was a bit saucy. But his own competence when it came to business was poor. He was always getting involved with new schemes but so often they ended in failure. This could bring out a streak of antisemitism in him, where he'd claim to have been ripped off by the Jews in his business dealings.' Latham Brown was another of his doomed enterprises. At an Extraordinary General Meeting in December 1960, the shareholders agreed to wind up the company because it 'could not, by reason of its liabilities, continue in business'. It was taken over by another paint manufacturer called Hunterseal, which itself was liquidated in 1976. As for Giles Baring, he was declared bankrupt in 1963. Before his death in 1986 he ended his days working in a garden centre and living in a bungalow in Eastleigh. 'It was not the world into which he was born, but there was no trace of any bitterness about him. I will always remember being struck at how contented he was in his final years,' said his grandson,

Beyond Baring's inadequacies, there was a deeper problem about Edrich's faith in amateurism as the key to the England captaincy. Despite all the hopes he invested in it, this belief was based on wishful thinking. The reality was that Edrich never really had a chance of the job, for, whatever his fine qualities, cricket's officialdom regarded him as too unreliable and irresponsible. His behaviour on his two England tours had shown that there would always be a risk of a diplomatic incident or a scandal. The MCC report for the 1946–47 trip revealed that he was the only member of the party who was fined £20 for indiscipline. Indeed, the cricket writer Scyld Berry revealed that Len Hutton once confided in him 'with an almost audible tut' that 'Compo and Bill should have been sent home' from the tour because of their conduct. Unchecked by the remote Hammond, the hedonistic culture was noted by the Australian press, which took delight in blaming England's defeats on 'too many parties'. In an interview quoted in Michael Marshall's *Gentlemen and Players*, Edrich complained that he had been misjudged, but his jocular tone implied otherwise, 'Yes, I set out to have a good time, and it's true that Denis Compton covered for me many times in Australia. And yes it's true that I enjoyed my drink. But the story that I dived overboard on the ship going to Australia for a bet so that the captain threatened to put me in leg irons is quite untrue. For a man who has had as many marriages as I have, it's been quite a quiet life.'

During the period from the summer of 1947 until the end of the 1951–52 India tour, England had no fewer than seven amateur captains, including little-known figures like Ken Cranston and Nigel Howard, yet Edrich was not once considered for the job. Crawford White, Edrich's biggest cheerleader in the press, came to recognise in private that the cause was in vain, telling his fellow journalist Norman Giller that 'the selectors would never consider Bill for the captaincy because of his well-known reckless lifestyle'. Always shrewd in his judgements, Trevor Bailey wrote that the blame for Edrich's exclusion could be put down to 'an unconventional outlook, a certain wildness of spirt and an impetuosity which would have been worshipped in Dublin and a refusal to conform to the standards laid down by others'.

Deprived of the post he wanted, Edrich would have to find another way to write himself into the history books. The summer of 1947 would see him do so in magisterial style.

7

TRIUMPH AND COLLAPSE
1947–1948

'Every time I have been to Lord's so far, I have had to sit through
Compton and Edrich. Doesn't anyone else bat in England?'

Sir Charles Aubrey Smith

The winter of 1946–47 was one of the bitterest of the century in Britain. Amid heavy snow and freezing temperatures, the country started to grind to a halt. Railways were paralysed, food supplies threatened and factories shut. The enveloping gloom was deepened by electricity cuts, which meant that lights in the homes and on the streets had to be turned off. Unemployment soared, coal reserves shrank. The Labour government of Clement Attlee tightened the food rations and urged households, with limited success, to consume imported whale meat. Even mid-week football and greyhound racing were banned in February. The mood of crisis was worsened by the continuing impact of the war, which had almost bankrupted the public finances and left the urban landscape devastated in a number of major cities. Returning from America, the writer Christopher Isherwood found the sight of the Blitz-ravaged capital 'powerfully and continuously depressing'. In Australia, Bill Edrich followed the news with some alarm. An instinctive Conservative, he felt that ministers were 'sliding the blame from their own to someone else's shoulders'.

What followed in the summer of 1947 was an uplifting antidote to this icy ordeal. For a few golden months, the privations of a war-torn land were forgotten as a mesmerising, record-breaking cricket season unfolded. At packed grounds under apparently perpetual blue skies, the public were treated to a festival of run-making such as had never been seen before and almost certainly will never be seen again. There was a dream-like quality to the staggering batting performances that occurred week after week, to which no scorebook could do justice. Hardened austerity gave way to generous stroke play, frozen hands to flashing blades. This was more than a vintage year in the long story of English cricket. It was an unforgettable moment that wrote its own unique chapter in the sporting heritage. As John Arlott said of the memories evoked by the summer of 1947, 'A wealth of nostalgia lies in recalling it. To have seen it is to count oneself a member of a club within which there is no disagreement, only a consciousness of riches shared.'

At the centre of this epic were the figures of Bill Edrich and Denis Compton, the two Middlesex and England cricketers whose names became synonymous with glorious deeds that captivated spectators and rewrote sporting history. Their dominance was astounding and did not fade even in September. So intertwined were they in the public consciousness that they became known as 'The Middlesex Twins' or, to opponents, 'The Terrible Twins'. When the Oscar-winning actor and former England captain Sir Charles Aubrey Smith was on a visit to this country in 1947 from his home in Hollywood, he was asked what he thought of the state of English cricket. 'Can't say I'm sure. Every time I have been to Lord's so far, I have had to sit through Compton and Edrich. Doesn't anyone else bat in England?' Their grip on the public imagination stemmed not merely from the astonishing scale of their batting aggregates, but also from the style in which they made their runs. In an era of severe rationing and grey oppression, they brought a colourful freedom to the crease. Their swashbuckling approach meant that bowling attacks were demolished rather than merely resisted, deliveries were hit rather than negotiated. As the flood of their boundaries continued, the game of cricket cast off its habitual, self-enfolded concern about its future and became the nation's primary form of entertainment. If Britain was a sickly patient in the first months of 1947, Compton and Edrich represented a huge injection of adrenalin. Watching one game during this 'heavenly summer' at Lord's, Neville Cardus observed, as written in Heald's 2006 biography of Compton, how, in that 'worn, dowdy crowd', 'the strain of the long years of anxiety and affliction passed from all hearts and shoulders at the sight of Compton in full sail, sending the ball here, there and everywhere, each stroke a flick of delight, a propulsion of happy, sane, healthy life. There were no rations in an innings by Compton.'

There had been previous cricket seasons associated with stupendous individual batting feats, notably in 1895 when W.G. Grace achieved the milestone of a hundred first-class centuries, Tom Hayward in 1906 when the Surrey opener made 3,518 runs, and Jack Hobbs's captivating summer of 1925 that saw him make 16 centuries. But no pair of batsmen had ever enjoyed such an ascendancy. Together Compton and Edrich hit 7,355 runs, with each of them averaging over 80. Both of them were now in their early thirties and at the peak of their powers, combining their innate ability with experience and judgement. Edrich had come of age as an international star in Australia, while Compton was already established as an England great. Their repeated conquests of new statistical summits became part of the thrilling rhythm of the summer. The Sussex off-spinner Robin Marlar was in the crowd at Hastings in 1947 when Compton and Edrich were in sight of beating the previous records for most centuries and highest aggregates for the season. 'The excitement was matched only by the certainty those records would be unmistakably different in style, the pair seemed un-get-outable, their pursuit of runs positively gluttonous yet accomplished not with greed but with a smile.'

As a child, the television broadcaster David Frost was brought by his father to the 1947 Lord's Test against South Africa. In an interview in *The Independent* led by Danny Danziger in October 1993, Frost said: 'I can remember it as one of the happiest days of my childhood. There was something about England that summer, a sort of charmed atmosphere.' He was enthralled to see the pair in action, building another of their record partnerships, but Frost's hero was Edrich. 'He was short, stockily built and gutsy. I knew everything about him, in the way that children memorise statistics and facts. I knew his batting average, bowling average, each night I pored over the *News Chronicle* cricket annual.' In the years to come, Frost was to see countless other matches but 'there was never one with this magic'.

The capacity of Compton and Edrich to inspire hero worship was captured in a sublime 'Compton and Edrich' *Wisden* essay by Raymond Robertson-Glasgow, who focused on their unique appeal and the contrast in their methods. 'They go together in English cricket, as Gilbert and Sullivan go together in English opera,' he began, before he went on to describe them as 'champions in the fight against dullness and the commercial standard . . . They are the mirror of hope and freedom and gaiety; heroic in the manner of the heroes of school stories.' They could also communicate their pleasure to the public, Robertson-Glasgow argued: 'Compton and Edrich are of that happy philosophy which keeps failure in its place by laughter, like boys who fall on an ice-slide and rush back to try it again. They give the impression, whether batting, bowling or fielding that they are glad enough merely to be cricketing for Middlesex or England. And they seem to be playing not only in front of us and for us, but almost literally with us.'

Of their batting, he wrote: 'Compton is poetry; Edrich is prose, robust and clear. Far more than Compton, Edrich uses the practical and the old-fashioned methods and areas of attack. He likes the straight hit and that pull-drive which gave old E.M. Grace (brother of W.G.) so many runs. Old-fashioned, too, is Edrich's high backlift in preparation for the stroke. He gives the idea of a height and reach beyond fact.'

The disparity between the two players was regarded by John Arlott as one of the secrets of their popularity: 'Compton and Edrich were and are two vastly different cricketers and men. Had they been too much alike they would not have so captured the imagination. They are not to be compared; rather their differences should be relished, for the contrast between them made their dual performances more absorbing.'

Because of his gift for the unorthodox and the artistry of his stroke play, Compton was often described as 'a genius', a word that was never applied to the more rugged but conventional Edrich. 'Denis did have a greater variety of shots, some played off his backside,' recalled the Lancashire and England off-spinner Roy Tattersall. Compton was nimble in his footwork and often deft in his shot-making, whereas Edrich was less fluid in his movements and liked to use his bat as a bludgeon when on the attack. 'Edrich was never a graceful player,' wrote Jim Swanton, while Dudley Carew of *The Times* thought he could be 'impetuous and lacks the balance and precision which Compton, not naturally a particularly precise person himself, brings to his batting.' Lacking Compton's creativity, Edrich tended to be more predictable, while Ray Lindwall claimed that he could keep him quiet by bowling 'just short of a length on the off stump'. In his study of the 1947 season, John Kay of the *Manchester Evening News* wrote that in comparison to Compton's 'exquisite' batsmanship, 'to Edrich, we looked for a more vigorous exhibition. His batting was dominated more by brute force than science. For one so slight of build he hits the ball long and hard. Not for him the gentle caress or the apologetic leg-glance. He always seemed to be vigorously applying the willow.' The power of his driving was noted by Margaret Hughes, the first female writer to have a book published about cricket. Describing Edrich as 'like a small boxer, with furrowed brow and the light of battle in his eyes', she wrote that 'he drives the ball harder and straighter than other batsmen I have seen'.

Whatever their differences in style, they made a formidable alliance in 1947. According to John Warr, the post-war Middlesex pace bowler and later county captain, Compton's presence strengthened Edrich's search for success: 'He might not have achieved the record he had without Denis at the other end. But as a pair they made opposing attacks look so stupid.' It was a point acknowledged by Edrich himself, who said it was 'a joy and a privilege to have him as a partner, adding, 'Denis and I were never envious of each other. The more runs he scored the happier I was, and Denis was always encouraging me to keep up with him.' Recalling that season, Compton said: 'I just could not stop scoring runs, and most of the time good old W.J. was at the other end and also making the scorer work overtime. We used to challenge each other by saying, "first one out buys the first round". We got very thirsty with all the running we did.'

Yet in the face of all the adulation about the summer of 1947, some dissenting voices have argued that the feats of Edrich and Compton have been exaggerated because they were lucky to play on flat pitches in fine weather against generally ordinary bowling and unathletic fielding. In his autobiography, the former England captain Colin Cowdrey said, with unaccustomed forthrightness, that 'the cricket watched by big crowds just after the war gave a false impression. They saw a run harvest which delighted them, but I doubt if one in a hundred of them understood that what they were really watching was total batsman-domination of mediocre bowling.' It was an argument that infuriated both men. While admitting that pitches were excellent then and new ball attacks lacked penetration,

Compton argued that, on the other hand, 'captains demanded runs at a higher rate; the priority of batsmen was to entertain rather than remain, sometimes at the expense of their own wickets, and the battery of medium-paced bowlers and spinners we faced were accurate and controlled, capable of dictating proceeds unless a batsman took the initiative.' Edrich was even more aggrieved, telling the writer Norman Giller, 'they say that the bowling we faced was of a poor standard. Tell that to the likes of Alec Bedser, Doug Wright, Trevor Bailey, Roy Tattersall, Cliff Gladwin, Tom Goddard and Jim Laker, who were just some of the bowlers around at the time.' On Compton's notoriously poor reputation as a judge of a run, Edrich also claimed that, in his experience, 'Denis was nowhere near as bad as the stories suggest. In all the years that we played together, he never once ran me out.' What prevented trouble, said Edrich, was to keep alert when Compton was on strike and make clear calls. Edrich admitted, however, that Walter Robins, their county captain at Middlesex, came up with the memorable dictum that a call from Compton for a run was just 'an opening bid in negotiations'.

It was Robins, innovative and dynamic, who played a crucial part in driving Compton and Edrich to new heights in 1947 as he led the quest for Middlesex to win its first Championship since 1921, having been runners-up in every season since 1936. Fast scoring was a key factor in his vision, and he would not tolerate any of his players putting their own wishes in front of the team's needs. The quest for the title began in inauspicious fashion in a home defeat to Somerset at Lord's, but four big victories followed during the rest of May. Fresh from his triumph in Australia and emboldened by his new amateur status, Edrich was in magnificent form right from the start, hitting three centuries in the month, including a mammoth 225 against Warwickshire at Edgbaston. His bowling also continued its dramatic improvement since the guidance from Austin Matthews the previous year. In an innings win over Gloucestershire, he took 2 for 26 and 6 for 28, and then, a week later, 5 for 61 and 5 for 69 against Worcestershire. In fact, Edrich opened Middlesex's bowling for most of the season, which made his batting record all the more impressive. Of his bowling, Robertson-Glasgow wrote in *Wisden*, 'Edrich began as a muscular slinger, as but a moderate advance on village heroics; then he grew into knowledge of swerve and variety. He is never done with.'

The visitors to England that summer were the South Africans, led by Alan Melville, an Oxford Blue and one of the most elegant batsmen of his generation. In the run-up to the First Test, they played Middlesex at Lord's, where Edrich gave them a warning of things to come with his innings of 67 and 133 in a heavy-scoring draw. The opener of the series at Trent Bridge was the first time in his career that Edrich had been a certain selection for the Test side. Under the leadership of Norman Yardley, England looked in serious trouble at one stage when, following on, they were 48 for 2 in their second innings, but they were rescued by Edrich, who scored his second 50 of the match, and even more so by Compton (163) and Yardley (99), who put on 237 for the fifth wicket. After this initial draw, the Second Test at Lord's encapsulated the essence of Edrich and Compton and the enthusiasm of the public in 1947. More than 30,000 people crammed into the ground on the second day to witness the continuation of a record-smashing stand between Compton and Edrich, which had started in the early afternoon of the first day. They had come together with the score on 96 for 2 and were still there at stumps, with England 312 for 2 and Edrich having completed his third Test hundred. He was not dismissed until after lunch the next day, by which time he had made 189 and put on 370 with Compton, still (in 2023) the highest third-wicket partnership in England's Test history. *The Times* called Edrich's contribution 'a splendid innings by a splendid cricketer, who is always well and truly in the game'. He had batted for almost six hours and hit 26 fours and a six. *The Cricketer* magazine was just as fulsome: 'Edrich has developed into a great batsman, sound in defence with all the strokes. He is a superb hooker of the short-pitched ball . . . but of all his strokes, the pulled drive caught the eye the most. In making it he hits straight down the line of the ball and then, as he feels the ball on the bat, he turns his right wrist over and she goes off with a lovely sound.' Compton went on to his first Test double-century, and his innings was followed by a 10-wicket England victory. As South Africa struggled to avoid defeat in their second innings, Edrich took another three wickets, including the vital one of the dogged Dudley Nourse with the first ball of the final day, a rip-snorting delivery that demolished the middle stump.

Edrich did even better in the Third Test at Old Trafford, putting on 228 with Compton in just over three hours before he was eventually dismissed for

191. Lindsay Tuckett, the persevering South African pace bowler, reflected on the tough demands of bowling to the pair as quoted in Alan Hill's 1994 biography of Edrich: 'It was our destiny to be touring England when these two men reached the peak of their form. We were just unlucky to bump into them. The big thing about Edrich and Compton was that they worked so well together. Bill had usually been at the wicket for around half an hour when Denis came in. He would nurse his partner through the first 20 runs.' Of Edrich's batting, Tuckett said, 'He had a penchant for the on side. His on-drives and pulls were invested with resonant power. He thumped the ball hard, getting well over and on top of it.' Edrich's partnership with Compton, extolled *The Cricketer*, was a 'magnificent performance because the wicket was not at all easy, the ball often flying about in disconcerting fashion'. The magazine said that 'their superlative skill is apparent to all and we must not overlook their remarkable physical fitness'. This was particularly true of Edrich, who in addition to his batting, bowled no fewer than 57 overs in the match, taking 4 for 95 in the first innings and 4 for 77 in the second.

There was an interval in the Test schedule after Old Trafford, and Edrich again helped Middlesex's charge towards the Championship. In fact, just before the Third Test, he had played a crucial part in destroying Yorkshire's hopes of retaining the title with a dazzling century at Headingley that featured one dramatic spell of hitting against Frank Smailes. Good enough to have played for England the previous summer, Smailes saw five successive deliveries disappear for 22 runs from Edrich's bat. Just as significant was Middlesex's visit to Grace Road for the game against Leicestershire in mid-July, when his county took advantage of his new amateur status to make him temporary captain in the absence of Walter Robins on business and the usual deputy George Mann, who was injured. In the *Daily Mail*, the sports editor Geoffrey Simpson wrote excitedly about the national implications of the move. 'Many interested eyes will focus on Bill as he handles his team at Leicester. He may be an England skipper in the making.' Edrich did his credentials no harm in a pulsating encounter and breathtaking finish. Middlesex built a huge first-innings total of 637 for 4 declared, thanks largely to a double-century from Edrich, but then Leicestershire fought back in their second innings. When only 70 minutes were remaining before the close, the home side went into the lead with six wickets still left. A draw looked inevitable. But then Edrich galvanised his bowling attack and presided over a sudden collapse in Leicestershire's lower order. Left with 66 to win in 25 minutes, Edrich refashioned his own batting order, and opened with Compton in front of a huge, hushed crowd. The atmosphere, wrote Edrich, was 'more electric than anything of the sort I could remember in a Test match'. Middlesex won with four minutes to spare as the pair gave another display of controlled hitting. It had been an extraordinary game that typified the spirit of 1947, with a total of 1,405 runs scored. In his autobiography published in 1948, Wally Hammond praised Edrich's leadership at Leicester as 'brilliant' and called for him to be given the England job: 'In my opinion, England's strongest captain today is Bill Edrich.'

But far from advancing further in the esteem of the authorities, Edrich became embroiled in another of those controversies that littered his career. Towards the end of July, in the run-up to the Fourth Test at Headingley, Edrich maintained his scintillating form, hitting 79 in his first appearance for the Gentlemen against the Players at Lord's, 44 and 83 against Essex at Lord's, and 267 not out at Northampton, which was to be the highest score of his career. Performances like that kept Middlesex in the hunt for the Championship against their chief rivals Gloucestershire, who were putting up a tremendous challenge under the leadership of Basil Allen. Back on England duty, Edrich helped England to win the Test at Leeds by 10 wickets, a victory that secured the series. After the grandeur of his two big centuries at Lord's and Old Trafford, his contribution with the bat was a comparatively modest 43, but he took 3 for 46 as South Africa were bundled out for 175 in their first innings, a collapse from which they never recovered. Another wicket in the second innings brought Edrich's tally for the series to 16 at an average of 23. Revealingly, nine of those wickets were bowled and two were lbw, an indicator of both his pace and his fuller length. But now that the Test series had been won, pressure began to mount for the selectors to leave out Compton and Edrich from the England side at The Oval, so that they could play for Middlesex in the vital fixture against Gloucestershire at Cheltenham. This game, whose outcome would almost certainly decide the title, clashed with the final Test. 'Leave "Twins" out of Test team. They'll be needed for county decider,' declared the headline above an article in the *Daily Mail* by Alex Bannister, who wrote, 'I can't believe that Gloucester would want to meet their Middlesex rivals below full strength. If they beat a weakened team, theirs would be a hollow success. In the circumstances I should be prepared to see an England XI without even Edrich and Compton.' The authorities were unpersuaded. Such a move implied that England selection could be influenced by the County Championship race, a process that would devalue the integrity of both Test cricket and the national side, as well as patronise the visitors.

Then came an intriguing twist in the tale of Edrich's availability for the Oval. Playing against Kent at Canterbury, he was bowling with his usual whole-hearted effort when he felt something snap in his right shoulder and had to leave the field in 'considerable pain', to use his own words. After a rough night, he still felt 'half-paralysed' the next morning. But fortitude was always one of Edrich's foremost characteristics. Determined to do all he could for his county's cause, he scored 130 in Middlesex's second innings despite his drastically restricted ability to make strokes. That evening he met his youngest brother Brian, who was on the Kent staff, at the hotel where Middlesex were staying.

'Will you be out of the Oval Test?' asked Brian.

'It may not be a bad thing if I am. I can help Middlesex win the Championship,' replied Bill. Unfortunately, the remark was overheard by another hotel customer, who relayed it to Jim Swanton, the self-appointed moral arbiter of English cricket.

On the eve of Middlesex's next game, against Surrey, Edrich saw the orthopaedic specialist Bill Tucker, who later operated on Denis Compton's famously ravaged knee. Tucker told Edrich that he had 'torn the tendons right off the bone' and the injury would take a long time to heal. In the face of Bill's insistence that he had to play against Surrey, Tucker said he could give him an injection and strap him up to limit how high he could raise his arm. 'Try it out and see if you can bat. You certainly can't bowl or throw,' Tucker told him. Fortified by this diagnosis and improvised harness, Edrich told his Middlesex skipper that he could play against Surrey. Walter Robins accepted this and Edrich made 157 in a big win for Middlesex. Writing more than 30 years later, he named this as his 'best innings' of the summer because of both the quality of the Surrey attack led by Alf Gover and Alec Bedser, and the painful circumstances of its construction. Soon afterwards, Edrich was contacted by Jack Holmes, the Chairman of the Selectors, who noted his two recent centuries and asked him if he was fit for the Fifth Test. Edrich explained that he could 'neither bowl nor throw and that I was batting under difficulties'. The two men agreed that he should be omitted, his place to be taken by his Middlesex colleague Jack Robertson, who had also scored heavily throughout the 1947 season. The move prompted Swanton to write in his *Daily Telegraph* piece that Edrich 'says he cannot bowl or throw, and indeed bats under limitations, though two hundreds in three days might suggest his resource is well equal to the handicap. Equally undeniable and also natural is his keen wish to try to help his county while the Test is in progress. I confess I would have opposed very strongly a precedent which made selection for England dependent on fixtures in the Championship.' Edrich was furious. 'I had to face smiles and winks and a charge of malingering,' he complained, even though it felt 'as if I had been stabbed by a knife' through his shoulder if he jerked it. When he ran into Swanton at Lord's he said in a low, angry voice, 'I can tell you this, Jim, if that inference is not withdrawn, I shall sue.' Swanton duly had an amendment published that exonerated Bill.

In this unique summer of high drama, the deciding match at Cheltenham turned out to be an absorbing, low-scoring thriller, played in a Cup Final atmosphere on a wicket that Edrich described as 'a spin bowler's paradise'. Opening Middlesex's first innings, Edrich compiled a painstaking 50 in a total of 180, which was enough to gain a narrow lead of 27. Against the deadly turn and bounce of the veteran, 46-year-old off-spinner Tom Goddard, who took 15 wickets in the match, Middlesex struggled to 141 in their second innings, Edrich falling for just 5. But Gloucestershire, set 168 to win, never looked like completing a successful run-chase. Appropriately, given his commanding role in Middlesex's triumphant season, the victory was sealed when the final wicket fell to a catch by Edrich, who managed to cling on to the ball despite his shoulder 'feeling as if a red hot iron had passed through it'. The title was confirmed at the end of the month when Middlesex thrashed

Northamptonshire at Lord's, signalling the start of another party oiled by champagne, as Edrich recalled. 'During the summer of 1947 the Middlesex team must have set some sort of record for drinking celebratory champagne. Denis and I had a bottle of bubbly after most of our centuries and the entire team joined in when we won the Championship, even lovely Jack Robertson who was usually an orange-juice man.'

There were also celebrations for the milestones that Edrich and Compton passed that summer. For a long time it looked as if Bill would be the first to overtake Tom Hayward's aggregate of 3,518 runs in a season, set in 1906, but he was slowed down badly by his shoulder injury, so it was Compton who broke the record while playing for Sir Pelham Warner's XI at the Hastings Festival in early September. In the previous match of the festival, against the South Africans, Compton had surpassed Jack Hobbs's total of 16 centuries in a season. It was fitting that in the last match of this miraculous summer, between the champion county and the Rest at The Oval, Edrich should also overhaul Hayward's aggregate during an innings of 180 when he indulged in some sustained hitting, including 17 off one over from Goddard, and forged a partnership of 210 with Compton. The 'twins' were prolific to the last. In a tribute at the end of the season, *The Cricketer* said that: '. . . their brilliant play was a great attraction to the cricket-loving public and never before have there been such crowds at Lord's. It is true that bowling in England today is generally weak but these two are so intrinsically good that they would have made runs off bowlers at any time. The immortals do not only belong to the illustrious past of Grace, Ranji, Trumper and Hobbs. They are playing in our midst today.'

Hyperbolic language like that demonstrated the belief that Compton and Edrich would dominate English cricket for years to come, but it did not work out like that. In fact, the pair were not even members of the MCC touring party that winter to the West Indies under the captaincy of 45-year-old Gubby Allen, who was given the job because Yardley could not spare the time from his business. Compton pulled out because of his contract with Arsenal, though he actually played just 14 League games that season because of his increasingly dodgy knee, which even during the summer had been giving him agony. In advance of the

Ashes tour in 1948 by Don Bradman's Australians, the selectors also wanted to rest Len Hutton, another key batsman, though an injury crisis in Allen's squad meant that Hutton had to be flown out in an emergency. The refusal to send a full-strength side to the Caribbean, like the eccentric choice of Allen as leader, appeared to indicate a sense of dismissiveness from the MCC for the hosts. In August 1947, five months before the tour began, the West Indies authorities were alarmed at the news of Hutton and Compton's absence. This was a moment in history when there were deepening sensitivities about colonialism and the impact of empire. In the very weeks that the British cricketing public were transfixed by Compton and Edrich, India was gaining independence, while Burma became a self-governing republic just as Gubby Allen was leading his men from England.

One certain way that Britain could show respect for West Indian cricket would be through the selection of Edrich, as R.K. Nunes, Chairman of the West Indies Board of Control, put it. 'With Compton and Hutton unable to go, the visit of the English team would lose much of its public appeal if Edrich was also "rested,"' Nunes pointed out. Inevitably Crawford White of the *News Chronicle* put the case not just for Edrich's inclusion but also for his captaincy of the party, despite admitting how forlorn his demand was: 'Bill Edrich is the obvious choice. He knows all the answers. But the honest professionalism that he embraced until this year sticks hard in the gullet of a certain section at Lord's (where, oddly enough, the pseudo amateurism which riddles county cricket today is viewed with complete equanimity) and his appointment is unlikely.'

Charles Bray of the *Daily Herald* reported that the call for Edrich would meet a positive response, 'I understand that there are no business difficulties to prevent Edrich making the trip and that he personally is most anxious to visit the islands for the first time. It can therefore be taken for granted that he will accept the invitation.' But Bray's confidence was misplaced. At the beginning of September, the *Daily Mail*'s Alex Bannister reported: 'I expect Edrich to decline the tour. He would be well advised to do so in view of the visit of the Australians next year. An England team then without Edrich would be unthinkable. He should give a full winter's rest to the right shoulder injury which prevented him bowling and impaired his batting during August. To risk this valuable player on a tour of this kind appears to me a blunder.'

The very next day, 2 September, Edrich informed the MCC of his decision to refuse a place on Allen's tour, because he was 'anxious to establish himself in his business', which he had been unable to do in the summer. In addition, he had 'played cricket continuously for near 18 months' and felt 'a complete winter's break would ensure his feeling fit for the strenuous cricket ahead next summer when the Australians visit England'. Bill did not mention another factor: that as an amateur he would only receive expenses rather than pay, so the tour would have been unaffordable if he was to take leave from Giles Baring's company. Besides his work with Latham Brown, Edrich had other commitments, which included writing his autobiography, due out in 1948, and his work with his friend Ted Ward on concrete cricket pitches, an enterprise that he persuaded Compton to join. A snapshot of Edrich as the busy executive in the winter of 1947 came from a report in the *Leicester Mercury*: 'A quiet, modest little man came to Leicester today on business. He was just one of scores who travelled up from London to see "what's doing" in the Midlands and only a handful of people knew he was in town. The visitor is William Edrich, representative of a paint manufacturing firm. Edrich is "up to his ears in a variety of tasks", chief of which is writing a book.'

In the absence of Compton, Edrich and a host of other leading players, England did badly in the West Indies and failed to win a single match, never mind a Test. After the glories of the 1947 season, the expedition had been an embarrassment. But worse was to follow in the summer of 1948, as England were crushed by the juggernaut of Don Bradman's Invincibles, who went through the tour unbeaten and left English cricket profoundly demoralised. The golden memories of a year earlier were obliterated by Australia's absolute supremacy with bat and ball. Yet the 1948 season had started in a burst of optimism for Edrich as he again put county attacks to the sword. A big century against Sussex at Lord's was followed by a superlative 168 not out against Somerset, when he and Compton in just four hours put on 424 for the third wicket, a record for first-class cricket in England and just behind the 445 made by W.N. Carson and P.E. Whitelaw in 1937 for Auckland against Otago. Edrich recalled how, in his partner's innings, Compton found the bowling so easy that he could not help monopolising the strike: 'There was a chap called Miles Coope playing for Somerset and if you look at his bowling analysis you'll find he took 0 for 60. Coope bowled from the Nursery end and Denis kept hitting him on to the Grand Stand balcony, but kept the party to himself. I didn't get up that end for a single ball.'

Arthur Wellard, who had bowled for England before the war, was savaged even more brutally, taking 0 for 158. 'Where do you bowl at them?' he asked plaintively.

Bob Wyatt, the tough former England captain, once described Edrich as 'a great slayer of moderate bowling without being a really great player against bowling of the highest class'. That argument might seem to be contradicted by Edrich's record on the 1946–47 Ashes tour, yet evidence in its support could be found in the opening two Tests of the 1948 series. In a bleak re-run of his nightmare ten years earlier, he made just 38 runs from four innings as England went down to two heavy defeats. Nor did his bowling seem to pose any threat to Australia's batting line-up, for he took just one wicket for 146 runs. The former Test leg-spinner Bill O'Reilly, who had been so impressed with him on the 1946–47 tour, now wrote that 'his usefulness as a pseudo speed bowler is questionable at the best of times'. But the far bigger problem was Edrich's batting, which seemed unable to cope with either the pace of Lindwall and Miller or the late swing of Bill Johnston. The former Yorkshire and England fast bowler Bill Bowes felt that Edrich was 'still a great player but a little out of luck'. Others thought the difficulty was more serious. 'Bill Edrich seems to have relapsed into that pre-war Test form that made him one of the most discussed players of the time,' argued the *Daily Herald*. Even Wally Hammond, his loudest advocate, described some of his stroke play as 'half-hearted', not something of which Edrich was often accused. Writing in the *Western Morning News*, the editor of *Wisden*, Norman Preston, said that Edrich's batting at Lord's in the first innings 'never inspired confidence' against Lindwall before 'sheer speed upset his middle stump'. Preston went on, 'the continuous failures of Edrich and Washbrook have put England in a very sorry plight besides giving severe headaches to the selectors'.

At the start of the series, there had been renewed speculation about Edrich and the England captaincy in view of the doubts about Yardley's Test calibre. 'Opinion at Lord's is veering towards the appointment of Bill Edrich as England's captain against the Australians if Norman Yardley fails to find his form. There is still some opposition to Edrich but it gets weaker every day,' claimed the *Manchester Evening News*. Yet by the middle of the series he was fighting to retain his place in the side, something that would have seemed unthinkable only a year ago. 'Will Edrich and Washbrook be dropped?' asked the *Daily Worker* after the Lord's Test. But neither of those two players was in fact omitted. In a sensational move, the selectors axed none other than Len Hutton, reportedly for a failure of nerve. The decision had little logic beyond a desire by the selectors to shake up the England team and assert their authority with a dramatic gesture. All too predictably, Hutton's replacement, the Gloucestershire opener George Emmett, was out of his depth, failed in both innings, and was never picked again.

But Edrich and Washbrook seized the chance to capitalise on their survival in the Third Test at Old Trafford, both of them showing far more resilience than they had in the previous two matches. Lindwall and Miller were as ferocious as ever, and England, having won the toss and decided to bat first, were soon 28 for 2, at which point Compton joined Edrich. Determined not to allow them to settle, Lindwall released a barrage of short-pitched balls, one of which gashed open Compton's forehead as he went to hook. With blood pouring from his wound, he had to leave the field; his place was taken by Jack Crapp of Gloucestershire, who resisted stoutly before falling for 37. After batting three hours with 'stubborn concentration', to use the *Daily Express*'s description, Edrich went for 32 with the score at 117 for 5, when he gloved Lindwall to the keeper. With his wound stitched up and his head heavily bandaged, Compton now returned to play one of the great innings of his life as he dragged England up to 363 and was left unbeaten on 145. Edrich was especially struck by how Compton, despite his injury, stood up to Lindwall and Miller in full cry, 'They really went after Denis but he never flinched and played some glorious attacking shots.' For the first time in the series, England were on top when Australia faltered in their response, slumping to 172 to 6. At the fall of this wicket, Lindwall came out to bat. Within minutes, Edrich had the crowd roaring with enthusiasm with his daring mode of attack as he bowled to the new batsman. At the end of the first day, Edrich had run into Lindwall at an official reception and, thinking about the barrage unleashed on him earlier, had asked the Australian:

'How would you react if I fired bumpers at you?'

'Wouldn't worry me. I'd treat them with impunity,' replied Lindwall.

'We'll see tomorrow.'

Edrich was as good as his word. Lindwall received five bouncers in a row from Edrich, one of which almost parted his hair and another that rapped him on the hand.

'Hey, what's the idea Bill? I can bowl a bit you know.'

'No need to worry, Ray, just giving you your impunity balls.'

To the accompaniment of loud boos from the crowd, Lindwall and Miller showed no hesitation about retaliating when Edrich came in to join Washbrook near the start of England's second innings. Confronted by a torrent of short balls, Washbrook was hit on the head and Edrich on the elbow. According to Edrich's account in his 1950 book *Cricketing Days*, in the wake of these blows, 'Bradman came across and said to me, "I'm sorry about all this. When these boys get excited, I can't control them."'

I said, 'That's quite okay, Don. It's perfectly legitimate.'

But Bradman went over and talked to Miller, who toned it down a lot after that.

Margaret Hughes, the cricket reporter, found the Australians' display 'rather childish and slightly ridiculous. An attempt to intimidate Edrich is laughable and those who certainly did had no reason to doubt his tough courage.' Once Edrich had survived his trial by bumper he grew in fluency, hitting eight fours and a six as he reached 50, only to be run out soon afterwards by a direct throw from Arthur Morris at cover. He had put on 128 with Washbrook, but subsequently far too much time was lost to rain and the match petered out into a draw. Still, Edrich's bravery ensured he would keep his place, *Wisden* describing his innings as 'one of his best and most confident'. In a handwritten note at the time of Edrich's death in 1986, Hutton said, 'Although short of stature, Edrich played those great fast bowlers Lindwall and Miller better than any batsman of my time. His courage and sense of humour were of a very high order.'

The next Test at Headingley was a personal triumph for Edrich, but one of the darkest calamities for England in Ashes history. Hutton was restored to the England team and put on 168 for the first wicket with Washbrook, then Edrich batted through to the close, reaching 41 not out. The next day, he and the nightwatchman Alec Bedser had a remarkable partnership of 155 that took England past 400 and Edrich past the century mark. He was eventually out for 111, having batted for more than five hours and hit 13 fours and a six. Due to the collapse of the England tail and vigorous wagging by the Australian one, the home side had a lead of only 38. But they batted with purpose in the second innings, Edrich putting on 103 with Compton before he fell lbw to Lindwall for 54. A compelling description of Edrich's aggression against spin was left by John Arlott: 'He is almost frightening: his feet take him on savage tip-toes to the ball and his whole body is contorted with the blow he strikes.' Australia were set a daunting target of 404 on a pitch that was taking spin, and England seemed to have a great chance of victory. But everything went wrong for Yardley's team as Bradman led one of the most spectacular run-chases ever seen in Test cricket. England's only front-line spinner, Jim Laker, bowled badly, the part-time spinners worse. Godfrey Evans, the flamboyant keeper, missed a string of chances, as did many of the fielders. Compton was convinced that if Edrich, a safe, sometimes athletic catcher, had been at slip, England would have won. Unfortunately, when Yardley put Edrich at cover, Jack Crapp was placed at slip and missed a couple of dollies off Bradman's edge before he had made 10. With 13 minutes to spare, Australia won by seven wickets.

Although Edrich was generous about the Australians, praising them for the 'truly great game that they played', the loss was deeply dispiriting for England. Their despondency was compounded in the last Test at The Oval, when they were bowled out for just 52 and 188 in an innings defeat as Lindwall mercilessly exploited the damp conditions. In their own miserable end to the series, Edrich made 3 and 28 and Compton went for 4 and 39, 'mere shadows of the "terrible twins" of last year', in the words of one writer. At county level, however, Edrich had been in excellent form in 1948, averaging 60 and hitting six centuries in the Championship. But the halcyon days of 1947 had passed, never to be recaptured. And in his domestic life more self-inflicted troubles were brewing. Shortly before he went on the 1946–47 Ashes tour, Edrich spoke in an interview with *Australian Women's Weekly* of his wife Marion's anxiety about the couple's long forthcoming separation: 'We had just moved into a lovely new flat. My wife's parting comment was, "I know it's all to do with priorities but I do wish we wives could come."' Her apprehension turned out to be well-founded.

8

LEGENDARY CHARM
1948–1950

'He was actually a very kind, loving, gentle, caring person, though some thought he was a rogue and a drunkard. He had his faults and was a bit flamboyant, but I loved and respected him.'

Jasper Edrich

Bill Edrich's legendary charm towards women did not have universal application. During one gathering at the end-of-season Scarborough Festival, he was so captivated by the sight of the long-gowned, bejewelled Lady Enid Leveson-Gower, wife of the Surrey grandee and festival patron Sir Henry, as she processed into dinner, that he walked up to her, fell to one knee and exclaimed, 'Have I told you lately I love you?' Her ladyship was not amused. She lifted her head in contempt, then walked on, leaving Edrich genuflecting to an empty space. In similar vein, Rodney Edrich recalled, 'My mother, who was pretty austere and Victorian, once said to me, "I can't see what all these women are fussing about. If I went out with him, I would probably just go to sleep." His wicked wiles did not attract her at all.'

Understandably, some wives and husbands felt threatened or angry at the perpetual motion of his roving eye. The Middlesex leg-spinner Ian Bedford remembered an incident where he was given a lift by one of his colleagues, who explained that they were 'going to pick up Denis on the way, so you take a seat in the back and Denis will sit up front'. When the car arrived at Compton's home, he ran out, followed by his angry wife who said, 'Don't you dare have anything to do with that Bill Edrich. He's a womaniser and unfaithful and disgraceful. Don't you dare have anything to do with him.' Another Middlesex player of the 1950s,

Mike Murray, said in our interview: 'Bill was incorrigible. We had a young player called Ted Clark and he had a very attractive wife. They were at a Middlesex party and Bill was there. He manoeuvred her into a corner, and, leaning against the wall, told her his story about his great day at Massingham during the war. He was very foolish because he must have known that Ted was just five yards away, watching.'

But Bill Edrich never allowed the occasional rebuff or other couples' marital vows to deter him from his unceasing quest for passion and romance. 'He was always chasing the girls,' said the England tour manager Geoffrey Howard. Nor did Edrich's seniority as an international cricketer or his yearning for the England captaincy inhibit his style. He wanted the job, but not at the price of any restraint on his pleasure-seeking mission. Shortly before he died in 2022, the late Sussex captain Robin Marlar told me, 'Bill felt life was for living. He was quite different to Denis. Good times just happened to Denis, whereas Bill went out and sought them. He wasn't Rudolf Valentino but he was a pretty quick mover. Self-confidence was part of it.' Peter Parfitt, the Middlesex and England batsman, said that 'Bill was a big trier with women, put it that way.' The same point was made by England all-rounder Trevor Bailey, who said of Compton, 'I have never come across anyone who was so attractive to women. Bill Edrich was different. He was predatory when it came to women, a hunter who made a great deal of effort. Denis wasn't like that. He didn't have to do anything. They just flocked to him.'

The lyricist Sir Tim Rice told me that Edrich was his 'favourite cricketer' when he was growing up and had fallen in love with the game. So it was with a tone of affection and amusement that he related a story illustrating the tangles that Bill could get into, bordering on the spirit of a West End farce. Sir Tim's version of this tale in our interview ran as follows:

Bill was playing in a Test and at the ground ran into an old friend who invited him to dinner at his home on Saturday night. Bill looked forward to the occasion, but when he turned up, he found his friend in black tie. 'I am so sorry, I forgot that I have this event, so I have to go out,' he said. These were the days before mobile phones and a message he had left for Bill at the ground never reached him.

'But my wife will entertain you,' his friend added. It was not a prospect that disappointed Bill, always an admirer of womanhood in general and of this woman in particular. Her husband having left for his dinner, the friend's wife proceeded to 'entertain' Bill in the widest definition of the term. When the friend returned from his dinner, he found the house empty and Bill and his wife gone. Nor did the pair show up the next day. In a fury, the friend went down to the ground on Monday, and waited outside the main entrance to confront Bill, knowing that he would have to turn up for play that morning. A little sheepish after his extra-marital distractions, Bill was all too aware of this likelihood, so instead of using the main entrance, he donned a coat, hat and scarf and joined a queue of spectators going through the turnstiles. With his collar up, his trilby's trim down, he made it into the ground without being recognised. Soon afterwards he was in the sanctuary of the dressing room. It is perhaps the only case of an England player paying to appear in a Test for which he had been selected.

In a variation on this tale, the cricket historian David Frith picked up a whisper that the England selectors had been forced to draw up a contingency plan for one of the 1948 Tests by putting another batsman on standby in case Edrich had to withdraw because of a death threat from an irate husband. Both of these stories might sound apocryphal, yet Bill certainly did go through a domestic crisis during the 1948 series and the incident was to have a profound impact on the course of his life. Although some of the details were different, the essential thrust of a disappearing act with another man's wife during a cricket match is correct. The episode occurred when Bill and his second wife Marion were invited by his friend Harold 'Dick' Milnes to stay at the home he shared with his wife Jessy and their two young daughters in Castle Donington, when Middlesex played Derbyshire at the beginning of 1948. Dick Milnes, a solicitor, had first met Bill when they were on a staff training course at Camberley in 1943. It was ironic, in view of subsequent events, that at the time Milnes should have given Edrich legal advice on his divorce from his first wife Betty. The Derbyshire game was the second time that Dick and his wife had extended their hospitality to the Edriches that summer, for they had also stayed during the Trent Bridge Test. Against the backdrop of illicit lust and an eagerness to escape current domestic ties, Dick's second invitation turned out to be an explosive device that blew apart two marriages.

Both Bill and Jessy were impetuous, headstrong characters, whose vivacity was matched by their stubbornness. By the summer of 1948, Bill, not a man given to routine and placidity, was tiring of his relationship with Marion. When his autobiography *Cricket Heritage* was published that year, he dedicated the book to Marion, thanking her, rather prosaically, for her 'encouragement and help'. But that was one of the last acts of generosity he performed for his second wife. Their union fell apart completely during the trip to Castle Donington, when the chemistry of mutual attraction between Bill and Jessy could not be contained.

'Bill kept saying how unhappy he was and I was miserable too at that time,' Jessy recalled. The stormy nature of her marriage was confirmed to me by her daughter Penny. 'My mother was not very happily married to my father, so it was quite an opportunity when Bill turned up. She and father had terrible, terrible rows when I was little. He was very distant. They probably should not have married in the first place. They were too young; and then he was away in the early part of the war. After that, he got a job in Nottingham so we moved there. I don't think my mother liked the east Midlands. She came from Yorkshire.'

Born in 1918, Jessy was the daughter of Hubert Gomersall, the manager of the Bradford branch of the Halifax Building Society. Her ambitions were more artistic and she became an actress in repertory theatre in the mid-1930s, gaining favourable reviews for some of her performances. In August 1936, for instance, she appeared at the Playhouse Theatre in Jesmond in Agatha Christie's *Love from a Stranger* in which, according to the *Newcastle Chronicle*, Jessy 'played the part of the girl Ciceley with natural charm'. Her future on the stage looked even brighter when she graduated from the Royal Academy of Dramatic Art in 1937, but the major breakthrough never came and she never revived her career after becoming a young mother.

Yet the liveliness she brought to the stage was central to Jessy's personality and one of the reasons that Bill was drawn to her. 'She was the life and soul of the party,' said Penny. 'She was fun. She was the kind of person that people like to go to the pub with.' Bill's sister Ena had the same opinion. 'She was the most delightful person and loved by all. I felt her to be the sister I had always longed for.' Less generously, another relative described Jessy as 'held together by cigarettes, sherry and vodka'. The start of her relationship with Bill Edrich could not have been more awkward, as they boldly fled to London once the game at Derby was finished. 'We just ran away. It was complicated because my two daughters were then quite tiny,' recalled Jessy. Amid much recrimination and unhappiness, the Edrich and Milnes marriages were dissolved, Dick winning custody of the two children because of their mother's admission of adultery in court. Penny said of the legal outcome, 'That was really not very nice for my sister and I because when we were with my father, he was working all the time and he had to get a series of people to look after us. We did not have what is called a family upbringing, though my mother was a good mother. She was very unhappy she was not given custody.'

Bill and Jessy married on 13 September, 1949 at Marylebone Registry Office. On the certificate, his occupation was described as 'representative of a paint firm and amateur cricketer', while his address was given as Weymouth Street in central London. Soon afterwards, they moved to a cottage in Hatfield, Hertfordshire, where they began to find a new stability after all the upheaval they had endured. They were able to see more of Jessy's children, which pleased Penny. 'Bill was a very good stepfather to me, playing padder tennis (a playground version of tennis featuring a smaller court and wooden bats) and getting me to help him pick race winners from the paper. He was a very nice chap, a much better father to me than my own father to be honest. Both of us really liked Bill.' Her sister Jo, who is five years younger, agrees: 'He was always very nice. I guess I adored him from afar. I certainly preferred him to my own father. What comes to mind when I think about Bill – dog-tooth jackets with leather elbows, his pipe and a lovely smell of gold leaf tobacco. He always listened to the shipping forecast (boring) and the six o'clock news (no talking). I remember he laughed a lot and rarely threw a wobbler.' Referring to her mother's sociability, Jo continues: 'They adored lots of booze but in my time I never saw him lose it completely, just very merry.' Edrich became a father in his own right when Jasper was born. Jasper provided these memories of his parents: 'He was actually a very kind, loving, gentle, caring person, though some thought he was a rogue and a drunkard. He had his faults and was a bit flamboyant, but I loved and respected him. Jessy was dynamic; she had a hell of a personality. She liked a drink and company. When we lived in Hertfordshire, people were always popping in to see her. I would not say that she was the brightest person in the world, but she loved chatting and aspired to higher social circles.'

Indeed, Sir Tim Rice's father worked for the De Havilland aircraft company at Hatfield and he remembers his parents regularly seeing Bill and Jessy at local cocktail parties. Yet Jasper recalled that, because of its remoteness, the Hatfield cottage was surprisingly primitive:

Thanks to his work with Latham Brown, there were pots of paint all over the place. Electricity was provided by a generator in a shed, powered by a cylinder petrol engine, which you had to turn with a handle to start. It would go bang, bang, bang and would sometimes catch fire. We used to shovel soil in the bloody thing to dampen the flames. Dad could be quite enterprising – somehow, despite rationing, he managed to get drums of petrol for the generator. But he was not really practical at all. In fact he was useless, he could not fix anything.

Because of business commitments, Edrich did not go on the England tour of South Africa in the winter of 1948–49, and his marital chaos would not have persuaded the selectors to attempt a change of mind.

The turmoil in his personal life did not seem to have much impact. Edrich's form for Middlesex in the 1949 season was impressive, as his first-class batting average remained above 40, and once again he hit over 2,000 runs. 'Edrich was often the mainstay of the batting and he fielded splendidly in the slips but his bowling was almost a negligible quantity,' said *Wisden*. Middlesex came joint top of the table and shared the title with Yorkshire, but *Wisden* felt they should have done better; the team's performances were 'unpredictable'; their batting 'inconsistent'. It was also a story of unevenness at the international level. After just one half-century in the first two Tests against New Zealand, there were renewed calls for him to be dropped. 'Bill Edrich is not at his best and should be given a rest,' argued the *Sunday Dispatch*, while the *Daily Mirror* felt he had 'done little to warrant his retention'. But he played better in the last two Tests, taking his average for the series up to 54 and scoring a century in the final game at The Oval against an attack that included the accurate and hostile fast-medium bowler Jack Cowie. Of his innings, *Wisden* wrote that he 'began quietly but he also drove and pulled with refreshing vigour and reached his century in three hours'. His runs could not help to force an England victory. The Oval Test ended in a draw, like all the other three matches in the series, which Compton described as 'the most boring' that he ever played.

England's captaincy was in a state of flux that summer as the selectors, still under the chairmanship of Jack Holmes, considered alternatives to Yardley. Not only had his leadership against Australia been heavily criticised in 1948, but his availability was becoming limited because of his business duties. In the winter tour of South Africa the England team had been successfully led by George Mann, who retained the job for the first two Tests against New Zealand, then stood aside for the veteran Northamptonshire all-rounder Freddie Brown. A bullish leader, attacking batsman and versatile bowler, Brown was enjoying an astounding renaissance in the twilight of his career after he had taken up a job at the Northampton manufacturer British Timken, whose board wanted to create a new era of success at the county club.

In the absence of an established incumbent for the post of the England captaincy, the cry went up from some quarters for Edrich to be given the job, led as usual by Crawford White in the *News Chronicle*. Later in life Bill gave Graham Saville, the Essex batsman who played for Norfolk with him in the late 1960s, a potential explanation for his hold on White. As Saville put it to me, 'Crawford was a great friend of Bill, who allowed him to join his group on their nights on the town during England tours. Bill said that this was so that White would pick up the girl the rest of them did not want.' Whatever the truth about his motivation, White was indefatigable in Edrich's cause.' Describing Edrich as George Mann's 'obvious successor' now that he had been an amateur for three seasons, White said that he 'appears to every cricket follower to have every qualification for the job. Yet the hard fact remains that there is a strong body of influential opinion which feels that while he is a good team man he is temperamentally unsuited for captaincy. They feel so strongly that they would prefer to see professional Denis Compton take over.' The reluctance of the establishment to consider Edrich gnawed away at him. Even as a child, Penny saw how much he wanted the position: 'He was tremendously patriotic and I remember his disappointment at not getting the job. He would have loved to have been England captain.' But she admitted that concerns about him were understandable. 'He was a bit over-gregarious, shall we say. He did drink but he did not get nasty. He usually just started to sing. I would say that Bill was not an alcoholic but he just couldn't hold his drink. A couple of beers would send him over the top.'

Yet even if he did not have a clinical drinking problem, his consumption could land him in serious trouble. He had a minor scrape with the law in February 1948 when he was fined 30 shillings for speeding in Edgware, but much more damaging was an incident at Christmas 1949 when he was detained by the police for being 'drunk and incapable' at Piccadilly Circus following a drinks party. So intoxicated was Edrich that Inspector Rogers, who arrested him, had to call a doctor to check on his condition. Held in the police cells overnight, he appeared at Bow Street magistrate's court on 23 December and pleaded guilty to the charge. 'I am very sorry it happened and to have taken up your time,' he said sheepishly as he accepted a 10-shilling fine and an order to pay 25 shillings in costs.

But, in terms of his career, an even darker episode occurred the following summer in 1950 when England played the West Indies. Yardley was back as captain for the First Test but more ominous for Edrich was the appointment of the new Chairman of the Selectors in place of Jack Holmes. This was Bob Wyatt, whose severe appearance embodied his attachment to discipline and rigour, the very opposite of Edrich's permissive outlook. 'The ethical gulf between the two men was enormous,' said Trevor Bailey, a point that Edrich conceded, writing that Wyatt was 'a dour, reserved type of man, whose views on cricket were so different to mine that we automatically bristled at the sight of each other'. They had quarrelled during the war, when both of them were in the RAF side, and

Edrich grew exasperated at Wyatt's defensive approach to captaincy, telling him so to his face. Now the scene was set for a much bigger clash that would resonate for years to come.

Edrich had made a mixed start to the 1950 season; his four first-class centuries before the First Test, including 189 versus Glamorgan and 152 against Sussex, stood in contrast to a string of low scores in the County Championship. Yet in his role as a pundit, for which he was in increasing demand because of his forthright views, he exuded confidence about England's chances against the West Indies, despite the pre-tour hype regarding the strength of the visitors' batting, headed by Frank Worrell, Clyde Walcott and Everton Weekes, and the intrigue generated by their two young spinners Alf Valentine and Sonny Ramadhin. In an article in the *Sunday Dispatch*, which turned out to be badly ill-judged in hindsight, Edrich wrote, 'Not for one moment do I believe the exaggerated stories going around about them. I still believe that England will get the better of them.' Turning to the spinners, he argued that 'the slow department is the most suspect part of the whole side', not least because the young pair lacked experience. Edrich's theory was badly contradicted when England batted first in the opening Test at Old Trafford and were bowled out for 312, Valentine taking a haul of 8 for 104 on his debut. Edrich was one of his victims, lbw for 7. Only Godfrey Evans with a swashbuckling century, and Trevor Bailey with 82 not out, broke free of the web that Valentine wove. With a battery of their own spinners, England gained a substantial lead, then Edrich top-scored in the second innings, making 71 and helping England set a target of 385 on a wicket that was now turning significantly. The West Indies never looked like they would reach their target, and England won by the huge margin of 202 runs.

According to several accounts, including his own, Edrich had a rolling programme of celebrations during the Test. He once said, 'I have little time for the goody-goodies who say rather pompously that if one is playing for one's country one should get to bed early and not go to parties before or during a game.' At Old Trafford, he spectacularly lived up to his principles. There were drinks not only to herald England's progress towards victory but also to mark individual achievements. On the evening of the first day, Thursday 8 June, the milestone of Evans's maiden Test century 'really called for a party', as he put it. In a sign of the event's sustained exuberance, Bailey's memory is that the next morning Edrich turned up still in his dinner jacket for breakfast at the team's hotel at Alderley Edge, Cheshire. Then there had to be another party to mark his own 'bit of success' in making 56 not out at the end of the second day, Friday 9 June. Edrich denied that the occasion spiralled out of control. 'It was great fun and I suppose we were a bit rowdy. But then most athletes are and it wasn't terribly late – only about midnight.' Others stated that Edrich's nocturnal antics were much louder and went on longer. Bailey recalled that Edrich had to be put to bed by the porter and was 'so paralytic that he woke everyone up'. There were also claims, relayed in the authorised biography of Denis Compton, that Edrich was entertaining female company with such energy that the sounds echoed far beyond his room.

Batting the following morning, 10 June, he prodded and poked 15 runs in 40 minutes and had two narrow escapes before he fell to Ramadhin. What gave the saga of Edrich's insobriety so much impetus was that Bob Wyatt had been in the room next door and had been woken in the early hours of Saturday. He said nothing while the match was still underway, but once England had won, he demanded to see Edrich in a committee room at Old Trafford. As soon as Edrich turned up, Wyatt came to the point. 'Your batting on Saturday was not up to Friday's standard and the reason was obviously the party you went to on Friday night.' In his highly controversial reminiscence, published in the *Sunday People* in 1958, Edrich said, 'His words hit me like a bomb. I admitted the party but pointed out that I was perfectly fit in the morning and batting at least in my best form on an awkward pitch.' Edrich thought the reprimand was the end of the matter, especially because Wyatt's selection committee, which also included the uncompromising former Yorkshire captain Brian Sellers, chose him for the next Test at Lord's.

But Wyatt had no intention of letting the matter drop. He told his official biographer Gerald Pawle that, while he was still contemplating his next step, his fellow selector Sellers, who had learnt to his disgust about the incident, 'came to me and announced in his usual forthright way that if I declined to report Edrich he would do so himself. That forced my hand because if anyone was going to report the matter then it had to be the Chairman of the Selectors.' Wyatt's report was duly sent to Lord's, triggering a chain of events that would result in the harshest disciplinary action against Edrich. At the time, in June 1950, the episode took place behind closed doors and the public were kept in the dark. But on his retirement from first-class cricket, Edrich was determined to present his side of the story, and he did so in a lengthy, incendiary article in the *Sunday People* to accompany his third and latest volume of autobiography. In the piece, Edrich downplayed the celebrations, pointed to his own second-innings score at Old Trafford, lambasted Wyatt's 'abominable' performance as Chairman and claimed that Wyatt had long borne him a grudge.

The 1958 article caused a sensation, as well as fury from key figures in English cricket. Walter Robins, the former Middlesex captain, complained that Edrich had presented an 'entirely erroneous picture' of a game where players 'are continually smeared by rows and jealousies'. In the *Daily Telegraph*, Jim Swanton called Edrich's column 'a shocker' and argued that Wyatt would have a good case if he sued Edrich, just as the MCC could justly 'institute an inquiry into the public defamation of one of their members'. Indeed, Doug Insole, the highly regarded captain of Essex, and Sir William Worsley, the Yorkshire patrician, both called on the MCC to take action against Edrich so he would see that 'members of the club disapprove strongly of the type of journalism in which he had indulged'. In a letter to Ronny Aird, who succeeded Colonel Rait Kerr as Secretary of the MCC in 1952, Insole said that Edrich's criticism of Wyatt 'is something which should surely not go unanswered . . . My own feeling is that some sort of admonition is called for', if 'only as a warning signal as to what might occur if further examples of this rather sinister journalism appear under Mr Edrich's name'. Sir William felt that Edrich's article 'left a very unpleasant taste in the mouth' and brought the game 'into disrepute'. It was, he argued, 'high time that something was done to stop this spate of scurrilous writing', perhaps through a warning to Edrich that 'his expulsion from the club' would result if he wrote any 'future article of this nature'. But the MCC 'after a lengthy discussion' agreed that 'it would be a mistake to take any specific action' or conduct an interview with Edrich, much as his conduct was 'deplored', since 'more harm than good might be done unless the matter was left alone'.

Wyatt also decided not to resort to litigation, but he wrote a public letter putting his side of the case. The letter, published in the *Daily Telegraph* on 3 June, 1958, was all the more powerful because of its mix of anger, bewilderment and hurt at what Edrich had written, which Wyatt said was 'scurrilous' and 'beneath contempt'. Edrich's suggestion, continued Wyatt, 'of a harmless party ending about midnight falls very far short of the truth. It is not my intention to go into painful details. I will merely mention that apparently Mr Edrich's watch was several hours slow and, taking into account other factors it is now rather surprising to me that he arrived at the ground in time to continue his innings.' Wyatt concluded, 'I have never been aware of any feud between myself and Edrich or any other cricketer. In fact I look back over more than a quarter of a century of first-class cricket with the happiest memories. It seems to me, to put it mildly, very sad that Edrich should now seek to surround first-class cricket with a spurious atmosphere of scandal.'

Much of the bitterness that Edrich poured out in 1958 stemmed from the way he was treated by Lord's as a result of Wyatt's report on his partying. Summoned to the office of the MCC, he arrived to find Plum Warner, the Treasurer Harry Altham and the Secretary Rait Kerr already waiting for him. 'It was pretty obvious something was afoot,' wrote Edrich in 1958. 'It turned out to be a court-martial with me in the dock. They said they had received a report from Wyatt that I had been drunk during the Test match at Old Trafford and asked me to answer the allegation. I repeated the statement I had made to Wyatt. I emphatically denied being drunk but admitted to being in high spirits.' Edrich was stunned by the next move, when Rait Kerr asked him to withdraw his name from the list of candidates for the MCC tour of Australia that winter, which was to be led by Freddie Brown. 'I refused on the grounds that I had been completely fit on the Saturday morning and had committed no offence.' His objections made no difference. When Brown's party to Australia was revealed, Edrich's name was absent.

Yet on the eve of the team's announcement, the signs for Edrich had looked promising. In his 1958 article, Edrich claimed to have heard 'that when my name had come up before the MCC Committee choosing the party for Australia, 11 had voted for me and two against'. Denis Compton detected that the mood was favourable when he attended a dinner at the flat of George Mann with some of the selectors. Compton recorded: 'I went home that evening convinced he would be in the side. So much so that in the dressing room the next morning, I took Bill to one side and said, "Don't buoy up your hopes because of what I say, Bill, but I was with three of the selectors last night and I formed a strong impression that you would be on the boat." Bill was delighted but when the news came that he had not been invited, I think my disappointment was greater than his.'

On the question of picking the touring party, the villain for Edrich was Freddie Brown, the England skipper. Walter Robins, who also sat on the selection committee for the tour, told Edrich that Brown and Sellers were the two who opposed Bill's inclusion, and the former effectively had a veto. 'The selection committee would not go against his wishes,' wrote Edrich of Brown in 1958. At the Scarborough festival, Edrich tackled Brown about his omission, and Brown denied any responsibility: 'If the choice had been left to me, I would have taken you.' But if Brown really said that, he was dissembling, for he was no admirer of Edrich and suspected him of being a poor tourist. 'I've enough on my plate without him,' he is reported to have said. As Gerald Pawle, Wyatt's biographer, put it, 'If Brown had expressed a wish to have Edrich in his side, he would undoubtedly have gone to Australia, but Brown was adamant about not taking him.' On the other hand, had George Mann or Norman Yardley been the captain for this Ashes tour, Edrich would probably been chosen. An outstanding leader, Mann believed that one of the requirements of a captain was to bring out the best in his players. Mann, whose own father Frank also captained Middlesex and England, urged flexibility and forbearance in dealing with the sometimes wayward Edrich and Compton. As quoted in Brian Rendell's dual biography of the father and son, George Mann believed, 'You didn't crack the whip with chaps like that. You had to give them their head and they never let you down.' Mann's philosophy was that 'if a player is picked for England, it does not mean he is naturally an easy or even nice person. What it does mean is that he is a bloody good cricketer. As a manager or a captain, you have to cope with misdemeanours and try to help players avoid them.'

Plum Warner heaped the blame for Edrich's exclusion on Brown, believing the skipper should have been less rigid. In a conversation with Philip Snow, the cricketer, colonial administrator and brother of the novelist C.P. Snow, Warner cited his own successful experience of accommodating the all-rounder Len Braund on the 1903–04 tour of Australia, despite his reputation for intemperance. 'He enjoyed the tour to the full and was a match winner. Brown should have taken the challenge over Edrich similarly,' Warner told Snow. Although Snow himself was taken with Brown's 'unflagging energy' and 'natural command', others were less enamoured. Peter Parfitt, the Norfolk-born Test cricketer who played with Edrich at Middlesex, told me, 'Freddie Brown was the biggest soak of whisky you could ever get. Dreadful man, dreadful. He was a bumptious sod. Not a favourite of mine at all. It was a pathetic side and Freddie Brown had a lot to do with that.' Just as antagonistic was the great fast bowler Fred Trueman, who described Brown as 'a snob. Bad-tempered, ignorant and a bigot.' His team for the 1950–51 Ashes certainly involved some strange choices, with too many inexperienced players. 'The worst-selected side I have ever seen,' said Alec Bedser. Normally a defender of the establishment, the *Daily Telegraph* said that the selectors 'have done a grave injustice to Edrich in passing him over. There is no reason for it.' This was part of a pattern of mediocrity in English Test cricket at the beginning of the decade, as *Wisden* spelt out at the end of the West Indies tour, which saw the visitors win by three Tests to one. 'Our troubles are shown plainly by the many changes considered necessary by the Selection Committee. No fewer than 25 men appeared for England in the course of the four Tests, not one man playing the whole series, whereas the West Indies were a real team with 12 players their total. In fact, England were little better than a scratch lot.'

The West Indies' superiority was graphically demonstrated at Lord's where they won a famous triumph at the end of June by 328 runs. Edrich, out in both innings to Ramadhin for 8, was part of the England procession that soon had calypsos being sung at the home of cricket. Afterwards, he confessed to Compton that he could not fathom Ramadhin's unorthodox style at all; in a vivid phrase, he said it was 'like someone is throwing a handful of confetti at you'. Calling for Edrich to be dropped, A.A. Thomas of the *Daily Worker* wrote that 'Ramadhin seems to bowl as he likes against the Middlesex all-rounder'. Even more scathing was the former Australian Test star Alan Fairfax who denounced Edrich's 'namby-pamby' play at Lords. But a back injury for Edrich pre-empted any decision by the selectors, and he withdrew from the Test side for the rest of the summer, appearing for Middlesex in a jacket made of plaster of Paris. Compounding this problem, his shoulder continued to give him trouble, which meant he could no longer bowl fast. But Edrich, deluding himself that he still had a chance of making the MCC side for Australia, claimed in August he was making 'good progress' in his recovery. With a whiff of desperation, he used a column in the *Evening Despatch* to make what amounted to a public appeal for inclusion, emphasising his reputation for resilience: 'If you are not confident, if you are afraid of a fight, you'd better never pack your bag for a tour like this.' But Wyatt and his colleagues were unmovable.

Only a few weeks earlier he had been mooted once more as a possible England captain. Without any grasp of how far Edrich had fallen in official favour, the *Sunday Dispatch* called for him to replace Yardley, who the paper said was not up to standard as a Test player. 'If we must have an amateur as captain, there can be only one choice: Bill Edrich. He is a brilliant cricketer. He is batting as well as he has ever done and his tireless enthusiasm in the field sets the ideal example to his teammates.' The paper also argued that he had done 'remarkably well' as a substitute leader in several games for Middlesex that summer. Indeed, the veteran Kent wicket-keeper Les Ames was impressed with Edrich's leadership when Middlesex visited Canterbury in August. Having set Kent a tempting target on the last afternoon, he kept the game alive by deliberately giving the home side runs if they fell behind the clock. His theory was that Middlesex were more likely to take wickets and win if Kent continued to chase rather than go on the defensive. His plan did not work; Kent won by six wickets, but Ames thought he had shown the right enterprising attitude. 'Without Bill's help the match would have fizzled out into a draw,' said Ames, who was also a selector in 1950, adding, 'he was always one for a good fight'.

Nevertheless, the defeat by Kent was indicative of a disappointing season for Middlesex. They finished in 14th place, their lowest ranking since 1930. In *Wisden*'s words, 'Edrich frequently stood in the breach when batters went badly', but there was a palpable sense of decline about him. Partly because of his back injury, he failed to reach 2,000 first-class runs, while his bowling average rose to almost 50. Now aged 34, time was catching up with him. In one very poignant moment, he generously went to St Pancras station to say farewell to Denis Compton and the Ashes team. According to Compton's moving account:

> From his expression, nobody could have imagined the disappointment he was hiding. Because of our close association, I sought him out just before the departure whistle sounded:

> 'I'm darned sorry you're not with us.'
> 'So am I,' came the reply.

9

TEST EXILE
1951–1953

'He has so much courage that he surmounted all handicaps and proved
himself completely fitted temperamentally, an essential attribute in
Nos 1 and 2.'

Don Bradman

Freddie Brown's tour was not the humiliation that England's critics expected.
Although Australia won the series 4-1, one of their victories was by a margin of
just 28 runs and another came when they had the good fortune to catch England
on a rain-affected wicket. Moreover, Hutton and Bedser confirmed their status
as world-class cricketers, while Brown proved to be a capable, big-hearted captain
and surprisingly effective medium-pacer. Victory in the final Test, England's first
against Australia since the war, was a just reward.

But the sense that the visitors had come closer to glory than most pundits
expected only made it all the more frustrating that the team had been so poorly
selected, particularly in the omission of Edrich. Compton, who had a disastrous
tour, averaging just 7.57 in the Tests, said that his partner's absence was 'the
biggest error' and with him in the side, 'I believe that England would have
brought back the Ashes', because he 'literally never knows, or never admits to
knowing, when he is beaten'. It was a sentiment with which Hutton agreed:
'Someone of his experience and fighting spirit might have turned the scales.' The
umpire Frank Chester, a seasoned judge, thought it had been 'a grave mistake to
leave him out' and 'the result could have been different', for Edrich was 'a bundle
of all-round talent, strength and pluck'. As a seasoned watcher of players close-up,
Chester believed that Edrich's resilience to pace was one of his most vital assets:

'He knew the value of moving into the line of the delivery. That was one reason why his drive past mid-on was so productive. He played the hook beautifully too and was the last person to be intimidated by bumpers.' Even when the Ashes series had begun in December, some voices were urging that the MCC fly Edrich out to Australia as an emergency to bolster the batting. 'His presence alone would have a heartening affect on the team and his fighting spirit would spread through the side,' argued Tony Horstead in the *Sunday Dispatch*.

There was no chance, however, of Edrich making an early return to the Test side in Australia, or during the 1951 season, when England hosted South Africa. Bob Wyatt was still on the selection panel, which was now chaired by Norman Yardley, and Freddie Brown remained captain for the whole series. Edrich began to realise that he was going to pay a very heavy price for his nights of frivolity at Old Trafford the previous summer. It was ironic that his qualities of gregariousness and conviviality with his England teammates should have led to isolation from them, just as his desire to celebrate would deny him further chances to do so in the immediate years to come. 'I'd done an indiscreet thing but it didn't warrant a punishment like that,' he said. His sister Ena believed Bill saw the ban not just as personally unfair, but also damaging 'to the fortunes of English cricket', something that really mattered to him because of 'his fierce nationalistic pride'.

The effective ban imposed on Edrich from June 1950 gave a lopsided appearance to the graph of his Test career, full of long absences and unusual gaps. Even taking the war into account, it is extraordinary that in an international career whose span ran from 1938 to the Ashes tour of 1954–55, during which England played 88 Tests, Edrich appeared in only 39 of them. Moreover, he went on just three overseas Test tours, though England made eight such trips between his debut and his final game. Official doubts about his behaviour were part of the reason, though injuries and loss of form were also an issue. Together, these factors meant that Edrich, for all his star quality, never quite fulfilled the enormous promise with which he had burst on the scene in 1937 and early 1938. His Test average of 40 was dwarfed by his England contemporaries Eddie Paynter (average 59), Wally Hammond (58), Len Hutton (56) and Denis Compton (50). Of others who played more than 20 Tests during his time with England, Peter May (average 47), Joe Hardstaff (47), Colin Cowdrey (44), Tom Graveney (44) and Cyril Washbrook (42) all had better records.

In Test exile throughout 1951, Edrich had to concentrate on his duties with Middlesex. He did so productively, averaging more than 45 in the County Championship and helping the team rise to seventh in the table. 'Edrich, free from back trouble, was in a class above the ordinary and he reached 2,000 runs in all matches. If the situation demanded caution or called for rapid progress, Edrich filled both roles with great distinction,' said *Wisden*, though Trevor Bailey in *The Cricketer* felt that 'he appears to have mislaid much of his old sparkle'. Now 35, Edrich was one of the veterans of the club, and his generous, open spirit was welcomed by the young players who had just started their careers. Fred Titmus, who made his Middlesex debut in 1949, thought him 'a great man' and 'full to the brim with the joys of life'. On the field, said Titmus, 'he was a magnificent, fighting player who was well aware of his limitations. He did not have a great variety of shots but he used the ones he possessed with tremendous verve and effectiveness.' Titmus also had experience of Edrich as a leader; that season Middlesex had embarked on a unique experiment whereby he and Compton had jointly held the club captaincy. It was a bold move, making Compton the first professional captain of Middlesex. The club initially announced that the two men would share their responsibilities during each game, but then, partly because Compton's troublesome knee required him to take regular absences, it was decided that the captaincy would alternate between the two men. 'Neither player would be in charge for a long period,' said the club at the end of April. Learning his craft as an off-spinning all-rounder, Titmus thought that Edrich was a deeper thinker about the game and 'much more serious' than Compton. 'I liked Bill because he let me bowl a lot. He was a good skipper who never got in a flap and never lost his temper. If he wanted to tell you off he did it tactfully.'

By now, Bill's younger brother Geoff was well-established in the Lancashire side, scoring 1,693 runs in 1951, along with seven centuries, and 2,067 runs in 1952. So impressive was his form that there were calls for him to be selected for England. Although they went unheeded and Geoff never won a Test cap, he did tour India with a Commonwealth team in 1953–54. Like Bill, he was a superb close fielder, but it was their resemblance in batting styles that struck Jim Swanton, who wrote, 'There is a good deal of his distinguished brother in Edrich: a similar physique, to begin with, a similar predilection for the drive and among other mannerisms that trick of remaining poised after the stroke with the bat following fully through and pointing in the direction of the ball.' Fierce competitors from childhood, Geoff and Bill never gave an inch when they came up against each other, as *The Cricketer* noted of a Championship match in late May:

> Little brotherly love was shown when Middlesex met Lancashire at Lord's. Indeed the duel between the two Edriches was fascinating to watch because of its friendly but keen rivalry. Geoffrey, the Lancashire batsman, could blame William John for missing his century by seven runs in the first innings. William, fielding at slip, seemed to sense a cut from Geoffrey almost before the ball had left the bowler's hand. Frequently he moved several places to his right before the stroke was made and sure enough the ball would find its way to him. Against another fieldsman with no such telepathic intuitions, Geoffrey would have obtained another 20 or so runs which would have taken him well past his century. Younger brother Geoffrey had the last laugh. When Middlesex looked like saving the game in their second innings he held a stinging drive at silly mid-off and dismissed William. That was the turning point in the game and Lancashire went on to win by ten wickets. To rub it in, Geoffrey made the winning hit.

The two other Edrich brothers had not attained those standards. After four seasons with Lancashire up to 1948, during which he won his county cap but never averaged more than 27 with his bat, Eric played out his career with Norfolk at the beginning of the fifties. At Kent, Brian was awarded his cap in 1949, prompting Bill to send him a telegram, 'Congratulations. Next step England', though Brian was nowhere near international class. On the domestic front, he went on to make 22 appearances that season, including an astonishing performance in the game against Sussex at Tunbridge Wells in June, when he hit 60 and 193 with his aggressive left-handed strokeplay, then took 2 for 45 with his off-spin as Sussex successfully chased down their target. Those second-innings heroics were to be the high point of Brian's career, and he bowed out in 1956 with a first-class batting average of just 20. But there was another Edrich, still at Bracondale School, where he was captain of cricket, who would eventually eclipse them all. A cousin of Bill, who first played for Norfolk in 1954, John became one of the all-time England greats, always at his best against the finest opponents. To Bill's courage and grit, John added ferocious discipline, concentration and a phlegmatic temperament. Geoffrey Boycott, who was a regular opening partner of John Edrich for England, told me John was 'a wonderful man' whereas he felt that Bill let himself down with his drinking, which 'must have been exasperating for his many friends and supporters'. Interestingly, John and Bill were never close. Peter Parfitt, the Middlesex and England batsman who knew them both, told me, 'John and I played for Norfolk as schoolboys. John always said that he went to Surrey rather than Middlesex because he thought that with Bill being there, he would get preferential treatment. He didn't want that, so he signed for Surrey. He was quieter than Bill, who liked to party.'

The legacy of Bill's fondness for a party in 1950 still kept him out of the Test side two years later. During the 1952 season he continued to be joint captain of Middlesex with Compton, the experiment having been deemed a success by the club in its first year. According to Middlesex's annual report, it was 'an extremely workable and satisfactory arrangement. Full credit must go to the joint captains, who co-operated whole-heartedly on all occasions. Whatever the differences in their methods, they always went for a result.' Middlesex started the season well but stumbled in the second half of the summer, with the result that they were flattered by their fifth place in the Championship table. *Wisden*'s verdict was that 'the sharing of the captaincy satisfied few people. Matches were lost which, with more tenacity, might have been saved.' Compton himself felt that the concept was no longer working. 'I was never really cut out for the captaincy business. Let's be honest, I was never the best organised person on the planet,' he once admitted. With hindsight. Bill agreed. 'The idea that we should work in harness was always a non-starter. Denis always found it hard enough to look after himself in getting from A to B and his late arrivals at cricket grounds were legendary. It didn't make much sense expecting him to exert discipline.' From the fringes of the first team, the brilliant young keeper John Murray, who made his debut in 1952 and went on to become a fixture at the club over the next two decades, felt that the split in responsibilities promoted a lack of purpose, as quoted in Christopher Sandford's 2019 biography of Murray: 'It was all great fun in its way. But you wouldn't confuse it for a modern sports outfit. There was never any sort of team meeting. Denis and Bill were great players but let's just say that they didn't exactly fire on all cylinders when they happened to be somewhere like Buxton or Ashby-de-la-Zouch on a wet Wednesday morning. Neither of them ever talked about "having a strategy" or "sharing a vision". You never heard anything about therapists or dieticians. We trained on cheese sandwiches and fags.'

The distractions could undermine both solidarity and bank balances, as Bill Higginson, a young Middlesex player, recalled of one rain-affected match: 'I found the card school, as a teenager, of great interest. I watched intently until the pile of cash and notes was added to with personal cheques. The eventual conclusion, I noticed, was a resounding win shared between "the Twins". Lesson learned, I never gambled on anything from that day.'

In other circumstances, Edrich's form in 1952 might have merited an England recall, as he hit 2,281 first-class runs and six centuries. His bowling also revived after years of decline; he took 41 Championship wickets at an average of 28, and even had a ten-wicket haul against Warwickshire at Lord's. Mike Murray, a distinguished future Chairman, Treasurer and President of Middlesex, made his debut as an amateur in 1953 while working for Lloyds Insurance, after Bill had given him a trial in the nets. In our interview, he recalls: 'I faced him in the nets and he was still quick, though I always enjoyed playing fast bowling. I never saw any decline in the quality of his play as a batsman. He had great guts, and was very strong hooking and pulling,' recalled Murray. 'I got on well with him. He used to come to my office and pick me up when we had winter nets, even though he was a legendary player. He loved the game.' But Murray admitted that 'drink played a big part in his life. Before he'd had too much to drink he was very modest and unassuming, quiet and not boisterous. But when he'd had too much to drink, he would become the absolute reverse of that; he became aggressive and noisy. That was when more of the adverse things happened in his life.'

The 1952 season took place against the backdrop of two crucial developments in the governance of Britain, which signalled the reassertion of traditional conservatism. The first was in the winter of 1951 when Winston Churchill returned as Prime Minister, replacing Labour's Clement Attlee, who had headed perhaps the most radical administration in modern British history. The second was the accession of Queen Elizabeth to the throne on the death of her father in February 1952, which reinforced the hold of the constitutional monarchy on the public's imagination. Yet in the world of English cricket, not an arena noted for being progressive, a far-reaching change was underway. This was the decision to finally appoint England's first professional captain. It was a move that would have been unthinkable only a few years before. But the post-war emphasis on social mobility, combined with the reduction in the pool of amateur talent, England's dismal recent record in Tests, and the decline in the integrity of amateur status through the creation of sinecures to maintain the illusion of unpaid players, laid the ground for this break with the past.

The move came about because of the desire of Freddie Brown, now aged 41, to 'make way for a younger man' as Test leader in advance of the summer's series against the visiting Indians. With the Australians touring in 1953, the selection committee, headed by Yardley, had a vital duty to ensure the right captain was in place for next year's Ashes. The quest to fill the vacancy sparked a frenzy of speculation in the press featuring an array of names such as David Sheppard, the young Sussex batsman training for the Anglican Church; Tom Dollery, Warwickshire's professional captain; Reg Simpson, the elegant opener and amateur captain of Nottinghamshire; Trevor Bailey of Essex; Charles Palmer, the secretary and captain of Leicestershire; Denis Compton; and the Derbyshire amateur Donald Carr. But for many commentators there were only two realistic candidates: one was Len Hutton, the world's greatest batsman whose strategic advice had been essential to England's captains for years; the other was Bill Edrich, whose qualifications had been boosted by his joint leadership of Middlesex, though most of the press were not aware of the unwritten ban that was in place. Crawford White, as Edrich's loudest advocate, predictably banged the drum for him and in the *News Chronicle* came up with an unscientific survey that purported to show a floodtide of support for the Middlesex all-rounder among the game's key figures: 'A poll of past and present cricketers which I have just compiled on the question of Freddie Brown's successor as England's captain produced an almost unanimous answer: Bill Edrich. Sixteen of the first 20 I approached did not hesitate. Edrich was their man. They felt that Len Hutton's great career should be honoured and there might be value in the experience and leadership of Tom Dollery. But even those who did not give Edrich their vote agreed that he was the type of player we need for the Australians next year . . . I must confess surprise at the strength and enthusiasm of the support for Edrich. Although I knew he was respected for his fighting, sporting play, I did not realise he still had such solid player backing for this responsible post. And I am surprised by the limited support for Len Hutton . . . Another reason for Edrich over Hutton was that most liked his cheerful boldness in attitude compared with Hutton's typically Yorkshire conservatism.'

Charles Bray in the *Daily Herald* also felt the only choices were Hutton and Edrich: 'None of the others can compete with Hutton or Edrich for experience of Test cricket, sound knowledge of the finer points of the game and sheer playing skill.' In the *Daily Express*, Frank Rostron favoured Hutton because he had 'virtually been captaining teams for years', buttressed by his 'agile mind' and 'one of the shrewdest brains in cricket'. In contrast, Edrich was 'just a little past his best'.

Given that the selectors had refused to pick Edrich for the past two years, it was hardly likely they would now make him captain. The *Daily Worker* read the position more correctly than some excitable pundits with axes to grind or heroes to cheer. 'Len Hutton is the popular choice. The Yorkshireman knows cricket inside out and has the advantage of being England's outstanding batsman.' In contrast, 'Bill Edrich has never been popular with the selectors, even when he was on brilliant form.' In the end, there was an inevitability about the appointment of Hutton, given his high reputation as both a player and an analyst of the game. Like many other papers, *The Guardian* welcomed the decision, calling him 'a cricketer of great experience and judgement', who 'is an integral part of our Test side', in contrast to men like Bailey, Sheppard and Edrich, 'none of whom is an automatic choice'. The *Daily Herald* felt that the era of 'stupid snobbery' in cricket was passing, while *The Times* praised the selectors for 'ending an anachronism' that was at odds with the new age of equal opportunity. 'They have shown a boldness that one had not expected of them yet,' said the paper. From his pulpit in the *Daily Telegraph*, Swanton praised Hutton as 'a thoughtful cricketer', but hoped he would not be too cautious.

Many years later, in 1978, Edrich wrote that Hutton's appointment was 'a triumph of common sense', not least because 'he possessed a deep knowledge of the game and was liked by his players'. But at the time, Edrich experienced another wave of disappointment at the news; 'he was very keen to be captain of England', said Mike Murray. It was a sad irony that Edrich had ditched his professional status, probably missing out on a five-figure sum, in order to win the England captaincy, only for the job to go to a professional. Yet Hutton's elevation turned out to be a tremendous gain for Edrich. The new captain's faith in him overrode concerns about his conduct and paved the way for a revival of his Test career. 'I had always admired his qualities as a cricketer' and had 'frequently championed his cause', wrote Hutton. Still ostracised in 1952, Edrich was to become a key ally of the new captain the following year. From the start of the 1953 season, Edrich strengthened his case in two striking ways. First he managed to acquire a new image of responsibility as he took sole charge of Middlesex with the end of the ill-starred experiment in a joint captaincy. He proved a far better leader on his own than he had done in league with Compton, *Wisden* declaring that he 'led Middlesex excellently'. Mike Murray said that he was 'a very popular captain because he played in the style of Walter Robins: aggressive, setting targets, the opposite of Yorkshire'. The other way in which Edrich helped his cause was by his outstanding form as a batsman. Having made a string of half-centuries in Middlesex's opening fixtures, he then hit 166 against Essex at Westcliff-on-Sea in mid-May, followed by centuries against Leicestershire and Lancashire before the end of June. Pressure grew for his recall to the Test side, made all the more intense by the weakness of England's batting in the first two Tests against Australia. In the rain-ruined draw at Trent Bridge, they had collapsed to 144 in their first innings in the face of a hostile spell from Ray Lindwall at his fastest. Then at Lord's, set a target of 343 to win, England's second innings had collapsed to 12 for 3, and they only escaped with another draw thanks to an epic defensive partnership by Trevor Bailey and Willie Watson. It was obvious that England's top order had to be reinforced, and by early July Edrich had emerged as the man with the strongest credentials to do just that. The former Australian batsman Sidney Barnes declared that 'Edrich is a must' and revealed that 'the Aussie camp is hoping' that he would continue to be left out. From an England perspective, the Kent leg-spinner Doug Wright wrote that to play Australia, 'you need fight and guts. That's why I would not hesitate for a second about Bill Edrich . . . He isn't very big but what there is of him is packed with just the spirit we need.'

With perfect timing, Edrich then hammered 211 against Essex at Lord's, just as the selectors were about to choose the England team for the Third Test at Old Trafford. 'Bill Edrich, Test man past and surely Test man again,' wrote the *Daily Express*, adding, 'This was Bill's fourth three-figure knock of the season, his second in successive games and the 74th of his career. And – Test selectors please note – he had no featherbed wicket.' Edrich was duly chosen, taking the place of opener Don Kenyon who had failed in all four of his innings against Australia. It was exactly three years since Edrich had last played a Test, and there followed a dramatic episode on the eve of the Manchester Test, when it looked as if he might be considered as England's emergency captain, Len Hutton having been afflicted by fibrositis in his right shoulder. Interestingly, Winston Churchill suffered a severe stroke in Downing Street on 23 June, just a fortnight before the England selectors announced the team for Old Trafford, and because there was a pact with the press to keep the seriousness of the Prime Minister's illness a secret from the public, Hutton's ailment received almost as many column inches of coverage. In a mood of over-heated conjecture, the names of Edrich, Bailey and Washbrook were circulated as potential substitutes for Hutton. 'Who is there to lead us to victory?' asked Ross Hall of the *Daily Mirror*, continuing: 'Could the man be Bill Edrich who until his selection for the Third Test has had to wander around for three years in a selectorially-created wilderness? His appointment would be sensational but at the same time I think it would be sound common sense. Edrich's qualifications? He has merited his place in the Test team on his batting ability. He has skippered Middlesex with great success. Against Edrich? He has been so long out of favour it might be too much to expect that after going so far as to bring him back in to the England team they'd be prepared to go any further by awarding him the greatest of cricket honours.'

The panic soon ended. Hutton responded well to treatment at his Pudsey home and was able to lead England in the field when Australia batted first at Old Trafford. In damp conditions, a magnificent century by Neil Harvey saw the visitors reach 312, then Hutton and Edrich came out to open for England for the first time since 1938. In *The Cricketer's* report, Edrich 'looked the part' by 'getting behind the ball and meeting the fastest of Lindwall's expresses with a dead straight bat'. It was not pace that did him but the unorthodox quick leg-spin of Jack Hill. Edrich's comeback had not been auspicious, lasting just 24 balls for six runs. Nor did he bat again in the match, which had too many rain interruptions to secure a result, though Australia bizarrely manufactured a frenzied last hour with a sudden collapse to 35 for 8.

Edrich retained his place for the Fourth Test at Leeds, with the fate of the Ashes hanging in the balance. He and Hutton both failed as England made just 167 in their first innings, allowing Australia to build a substantial lead, but Edrich top-scored in the second innings with a typically robust, defiant 64 that lasted four hours. Assessing his performance, the former Australian batsman Jack Fingleton wrote: 'Edrich has lost the keen edge of his eyesight but he still retains the same old debonair spirit as he moves inside short balls and pulls and hooks with all his might. No ducking for Edrich. He meets a challenge with a counter-challenge.' A report by the Press Association said that 'Edrich batted splendidly for four hours in making his 64. He thoroughly justified his return to the England side and showed that experience plus grit plus skill makes a formidable combination of virtues.' His innings, backed up by 61 from Compton and some obdurate stonewalling by Bailey, enabled England to set Australia a tricky target on the last afternoon of 177 runs in 115 minutes. It was during this chase that Edrich caught a glimpse of Hutton's highly strung nature, which seemed to cause the dry Yorkshireman to freeze under the strain of the contest. Hutton had hoped that his two spinners, Tony Lock and Jim Laker, would put Australia on the defensive, but just the opposite happened as their batsmen, led by Neil Harvey, went daringly on the attack. Yet Hutton kept Lock on, believing he was the key to victory despite the unstoppable flow of runs. In his 1959 book *Round the Wicket*, Edrich recalled how alarmed he became at the signs that Hutton had 'lost control' of the game and 'cracked when the heat was on'. To Edrich, the solution was obvious: replace Lock with Trevor Bailey. According to Edrich's account, this was the point when he performed one of his most valuable services of the summer for England. 'At last, I could stand it no more. I went up to Len and said, "Len, for God's sake, put Trevor on." Bailey joined us at that precise moment. Len looked at us vacantly for a moment, as if he could not comprehend what was going on.' But a few minutes later, Hutton did as suggested and brought on Bailey to bowl down the leg side. The Essex all-rounder executed his orders to perfection. His highly accurate leg theory bottled up one end, prevented an Australian victory and ensured that England went to the final Test at The Oval all square. Afterwards, the Australians were livid, feeling they had been cheated by underhand tactics and, in Godfrey Evans's words, 'the worst kind of negative cricket'. Yet without such action, which under the Laws was perfectly legitimate, the Ashes would have been lost and the series would have ended in an anticlimax. As it was, the outcome would be decided at The Oval.

No match in English Test history was ever infused with higher expectations than the Fifth Test of 1953. In fact, the *Sydney Morning Herald* called it 'the Test to end Tests'. The recent Coronation, along with the conquest of Everest, added to a sense that it was England's destiny to recapture the urn. Indeed, Princess Margaret, who was reputed to have had an affair with the dashing Keith Miller, told Lindsay Hassett during a Buckingham Palace reception at the time of the Coronation, 'You must admit, Mr Hassett, that it is surely our turn.' But there was little clear pattern from previous Anglo-Australian Tests at The Oval that could point to a probable England victory. The only valid welcome comparison was the 1926 victory built on majestic centuries by Jack Hobbs and Herbert Sutcliffe, the captaincy of Percy Chapman and the left-arm spin of 48-year-old Wilfred Rhodes.

Bill Edrich was not nearly so advanced as to be considered a veteran, but he was still the oldest player in the England side. At the start of his Test career, his temperament had come under ferocious scrutiny and had been found wanting. But his experience and determination ensured there were no such accusations in 1953. 'In the three Tests in which he played, Edrich never failed England in his prime duty of seeing off the opening attack,' wrote Freddie Brown in his autobiography *Cricket Musketeer*, praise that was all the more meaningful given his role, as the previous Ashes captain, of keeping Edrich out of the 1950–51 tour. 'Edrich showed the way,' proclaimed the *Daily Mail*, with his 'punchy, attacking' brand of cricket that 'answered his captain's call for a spirt of aggression'.

Before the match began, Australia made a serious mistake by failing to include a front-line spinner; this on a pitch that in the 1950s was famously conducive to turn. The error was made all the worse when Hassett won the toss and batted, which meant that England's second innings would take place on a wearing wicket. Against a well-balanced England attack headed by the young tearaway Fred Trueman, Australia struggled to 275, a total that would have been much lower if England had held their chances. Bill Edrich joined in this fielding malaise with a bad drop, but he partially redeemed himself with a brilliantly athletic, one-handed catch low to his right to dismiss Alan Davidson off Jim Laker. When England batted in response, he opened with Hutton, putting on 37 in a partnership that blunted the Australian attack, though his own total was a modest 21 as he fell lbw to Lindwall after looking very secure. Hutton went on to make 82, helping England to gain a narrow but crucial first-innings lead of 31.

On an increasingly dusty pitch, Australia collapsed in their second innings to the Surrey spin twins, Jim Laker and Tony Lock, again emphasising what a howler Hassett had made in not picking a spinner. Set just 132 to win, England finished the third day on 38 for the loss of Hutton, with Edrich still at the crease on 16 and Peter May on 6. 'Breathe deep, Englishmen. The scent of victory is in the air. We caught these Australians on a dustbowl and we rubbed their noses in it,' exclaimed the *Daily Mirror*. The next day Edrich and May initially made slow progress against the accurate Australian bowling, but, with so much time left, the run-rate was irrelevant. What counted was England's steady accumulation of runs without any dramatic loss of wickets. That is exactly what Edrich and May achieved. When May was eventually dismissed, only another 44 runs were needed. It was the perfect platform for the legendary Middlesex pair to guide England home amid a national tidal wave of sentimentality. If 1947 had been a miraculous year in county cricket, 1953 was by far the highest peak Edrich ever attained at the international level. Having presided over the successful run-chase that saw the return of the urn after 19 years, he and Compton, in the words of *Wisden*, had to 'fight their way to the pavilion' as 'the crowd swarmed on to the field'. The two men were united in triumph at that moment, but it was Edrich's batting that had been the crucial factor in this famous victory. His unbeaten 55, painstakingly but heroically compiled, had denied Australia any chance of a come back. 'But for Edrich England might have had a most undignified struggle to win,' wrote Ross Hall in the *Mirror,* while *Wisden* said that he had 'batted splendidly'. Perhaps the most notable tribute at the end of the series came from none other than Don Bradman, who was impressed that Edrich succeeded as an opener even though he did not play in that position for Middlesex. 'He has so much courage that he surmounted all handicaps and proved himself completely fitted temperamentally, an essential attribute in Nos 1 and 2.'

The Australians had been so bitter after the Leeds Test that the post-match drinks, unusually, had an edge of friction about them. But that discord then vanished as the Oval celebrations went on long into the night, led inevitably by Edrich and Compton. Of this pair, Ray Lindwall once said, 'We thought we had some high livers in the Australian camp, but Bill and Denis had such a capacity that we wondered how we got to the ground the next day. They made cricket such fun both on and off the field.' Such remarks helped to reinforce Edrich's image of indestructibility. But even with his ironclad constitution, Edrich could sometimes find the journey from the pavilion to the middle a struggle after a heavy night. John Murray recalled just such occasion, as quoted in Christopher Sandford's 2019 biography of the great keeper: 'He went out at Lord's once to toss up at the start of play and he was leaning on the other lot's captain just to get out there and back. He won the toss, staggered in and said, "We're batting."' Reputedly he scored a century that day. Len Hutton's son Richard, who also played for Yorkshire and England, related to me this story from Bill's time as captain:

In a match against Lancashire at Old Trafford, the weather prevented any possibility of play until the third day. The Middlesex team were billeted at the Lymm Hotel in Cheshire, a smart location with well-stocked bars. At the conclusion of Sunday lunch after two days of heavy drinking, Bill insisted on pouring the coffee. In the process, not a single drop reached any cup. When play was eventually possible, Bill and Cyril Washbrook went out to toss; Bill was unable to support himself without Cyril's support.

When Bill batted he knocked up a quick 70 but was reported to Lord's for ungentlemanly conduct.

Bill was fond of saying, 'Some people like a party and some don't. I like a party.' In his hands, any occasion could be turned into an arena of intoxication. He and Denis were once invited to Dublin to open a new cricket pavilion in the city, and they both prepared for the ceremony by indulging in several rounds of Irish coffee. Soon, recalled Edrich, 'Denis and I were flying higher than one of my old Blenheim bombers.' Despite some heavy slurring, Compton just about managed to deliver a speech, but by now Edrich was swaying. Fred Titmus was among the guests and recalled, 'There was an air of growing alarm as Bill rose to his feet and silence fell on the assembled gathering. He proceeded to sing "Molly Malone" perfectly in tune and sat down again to tumultuous applause without even troubling his audience with a speech.' Edrich himself recalled that 'it was the best reception I ever got'.

One of Bill's favourite indulgences of the season was the Scarborough Festival at its close, because of its scope for celebration and inebriation. Dances and black-tie dinners were held at the top hotels, whose very names like the Grand, the Balmoral and the Royal were evocative of opulence. Town bands played on the seafront, which was bedecked with flags. Huge crowds attended the matches at the resort's ground on North Marine Road, where liveried staff brought out refreshments in the intervals. The holiday atmosphere, centred on a leisurely schedule and lavish hospitality, was remembered by Godfrey Evans who said, 'We didn't start the cricket until 12 o'clock. Lovely hours they were. We would call in at the Royal at eleven o'clock to quench our thirst. They served some nice draught bitter. It was just a nice gentle stroll from the bar to the ground.' The year 1953 was a particularly vintage one for Edrich, not just because of his England recall and the Ashes triumph, but also because of his success in hitting a big century for the Gentlemen against the Players in a gripping run-chase to win by five wickets.

In a further indulgence at the festival that autumn, turning out for T.N. Pearce's XI against the Australians, Edrich was so hungover from the night before that at the fall of an Australian wicket, he curled up on the grass at fly slip and went to sleep. He was left dozing in that position until lunchtime. On another occasion, on the morning of a festival match, he was in such a poor state from the previous evening's social whirl that he had to be padded up by his teammates and then escorted out to the middle by Reg Simpson. At the festival in 1955, Edrich crawled back to the Balmoral Hotel shortly before dawn began to break over Scarborough. Exhausted and still in his dinner suit, he stumbled into what he thought was his room, and, without undressing, lay down on the bed. Suddenly he was woken up by the affectionate tickling of his ears. In his confused state, he raised his head, only to make out the drowsy but distinguished figure of Antonia Yardley, wife of the former England captain and chairman of selectors Norman, who slumbered next to her. Semi-conscious in her darkened hotel room, she had mistaken the inert form of Edrich for the family dog, who always slept on their bed in their home. Mrs Yardley let out a piercing scream, her husband shot upright and Bill Edrich scarpered. He hit another century for the Gentlemen that day.

Bill's third wife Jessy, who often accompanied him to Scarborough, revelled in the festival, if not quite to the extent of her husband. 'You were queen for a fortnight,' she said. But for Jasper, Bill's son from his marriage to Jessy, the memories of Scarborough are not entirely happy. 'They were always fighting and then making up. They went together to the festival and often had a rip-roaring time. But I once went with them and I remember one night, about three or four in the morning, there was wrestling in the bedroom. They'd had a few drinks. In fact, most of their rows were alcohol-related.'

10

TRIALS AND TRIBULATIONS
1954–1958

'Bill had plenty of guts, and a lot of tenacity, but when I arrived he was a bit of a shadow of his former self. Still, he was a very good chap, great fun even when he was pissed.'

Charlie Robins

Sitting in the courtroom, Jessy Edrich nervously twisted her gloves in her hands and fingered a gold bracelet. Her gaze was fixed on her husband, who stood in the dock as he waited for the foreman of the all-male jury to deliver the verdict. Normally so animated, Bill looked tired and slightly shrunken, the long cross-examination having taken its toll. She knew, as much as he did, that his future was at stake. If the outcome of the trial went the wrong way, his career could be brought to a halt.

That would have been a remarkable turnaround in his fortunes, for less than a year earlier Bill Edrich had been celebrating the return of the Ashes at The Oval. The mood of jubilation had continued for weeks and infused the merriment of his stay at the Scarborough Festival. But it was precisely his uninhibited attachment to alcohol that had led him to the embarrassing position of standing in the dock as a defendant in the Middlesex Sessions. For Edrich, the journey into court had started on Friday 11 June, 1954 at Lord's, where England were playing Pakistan in the First Test of the summer. While not possessing the grandeur and heritage of the Ashes, the 1954 series was an important landmark in international cricket's development, for it was the inaugural contest between the two countries. Sadly, amid the excitement of a new beginning, heavy rain washed out the first three days of the Lord's contest, so Bill spent much of his time with business associates and friends in the private hospitality box hired by Giles Baring, the managing director of Latham Brown. According to his later testimony in court, he had a beer with his lunch at Lord's, then another three and a half pints, plus a single whisky, in the afternoon.

Once play had been formally abandoned for the day, he drove out of the ground in his car and travelled to the Golfers' Club in Whitehall, where he met two business friends and had another three glasses of beer and a whisky. Leaving the club at 8.45 p.m., he then embarked on the trip home to Hatfield. He successfully negotiated his way out of central London, but trouble began at just after ten o'clock when he reached Bignell's Corner on the Barnet bypass. What happened next was fiercely disputed and became the crux of Edrich's trial. On the road in front of him, stopped at a set of traffic lights on red, was a car driven by Sidney Clare, a company director from Croydon, who had three other passengers in his vehicle. In court, Clare recalled, 'I heard a squeak of brakes and then something collided with the rear of my car with a glancing blow. I saw a car pass me immediately after the impact and I followed.' For his part, Edrich claimed that as he overtook the car at the lights, he sensed 'a slight bump. It felt much like two bumpers touching and I did not attach an awful lot of importance to it. I did not stop, though I now realize that I should have, no matter how slight the accident.' The chase continued for about half a mile, and for the last 100 yards the two cars were alongside each other. Looking directly at Edrich, one of Clare's passengers repeatedly signalled for Edrich to pull over and stop. Eventually Edrich did so, and the men all got out of their respective vehicles. By now Clare was furious, and his indignation was worsened by the signs of Edrich's apparent intoxication. Trying to stand on a grass verge, Edrich was unsteady on his feet and his speech was slurred. Far from showing any contrition, his manner was 'slightly aggressive' and 'uncooperative' when Clare asked him, 'Do you usually crash into people and drive on?'

'What damage is done?' he replied, and reportedly showed little interest when Clare pointed out the dents in the rear of his car.

One of the passengers then telephoned the police. Two officers turned up quickly and asked Edrich if he had been involved in an accident. 'As far as I am concerned there has been no accident,' he said. When the officers pointed to the damage on both cars, he told them, 'I don't know anything about that.' To the police, even more incriminating than his dismissive answers was his demeanour. They said he was 'swaying backwards and forwards, his breath smelt strongly of drink and he had difficulty putting his pipe in his mouth'. Having cautioned him, they told Edrich he was under arrest, at which the England star visibly bristled: 'You know me, don't you? I am Edrich, I am playing in the Test at Lord's.' He was then helped into the police car before being taken to Barnet police station, where he was examined by a doctor, Charles M. Scott, at 11.15 p.m. In his evidence, Dr Scott said that he found Edrich was 'unable to stand without swaying considerably and was unable to walk straight. His pupils reacted slightly, his tongue was furred and there was a strong smell of alcohol.' Dr Scott concluded that Edrich had been 'driving under the influence of alcohol'.

One of the inspectors at Barnet station, Thomas Cowling, said that Edrich was 'very talkative' and 'made disconnected statements about calling a solicitor'. Edrich's memory was different. He recalled that he talked about the weather and the Test against Pakistan, 'in order to impress the police that I could carry on a reasonable conversation', though he felt his loquacity was used against him.

But there were two events on the night that were to work in his favour. One occurred after the police told him that he could call his own doctor to conduct a second examination. Although his usual consultant was not available, on the grounds, said Edrich, that he was having 'dinner with Denis Compton', Edrich managed to get hold of another doctor of his acquaintance from Hatfield, William Jones, who conducted his own test from 12.35 a.m. and pronounced Edrich 'fit to be in charge of a car'. Any eccentricities in Edrich's behaviour Dr Jones ascribed to the shock of the incident. 'He struck me as a person in extreme nervous agitation.' The second event was when Jessy arrived at the station to take him home. As she later testified in the witness box, she 'saw no sign of him having had too much to drink'. Cynics might respond with a variation on the famous line of Mandy Rice-Davies's during the Profumo scandal: 'Well, she would say that wouldn't she?' But Jessy's expression of loyalty, made all the more potent by her acting skills, undoubtedly strengthened Edrich's credentials as a man of decency.

In view of the seriousness of the case, Edrich needed all the help he could get. He was formally charged on two criminal counts: driving under the influence of alcohol; and dangerous driving. Pleading not guilty at Barnet magistrates' court, he opted for a trial by jury at the Middlesex Quarter Sessions and was granted bail of £10. His relative Rodney Edrich, who was a respected magistrate in East Anglia, thought that, despite the risks of a tougher sentence in a Crown Court, Edrich's move was a shrewd one. 'Famous defendants, especially sportsmen, nearly always went for a jury trial because they knew that 12 good men and true could be bowled over by their prestige,' he told me. Bill's decision was heavily influenced by his solicitor Monty Garland-Wells, who had successfully played first-class cricket between the wars for Oxford University and Surrey, captaining the south London club in 1939. During the war, Churchill's government and the Chiefs of Staff used 'Garland-Wells' as a coded term for Field Marshal Montgomery, rightly believing that the Germans would never crack such an obscure cypher.

Edrich's trial was held in early July 1954, presided over by the Deputy Chairman of the Quarter Sessions Captain Edward Montagu, a barrister and former Royal Navy intelligence officer. Twice portrayed on the screen, he was the imaginative architect of Operation Mincemeat, the brilliantly executed deception operation of 1943 that misled the Germans into thinking the Allies were planning to land in Greece rather than Sicily. The prosecution, led by Evelyn Russell, appeared to have a formidable case, including the testimony of Sidney Clare and his passengers, the police and Dr Scott. But Edrich and his team, headed by the barrister for the defence G.D. Roberts QC, put up a strong fight. At his charming, self-confident best, Edrich was an effective witness who managed to sow doubts in the minds of the jurors. He not only pointed out that in his 18 years of driving he had just received one speeding ticket, but also fiercely denied that he needed help to walk to and from the police car, while his reflections on the actual scrape managed to insinuate that the other driver was partly to blame. 'I might have made a slight error of judgement but whether the other car ran back a little I cannot say,' he explained. He even enjoyed some banter with his defence counsel at one stage. Referring to the accusation that he had been 'swaying' while he stood on the grass, Roberts asked him, 'How do you normally stand? On your toes?'

'Yes, I am always on my toes,' Edrich replied.

Roberts also delivered a powerful speech to the jury that emphasised the grim consequences of a guilty verdict for Edrich and suggested that he had already paid his dues: 'He just touched a car in passing and did not stop. There is no question that he should have stopped but he has been bitterly punished already. The arrest, the appearance at the magistrates' court, the unwelcome publicity which this man – so much in the public eye – has received, the ordeal of sitting in the dock which has found so many disreputable criminals.'

In portentous terms, Russell concluded, 'to some extent this man's future is in your hands'. Yet Edrich was perhaps given even more help by an extraordinary and unbalanced summing-up from the judge. In contradiction of so much that had been said at the trial, Montagu claimed that 'no one has suggested that the defendant was drunk in the normal sense of the term or that he was very much under the influence of alcohol'. On the accusation that Edrich's speech was slurred, Montagu said, 'Although you may think he has a naturally soft voice his diction is extremely clear.' After that it was little surprise that the jury failed to reach a verdict, despite 80 minutes of deliberations. Montagu urged the foreman to see if further discussions might bring an agreement, but was told there was no hope.

A second trial had to be held at the end of the month. This time Edrich was acquitted of the drink-driving charge, but found guilty of dangerous driving, a conviction for which the judge Eric Neve, the Chairman of the Sessions, handed down a fine of 10 guineas and an additional demand for £10 in costs. Witnessing the scene at the end of the trial, the *Daily Mail* reported, 'First to congratulate him was his wife who kissed him as he stepped from the dock. She had given evidence for him. "I am very relieved about it," he said. "I have tried not to let it affect my cricket but obviously it is a very worrying matter."' It had been a financially as well as emotionally draining experience. In addition to the fines and court costs, he had huge legal bills. Later Garland-Wells, his solicitor, privately admitted, 'If you say the cost to Edrich of the whole case will be approaching £1,000, you will not be far wrong.'

Nevertheless, apart from the damage to his bank balance, the fallout from the case had not been too severe. Little harm was done to his already colourful reputation in the cricket world, especially since drink-driving was not in the 1950s the social taboo it became towards the end of the 20th century. Indeed, the widespread feeling in the game was not disapproval but amazement that Edrich seemed to have got away with the first, more serious offence.

Nor did his place on the MCC tour to Australia that winter of 1954 seem to be in jeopardy. Led by Len Hutton and managed by Geoffrey Howard, the side had already been announced before the conclusion of his second trial. 'One never knows what is in the selectors' minds where this gritty fighter is concerned. For my money, he would never be out of the side,' said the former England fast bowler Alf Gover at the start of the summer. Hutton was inclined to the same view, and his backing suppressed any reservations about Edrich's conduct or age. Some members of the public perceived a southern bias in the inclusion of Edrich and Compton with his ravaged knee, while the Yorkshire fast bowler Fred Trueman was excluded, reportedly because of his behaviour on the previous winter's tour to the West Indies. One England follower wrote to the MCC, 'You have left out the finest bowler in the country and still left in the old faithfuls Compton and Edrich who seem to be of no use to anyone at the present time. If Trueman had come from Middlesex, he would be on the list.' Another told the MCC that, 'You have a strange morality. You strain at the gnat of a bit of a temper in Trueman and swallow the camel of two alcohol-sodden adulterers. I needn't name them.'

But most commentators felt that the choice of the veteran Edrich was a sensible one, in view of the intense pressures of an Ashes tour. Alan Ross in *The Observer* thought that his 'experience and courage against fast bowling make up for his limitations as a stroke player . . . He gets himself solidly into the line of fire and never surrenders his wicket through indecision or lack of concentration.' In the *Daily Telegraph*, Jim Swanton argued that Edrich was now batting better than 'at any time since Compton and he rode the world together in 1947/48'. In a generous tribute to Edrich's character, Swanton added, 'His inclusion must be seen as a gesture of faith towards one who, in many ways, has given to his fellow cricketers a notable example of determination and courage. Edrich would be less than the man one takes him for if he did not respond wholeheartedly and in every way.' Behind this lofty prose, Swanton was referring to a specific recent example of Edrich's unparalleled, almost superhuman bravery that had sent a wave of admiration through English cricket. In mid-July, while the selectors made their deliberations, Middlesex played Northamptonshire at Lord's. In the Northants team was a young bowler who was beginning to build a reputation for extreme pace. His name was Frank Tyson.

Ted Dexter, the England captain of the early 1960s, recalled in *The Cricketer* in November 1978 that when he was starting out as a young batsman, he met Edrich: 'I found myself asking how to play very fast bowling. "Have you ever been hit on the head?" When I replied that I had not, he put a quick end to the subject by telling me not to worry about the possibility. "It doesn't hurt in the slightest," he assured me.'

But even Edrich could not be nonchalant against Tyson when he encountered him for the first time at Lord's. Going in to bat on a lively wicket pitch late on the second day, Edrich received a short delivery from Tyson and began to play his trademark hook, only to find that the ball was too quick. It flew off the top edge of the bat and hit him right on the jaw. In the description of *The Times*, Edrich 'fell like a log with a sickening cry'. With blood soaking into the pitch, Edrich was assisted from the field, though, typically, he refused a stretcher. He had to spend the night in hospital, where doctors confirmed that his jaw had been broken. But the next morning, despite the seriousness of the injury, which was manifested in the heavy bandages around his battered, swollen face, he returned to Lord's full of determination to resume his innings. Denis Compton said: '. . . anyone else but Bill would have accepted that cricket was out of the question for at least a month, but he insisted he was going to continue his innings that morning. None of us, not even the umpires, could talk him out of it. "Look," he said, "I have seen comrades blown out of the sky and others who have carried on flying with terrible wounds. I am not going to let the little matter of a fractured cheekbone stop me batting."'

So at the fall of the next Middlesex wicket, he marched out to the middle and took guard. Even as Tyson, who was still bowling, turned to start his run-up, Edrich did not flinch. 'He looked like a war casualty. His jaw was in a sling tied at the top of his head, his face was more black and blue than pink and his eyes were almost closed by massive facial bruising,' recalled Tyson. Edrich would have expected no concessions in the battle and Tyson gave none. His first ball to Edrich was a bouncer. Even in his wounded state, Edrich still had the guts to go for the hook. Once again, he was beaten for pace and this time was hit over the heart, but Tyson could only marvel at this show of defiance. 'You simply could not intimidate him,' he said. Edrich went on to stay for 70 minutes and make another 20 runs before he was caught in the slips. In his report of the day's play, Alex Bannister in the *Daily Mail* called Edrich 'the Middlesex Bulldog' and wrote that 'in years to come feats of courage and determination may be epitomised in the phrase, "as tough as Edrich"'.

That ruggedness was proved at the end of that month when Middlesex travelled to Northampton and Edrich took on Tyson again, even though his jaw had not yet fully healed. In another exhibition of raw courage against pace, he hit his sixth century of the season. The unique duel in late July between Edrich and Tyson had a significance far beyond the County Championship. 'The whole episode put the pair of them on the tour to Australia,' thought the Northants wicket-keeper Keith Andrew, a view shared by Tyson, who wrote in his diary that 'consigning Edrich overnight to a hospital bed' probably convinced 'the selectors of my outstanding speed'. Resilient to the last, Edrich seemed to bear no psychological aftershocks from the savage blow Tyson had inflicted, but the physical damage was clear as his brother Brian, still with Kent, remembered of a visit to Canterbury in August by Middlesex. 'I didn't recognise Bill when he played against us. The side of his face, where Tyson had cracked his cheekbone, had collapsed. But it didn't stop him playing.'

The drink-drive trial had shown Edrich at his worst: irresponsible, reckless and self-indulgent. The showdown with Tyson had revealed him at his best: skilful, valiant and selfless. Both sides were to be on display during the forthcoming Ashes tour, as his dedication to the team was matched by the usual catalogue of indiscretions. Indeed, even before the MCC's liner *Orsova* arrived in Australia, this duality was apparent. On the one hand, Hutton showed that Edrich was right back in official favour when he was named as a member of the tour's selection committee, alongside the captain, Peter May his deputy, Alec Bedser the senior professional and the manager Geoffrey Howard. Hutton later explained that it was Edrich's 'forthright views' and 'willingness to express them' that made him so valuable to the committee. 'Forgiveness of Edrich, who was cold-shouldered for the last Australian tour, has reached its peak,' wrote the *Daily Express*'s Frank Rostron. On the other hand, during the voyage from England, Howard caught a glimpse of Edrich's almost neurotic infidelity and the embittered chaos of his domestic life, despite Jessy's very public display of loyalty at his trial. In his diary, Howard noted of Edrich, 'On the boat he formed quite an attachment and he kept in touch with her throughout the tour. I was in his cabin one day, having a few drinks and there was a photo of his wife. And suddenly he said, "I hate my wife" and threw the photo out through the porthole. That was Bill.'

A far more public controversy involving Edrich and several women blew up once the tour was underway and the England team was in Adelaide. One evening during their stay, the dashing trio of Compton, Edrich and the specialist opener Reg Simpson went to a show featuring a troupe of glamorous, high-kicking female ice-skaters. The presence of the three sporting celebrities from England caused something of a stir in the theatre, and the cricketers were invited backstage, where, complete with beaming smiles, they were photographed with three of the performers. Soon afterwards, some English papers published the photo, including Rostron's *Daily Express*, fuelling the whispered gossip about the indiscipline of some England players. Howard, who had actually been present at the ice show, thought that the row was an absurd confection, as he told Ronny Aird, Secretary of the MCC, in a long letter of grievance on 12 November, 1954:

It is a monstrous piece of mischief-making. I was present when the photograph was taken and nothing more innocent was possible but I imagine that the interpretation put upon it was less so. I was a fool because I thought the photographer was a theatrical one and it never occurred to me that this thing might find its way into the English press but of course Master Rostron [a condescending reference to the *Daily Express* correspondent, Frank Rostron] nipped in and bought the negative in his inimitable way. Quite what good he thought it would do anyone I do not know but he is interested only in selling the *Daily Express*. English cricket means nothing to it. I am going to get the boys together tonight and tell them that they must not allow themselves to be photographed by anybody at private occasions of any sort and I hope that this sort of thing will not be repeated.

Aird assured Howard that the saga had made little impact in England, telling him that 'no one here has treated the photo at all seriously and I have heard of no reaction whatsoever'. That was not entirely true. Back in England, Jessy Edrich followed the press coverage of the tour intently and she kept a scrapbook of clippings about Bill, so the ice-show picture became the cue for an airmailed rebuke of her husband, as Frank Tyson recorded in his tour diary *In the Eye of the Typhoon*:

Some of the English press were in the audience and when they saw photographs being taken of the players linking arms and doing high kicks with a chorus line of scantily clad showgirls, they could not resist the temptation. They bribed the photographers and sent the shots off to their papers. The next day, the photos appeared – with Bill in a centre of beauties and one leg high in the air. Result? An angry, 'Please Explain' letter from Mrs Edrich. Moral? Never pose for suggestive photos with press in the vicinity.

On the playing side, Edrich's tour was not going to plan. In the MCC's opening first-class games, he failed to make any significant runs, much to the consternation of Howard, who told Billy Griffith, Assistant Secretary of the MCC, that he 'looked right out of touch'. Even when Edrich made a century in a minor, up-country game, Alan Ross of *The Observer* wrote, 'I have never seen him bat worse.' After another poor performance, this time against an Australian XI, Ross warned that 'Edrich is deep in some hateful nightmare and he will be a problem. Personally I would play him in the Tests even if he made no runs at all between now and then. His character and concentration are worth the easier strokes of his rivals and his stature grows in a crisis while theirs diminish.' In the midst of this dire run, Ross was impressed by the supportive attitude of Len Hutton, so often criticised for being distant, uncommunicative and bound up in his own problems. 'Hutton has shown great understanding in his handling of him,' wrote Ross. Far less appreciative was Charles Bray in the *Daily Herald*, who thought that Hutton's insistence on having Edrich in the team for the First Test was 'a crazy policy', given the Middlesex player's 'complete failure' on the tour so far.

Edrich had one advantage over some of his rivals in that he could bowl the occasional spell of either fast-medium or off-spin. Therefore, when Hutton decided to go into the First Test at Brisbane with a front-line attack made up entirely of pace, the presence of Edrich in the side potentially offered some alternative options with the ball. As it turned out, he bowled only three overs for 28 in Australia's mammoth first-innings total of 601 for 8, after being put in to bat by Hutton. Nor did Edrich succeed with the bat in England's first innings, making just 15 before he was caught at the wicket off Ron Archer. He did better when England followed on; his gritty 88 was England's top score, though the manner of his dismissal was anticlimactic as he missed a pull at a short ball from Bill Johnston and was bowled.

That was to be the high point of Edrich's series. In an enthralling but low-scoring Ashes summer, he failed repeatedly, much to the puzzlement of Hutton who had so eagerly championed him, but found his poor performances 'a mystery as well as a disappointment'. David Frith, later one of the game's greatest historians, saw part of the series as a teenager and felt that Edrich only held on to his place due to Hutton's sentimentality. Frith was in the crowd for the Second Test at Sydney, where Edrich was out for 10 in England's first innings of 228, and he later wrote, 'His dismissal at Sydney was not an elegant thing. He jabbed a lifter to gully off the shoulder of the bat, an image that still lives in my cluttered memory bank.' In fact, the memory of Edrich's unattractive style led Frith to describe him as 'the ugliest little batsman (in stroke play terms) that I had yet seen at a high level or was ever to see'. Edrich struggled to 29 in England's second innings, during which he was at the non-striker's end for perhaps the turning point of the series. Coming in at the unexpectedly high position of Number 7, Tyson had joined Edrich to try to push England towards a defendable total. Immediately, Tyson was confronted with the task of facing the fearsome Ray Lindwall, who wanted revenge after the England fast bowler, operating off a new shortened run, had bounced him out cheaply in Australia's first innings. To that end, Lindwall unleashed a very fast, short-pitched delivery that struck Tyson with an agonising thud on the back of the head. In the account that Tyson wrote in his diary, 'I sank to the ground and lost consciousness. I was dimly aware of the players gathering around my prostrate body. Instinctively I heard my fellow batsman Bill Edrich saying, "My God, Lindy, you've killed him!"' Now in Australia's second innings, Tyson was on a mission of vengeance, fired by his anger at Lindwall. Bowling with a hostility not seen from an Englishman in Australia since Harold Larwood in the 1932–33 Bodyline series, he ripped through the Australian line-up to bring an England victory by 38 runs.

Hutton's fixation with pace had been vindicated. England chose the same side for the Third Test at Melbourne, much to the exasperation of Reg Simpson, who complained that Edrich should go 'because of his continued lack of success'. But Hutton, like Hammond in 1938–39, would not budge, certain that Edrich would come good. The strange aspect of the England skipper's faith in Edrich was that he did not wholeheartedly approve of Edrich's lifestyle. There was a telling moment on the eve of the Melbourne Test when Hutton was having an after-dinner coffee in the lounge of the Windsor Hotel with the versatile England bowler and fellow Yorkshireman Bob Appleyard. As the two men engaged in quiet conversation, Edrich,

Compton and Godfrey Evans came past, dressed up for a night on the town. Hutton said, 'Look at those three. They're going out and the excuse will be that they need to relax before the match. But this is just the time to be thinking about the match.' Tyson thought that Hutton was too soft on the three party enthusiasts, as he said in an interview in 1987: 'There was undoubtedly a need to instil a bit of discipline in the England dressing room. Denis, Godfrey and Bill were all delightful characters but they could be real blighters and laws unto themselves.'

For his part, Edrich thought that, as a captain, Hutton had severe defects: 'he was not a good mixer'; he was 'unable to assess' the characters of his team members; and 'his reactions were slow when things began to go wrong for his side'. Edrich spelt out these points in the sensational batch of articles published in *The People* in 1958 that had so angered Lord's, in advance of his explosive book *Round the Wicket*. Other aspects of Hutton's leadership came in for the same kind of treatment as Bob Wyatt's chairmanship of the selectors. 'I saw Len Hutton crack under the strain', ran the headline of a scathing article about Hutton's alleged nervous collapse on the morning of the Melbourne Test, which was indicative of his wider inability to handle the strain of the Test captaincy towards the end of his career. So allegedly broken was Hutton at this stage of the series, claimed Edrich, that 'he insisted he was physically ill even though a doctor could find nothing wrong with him'.

In his account, Edrich's involvement in this episode started at ten o'clock in the morning when Geoffrey Howard warned him that Hutton may have come down with flu. Visiting Hutton's room, he found Len 'still in bed, looking pale and worried'. Edrich persuaded him to have some coffee and sandwiches, though Hutton continued to insist that he was too ill to get out of bed. Then Godfrey Evans, the epitome of optimism, arrived to join Bill and Geoffrey. Together the three men cajoled, pleaded, chided, reasoned and implored. In particular, they warned Hutton of the disastrous impact his absence would have on England's morale and the boost it would give to Australia's. Eventually Hutton relented and agreed to go to the ground, even though he still felt he would be unable to play. Once he was there, however, 'the dead-look went out of his eyes' and he took an interest in seeing the pitch. After his examination, from which he concluded that it would 'crack up', he walked back to the pavilion, still accompanied by Edrich, Howard and Evans. On reaching the steps, he lingered for a moment, then said 'All right, I'll play.' Edrich and Evans felt like yelling out in relief. 'We'd won our argument, convinced a man who thought he was ill that he was fit enough to play,' wrote Edrich.

There is no doubt that Hutton felt like dropping out on the morning of the Test, as Geoffrey Howard confirmed in his diary. According to Howard, Hutton was dismayed by the doctor's verdict that he was able to play. 'He wanted to be told he was unfit,' said Howard. Hutton's febrile state may have been a combination of fibrositis and psychosomatic dread at having to tell Alec Bedser, England's stalwart for so long, that he had been left out of the side. Godfrey Evans also wrote that 'Len seemed to be on the verge of cracking up', and it was to Edrich that the long-serving keeper gave the credit of persuading Hutton to play. Ignoring the harshness of his later words, Edrich certainly performed an invaluable service, perhaps his greatest contribution of the tour, in helping to ensure that Hutton remained their captain. As Tyson put it in his own diary, 'If our captain abandoned ship, it would be a devasting blow to our chances of victory.' The Melbourne Test was another triumph for both Hutton and Tyson, who took 7 for 27 in Australia's second innings as England won by 128 runs. Further crucial contributions were made by the young batsmen Colin Cowdrey and Peter May, as well as by the Lancashire paceman Brian Statham. But once again, Edrich failed in both innings, making a total of just 17 runs. 'His bat seemed to have developed not only edges but holes,' wrote Alan Ross.

Despite his dismal form, Edrich continued to enjoy himself in his usual fashion, led by his extra-curricular romances and an unceasing round of parties. Geoffrey Howard recorded that at one Saturday night gathering of the England team at its hotel, Edrich turned up after he had been 'to the races and was full of grog'. At one point 'Bill got up to speak but the words wouldn't come out. He was smiling away, talking nonsense and young Colin [Cowdrey] was sitting there, thinking, "What's wrong with him? This isn't the man I know."' Now in the twilight of his career, Edrich often acted on extreme impulse. Tom Graveney, who said he was 'never surprised at anything Bill did', recalled an occasion at the team hotel when Edrich 'was politely asked to extinguish his cigarette, he did so by jumping fully clothed into the hotel swimming pool'. When the team manager Geoffrey Howard handed him a huge invoice of £45, mainly to cover all the phone calls that Edrich had made to the woman he had met on the boat, he took the demand in his stride and signed it without a word. Howard admitted that Edrich sometimes had to be 'rescued' after his wilder adventures or heavier hangovers, so that he ended up on the right train, bus or ground, but 'he always co-operated in the nicest possible way'. In addition to his crooning, he liked to perform a conjuring trick that involved a metal tray, a raw egg, a glass of water and an egg cup. In the style of Tommy Cooper, the party piece was at its most entertaining when it descended into a farce accompanied by flying egg yolk, as it usually did. At an up-country match in Western Australia, the England team, minus Edrich, arrived the night before to take up their accommodation. It was not until just before the start of play next day that Edrich turned up, confessing that he and his driver had 'run into a bar en-route'.

But the biggest party of the tour was held at the Pier Hotel in Adelaide, after England had won back the Ashes with a five-wicket win in the Fourth Test. Once again, Edrich contributed little with the bat, hitting just 21 runs in his two innings, but he certainly made his presence felt in the celebrations. In one of the memorable highlights of the evening, he climbed up a 20-foot-high marble column in the foyer, and, glass of champagne in hand, sat on its pinnacle while he sang to the astonished, cheering throng below. His tour was effectively over. He played two more first-class games for the MCC, one in Melbourne and one in New Zealand, but he was dropped for the Fifth Test, his place as Hutton's opening partner taken by Graveney, who scored a century in a rain-affected draw. Tyson, for one, thought that the decision was long overdue. 'Bill only kept his place in the team because of his senior status,' he wrote. The verdict of John Kay, the cricket reporter of the *Manchester Evening News*, was that 'Edrich, the biggest batting flop of all, made this tour four years too late. At the same time he counselled wisely and Hutton leant on him quite a lot.' In a private letter of 15 March, 1955 to his friend, the Lancashire committee-man Tom Higson, Edrich said that 'the tour has been very successful, although my own performances have been far from satisfactory'. He was full of praise for the 'outstanding achievements' of the young quartet of May, Cowdrey, Statham and Tyson, who he thought would be the 'nucleus of the side for a few years to come'. Interestingly, while all the media had focused on Tyson, Edrich thought that Statham 'bowled best of all' and 'never seems to tire even in the most trying circumstances'.

The tour was Edrich's last experience of Test cricket. In the stark words of Tom Graveney, he was 'Finished. Exhausted. Shot his bolt.' But he was not yet finished with Middlesex. He continued to lead the club in 1955, taking them to fifth place in the title race, though *Wisden* labelled them 'one of the most inconsistent sides in the Championship. At times they appeared capable of beating almost anyone, yet on other occasions, they looked a poor team.' As in Test cricket, his batting at county level was no longer the force it had been in his post-war heyday, and his average in the Championship fell to just 26.44, with only one century. Nor did his 30 overs yield a single wicket. One young player who came into the Middlesex side at this time was Charlie Robins, the son of Walter. As he told me: 'Bill had plenty of guts, and a lot of tenacity, but when I arrived he was a bit of a shadow of his former self. Still, he was a very good chap, great fun even when he was pissed. He was a very good bloke, a better bloke than Denis. There wasn't a nasty streak in Bill, whereas there was a rough streak in Denis, who was not the laughing cavalier they made him out to be. I know which one I preferred to spend time with.'

Robins found Edrich as a captain 'pretty conventional; he did not do anything out of the ordinary. But he stayed in the job too long.' In Robins's view, this meant that his successor John Warr, who had played on the 1950–51 Ashes tour, was 'too old' when he took over. Another first-class captain of this era, Sussex's Robin Marlar, agreed with this analysis. 'John Warr had a much better cricket brain. I wouldn't have said that Bill was the greatest tactician of all time. At Middlesex, he was dozy. He just carried on and was looking forward to retirement, so he sort of switched off.'

Despite these apparent weaknesses, Middlesex stayed in fifth place in 1956, while Edrich, now aged 40, showed a significant improvement in his batting form, raising his first-class average for the season to 33 and playing a number of defiant innings in his classic, rigorous style. A sweeping victory against Derbyshire at Chesterfield saw him pulverise an attack led by Les Jackson and Cliff Gladwin, two of the finest new-ball bowlers in England. The local paper, the *Derby Evening Telegraph*, described how Edrich dished out this 'humiliation' for the home side: 'This small, taciturn batsman has been in and out of form and in and out of the England team with incredible consistency. It has been whispered that Edrich was perhaps "dropping behind this season". Some "drop". He was at the wicket six hours, chopped, cut, drove and hooked his way to 208 and handed out a few lessons in the gentle art of forceful restraint. He hit four sixes and 32 fours, treated all the Derbyshire bowlers with almost indifferent ease and in doing so pushed his side into a position which is, to say the least, formidable.'

Later in the summer, he showed magnificent defensive skills on a typically bowler-friendly wicket at The Oval against the Surrey spin twins Jim Laker and Tony Lock, who had spent much of the summer demolishing the Australians. The *Daily Telegraph* called his 82 'a great innings', explaining that 'for over three hours, Edrich, as always greatest in adversity, concentrated all his craftsmanship and experience against the turning ball while nursing his young partners'. The Surrey opener Micky Stewart played in that game and gave me these memories of Edrich's style: 'Bill was a very up-front, physical cricketer but played with a smile on his face – most of the time. I remember him as a very pugnacious, determined player. That is what he was like as a person, a top bloke. He was a fine player of pace and would not give an inch. Because of his height, he was great on the back foot. His captaincy was the same as his batting, all up front.'

One key Middlesex player who made his debut in 1956 and went on to become a fine Test batsman was Peter Parfitt. In fact, Parfitt's Test record is almost uncannily similar to Edrich's. He played 37 matches, Edrich 39. He averaged 40.91, Edrich exactly 40. He scored seven centuries, Edrich six. He took 42 catches, Edrich 39. The bonds between the two men extended far beyond statistics. Parfitt also hailed from a farming background in Norfolk, played cricket for the county and appeared in his youth for Norwich City reserves. Through his Norfolk connections Edrich knew of Parfitt's talent and was instrumental in bringing him to Middlesex without even a trial, a process that reflects how much confidence the club had in its captain's judgement. 'I idolised Bill, just idolised him. For me to follow him to Middlesex was just wonderful. He was a fantastic character,' said Parfitt in our interview. But on his debut, he was in for a shock:

My very first game for Middlesex was away at Oxford University and we were in the hotel on the first morning. I came down for breakfast and Bill arrived several minutes later. Once at his table, he called the waiter over:

'Waiter, would you please bring me a bottle of champagne?'

'I'm terribly sorry, sir, but . . . erm . . . well . . . the bar is not open.'

'It is open, I'm a resident and will you please get me a bottle of champagne.'

The poor lad had to go off and get a bottle. And I thought, 'Bloody hellfire, what have I let myself in for?' It was not a special occasion. He had probably sat up to 2 or 3 o'clock in the morning, so he may have felt a bit jaded.

Describing his captaincy as 'astute', Parfitt continued:

I wouldn't say that he ruled the roost with a rod of iron. He didn't but he was a disciplinarian. You didn't come back at him on anything. If he told you to do something, you did it. He was a stickler for high standards. I remember we were playing Gloucestershire and I was on 48 shortly before lunch. George Lambert, their quick bowler, sent down a bouncer on the leg side. I went to hook it and it just shaved my glove. They all went up. Well, I was as green as grass and just stood there. I can remember Peter Rochford, their wicket-keeper, walking past me at the end of the over and asking, 'You hit that, didn't you?'

Like a bloody idiot, I said, 'Oh yeah, I did. I got a glove on it.'

'Well why didn't you fuck off then?'

When I got back to the pavilion, nearly everyone had gone to lunch upstairs, except Bill. He was sitting there in his blazer:

'Peter, can I ask, did you get a nick on that, off George Lambert?'

'Yes, captain, it just grazed my glove.'

'Right, when you play at this club, if you get a nick, you walk, the same as you walk if you hit it to cover point and get caught. We do not have people standing their ground after they have nicked the ball in this club.'

He was a stickler for it. He always walked himself, absolutely.

Of Edrich the cricketer, Parfitt remembered him as 'a very good catcher' in the slips and 'still a fine batsman. I played in the game where he got 200 against Les Jackson at Chesterfield. It was a magnificent innings. Bill was very strong on the leg side, a good hooker and he was also a good cutter of the ball. He wasn't classical like Len Hutton or creative like Denis. He was a dogged player, who really took some getting out.' Parfitt also felt that Edrich 'worshipped Denis in terms of rating him as a player', but, like Charlie Robins, Parfitt found that Compton 'had a hard streak, no doubt about that. I once batted with him against Somerset at Glastonbury and I never saw the bowling. He would take a single off the fifth or sixth ball every over, then call down the wicket and say, "Sorreee".'

Towards the end of 1956, there were rumours that Edrich was to retire from the captaincy and hand over to John Warr. 'It's news to me. I'm prepared to carry on for three or four more years,' he told the *Daily Herald*. He therefore remained in charge the following summer, but his decline as a player was beginning to accelerate. His first-class average fell to 22.92 and he did not score a century that season, while Middlesex dropped to seventh place, prompting *The Cricketer* to argue that there was 'something unsatisfactory' about Middlesex's approach. 'It is not easy to define but perhaps it is best to state that it gave a feeling of casualness.' There was also a sense of an era coming to an end, as Denis Compton played his final match for the county, against Worcestershire at Lord's in August. Fired by the spirit of the occasion, he scored a century in the first innings and looked like he was on the way to another when he was caught on the boundary. As he walked back to the pavilion, the large crowd gave Compton a thunderous, prolonged ovation, bringing Edrich to the brink of tears. 'Denis could not have stage-managed a better exit. I don't mind admitting that I had a lump in my throat the size of a boulder. Boy did we have a good drink that night,' said Edrich.

On his departure after 21 years, Compton was given a further testimonial of £1,200 by the club, which prompted Frank Rostron to complain in the *Daily Express* that, because of his switch of status back in 1947, nothing had been done for Edrich despite more than two decades of service to Middlesex. 'Take a bow, W.J. Edrich, professional-amateur and neglected twin, fated to the end to be overshadowed by Compton's glitter,' he wrote. Perhaps shamed by such comments, the Middlesex Committee in 1958 agreed to show Edrich its appreciation by presenting him with 'an antique dining-room suite'. For Rodney Edrich, such treatment illustrated how Bill was always in Denis's shadow. 'I think Bill got a raw deal. I hate the way he is made out to be a kind of drunken rake, yet Denis was just as bad and he wasn't as nice a person. I just find that very hurtful. I am afraid I am a Bill fan.'

Interestingly, Henry Blofeld, the renowned commentator who knew Edrich well, did not feel that Compton and Edrich were as close as conventional wisdom suggests. They were so entwined in the public imagination that two stands at Lord's, situated beside each other, were named after them, while in May 1951, when they appeared on the long-running radio show *Desert Island Discs*, they were not only cricket's first castaways but also the first guests to be shipwrecked together. Yet, according to Blofeld, 'they were very different sorts of people, not each other's kind naturally'. It is a point reiterated by contemporaries like Parfitt who said, 'I don't think Bill and Denis were great friends off the field.' Bill's son Justin agreed. 'I don't remember Denis coming to our house or anything like that or it being obvious that they were great friends. There's a lot of nostalgia about 1947.'

The years of Middlesex service were coming to an end. After finally handing over the captaincy to John Warr for the 1958 season, Edrich appeared only sporadically for the club, making just 13 appearances in the Championship and scoring just 335 runs at an average of 17. His last, and 86th, first-class century was scored at his beloved Lord's against Cambridge University, whose side included the aristocratic Ted Dexter, the future England captain. Unlike

Compton's exit the year before, there was to be no dramatic farewell, no standing ovation. Edrich's career with Middlesex ended on a note of bathos when he was bowled for a duck by Jim Laker in Middlesex's home game against Surrey. Soon after the close of the season, he announced that he had been invited by Michael Falcon, the chairman of Norfolk, to take over as skipper for the 1959 season. 'I am overjoyed at the chance to return to the county I played for as a young man,' he said.

It was also time for new beginnings elsewhere in his life.

11

ON THE DEFENSIVE
1959–1965

'The thing I remember most was his great sense of humour. He loved to
laugh and he was always fun in the dressing room.'

Henry Blofeld

The separation had been a long time coming. There had been too many drunken
rows, too many betrayals, too many humiliations. The good times of the past had
given way to the bitter words of the present. Trust had been replaced by anger.

The last straw for Jessy had been a letter she had received from a woman in
Australia revealing her affair with Bill during his recent trip there in the winter
of 1958–59, when he had accompanied Peter May's MCC team as a journalist.
There had been trouble on the previous trip to Australia he had made four
years earlier as a player under Len Hutton in the winter of 1954–55. Then the
press had carried some pictures of Bill cavorting with several ice-skaters, all
long legs and white-toothed smiles. Bill had assured her that the scene was
entirely innocent and that the press were trying to whip up a scandal where
none existed. There had been some frostiness after that, but they patched up
their relationship.

But the letter from this alleged lover, who worked for the Australian airline
Qantas, seemed a deadly strike aimed at the heart of her marriage. Jessy's worst
fears were confirmed when Bill, back from Australia, did not deny the affair but
almost took a perverse pride in being open about it. Yet again, the duality at the
heart of Bill's character was apparent. He was completely indifferent about his
marriage vows, but had his own code of honour about the need for frankness.
Inevitably, the atmosphere in the Hatfield cottage became impossible. Relations

between Jessy and Bill had utterly broken down, to the dismay of his family and many figures in the cricket world where she was a popular figure. 'I remember calling at Hatfield to see her; she was a lovely lady,' said Peter Parfitt. Sir Tim Rice has happy memories of a visit to Lord's in 1956 organised by Jessy complete with a delicious picnic. Bill's own sister Ena wrote in her memoir that 'once again, Bill chose the foolish path of dalliance and Jess was informed by letter. There is no doubt it broke her heart. We all had such hopes for this marriage. After all, Bill and Jess had been together ten years and had produced a fine son, Jasper.' With Jessy's two daughters at boarding school, it was Jasper who was the prime witness to the painful disintegration of the relationship, as he recounted: 'They'd had a lot of happy moments but also a lot of sad moments. When he was playing in England, my mother would often go and watch him, and she also kept press cuttings of the 1954–55 tour. He liked a drink and she usually had a gin and tonic on the go.' But Jasper recalls how the mood turned sulphurous after the letter's revelation of the affair in Australia, about which one newspaper dropped hints through the publication of a photo of Bill in public with his lover. 'I remember when he came back from Australia, he'd been having an affair with a woman out there. We were sitting down to breakfast one morning and a newspaper arrived through the letterbox and landed on the doormat. My mother picked it up. On the front page was a picture of all the people on the tour and my father was sitting next to this lady. My mother got into a rage, tore the paper in half and threw it across the table. That's the way we were then. I got a bit upset.' The thrust of this story is corroborated by Penny, Jessy's older daughter, 'Their break-up came after the Ashes tour. To be honest, he had an Australian girlfriend who was going to come here. My mother booted him out. She was not having it.'

In July 1959 Jessy and Bill confirmed their split, as the *Daily Mirror* reported: 'At the little wooden cottage they used to share on the outskirts of Hatfield, Mrs Jessy Edrich, 41, told me, "We've decided to live apart. The separation is unofficial because nothing is settled yet."' Bill had temporarily moved into a hotel in the nearby town of Hoddesdon, where Jack Belton, a great friend from his RAF days, lived and ran his business. Speaking to the press, Bill explained with a degree of circumspection. 'I can't say for the moment whether divorce proceedings will be taken.' When asked whether, in view of his three failed marriages, he considered himself unlucky in love, Edrich grew even more reticent. 'If the answer is for quotation, I don't think I better speak.' But divorce did swiftly follow, in November 1959, when Jessy was granted a decree nisi on the grounds of her husband's adultery with an unnamed woman. As in his previous two divorces, he did not contest the lawsuit. Jessy, who went on to run a successful boutique dress shop and find happiness in a more stable relationship, later told Ena, 'Though I loved Bill, I just could not live with him.' Jasper's memory is that his mother 'was very relieved at the end of her marriage to Bill'. Jo, Penny's younger sister who was at boarding school at the time, also experienced the finality of the break: 'I remember learning about the divorce from the newspapers. I cannot remember how I felt and since then, I never heard from or saw him again. Looking at those words, it's sad.'

Edrich's matrimonial record might not seem shocking today, but in 1959 divorce was still viewed with disapproval. It was only four years since, under heavy ecclesiastical and political pressure, Princess Margaret had felt compelled to end her relationship with Group Captain Peter Townsend because he had been through a divorce, just as her uncle King Edward VIII had been forced to abdicate because he wanted to marry the American divorcee Wallis Simpson in 1936. The concept of marriage as a moral, even sanctified, institution still had a strong resonance in British society, which is why the divorce laws were so restrictive and would remain so until Parliament passed the 1969 Divorce Reform Act, vastly liberalising the process. Before 1969, adultery was the most common grounds for the dissolution of an unhappy union, as in all three of Edrich's break-ups, and this helped to create a vast industry of deceit, intrusion and hypocrisy, involving private detectives, photographers, lawyers, hotel managers, journalists, chambermaids and prostitutes. The change in attitudes to divorce can be traced through Edrich's own later adult life. In 1959 there were 23,286 divorces, a figure that rose at the time of his death in 1986 to 153,963. Similarly, the divorce rate increased sixfold from 2.1 per 1,000 of the married population in the late 1950s to 12.9 per 1,000 in the mid 1980s.

The erratic nature of Edrich's personal life did not seem to put him off the institution of marriage. When his separation from Jessy was first revealed, he said, 'I have positively no intention of marrying again.' Yet he was soon retreating from that position after he met Valerie Terry, an independent-minded, professionally successful woman. The daughter of Constant Ponder, a Kent-based GP whom she described as 'undemonstrative, unemotional and severe', she had served in the WAAF during the war and then ran her own business as a consultant in the insurance industry. She had previously been married to John Terry, a media executive with whom she had two daughters, but that too was an unhappy relationship because of her husband's infidelity. In her private, unpublished memoir Valerie wrote how John 'had become involved with an attractive and very well-off girl' and 'asked me for a divorce, to which I reluctantly had to agree'. Her one comfort through this painful experience was the court's decision to give her custody of their two children, Jane and Judy, 'there being no question that John would make any demand for them'. Keen to make a new start in her life, she took a new job with the Australian Mutual Provident (AMP) Society, attracted by the possibility that she might be able to emigrate soon with the girls to Melbourne if she could win a transfer to the company's headquarters in that city.

But thoughts of moving to the other side of the world were banished after Valerie met Bill. One afternoon in September 1959, even before his divorce from Jessy had been finalised, she received a request from her AMP boss to call on some businessmen in Hoddesdon to discuss their plans for a new insurance consultancy. If they affiliated to AMP and made a success of their venture, Valerie's company could do well out of the arrangement. She was therefore determined to make a good impression when she reached Hoddesdon. She certainly triumphed on that score. The businessmen turned out to be Edrich and Jack Belton. Over lunch, Valerie pressed the case for joining AMP, and Bill seemed interested. But it was not the Australian company that had enticed him. Already he was working on a much more personal strategy, one that would require dishonesty followed by charm. He told Valerie that through his contacts, he could supply her with a list of local tomato producers, some of whom could be lucrative clients to her because this industry was booming, like many other parts of the British economy at the time. Valerie's account continued, 'I gave him my telephone number and waited for the names to be forthcoming. He called a couple of days later to say that he hadn't been able to find any tomato growers, but would I come out to dinner, which I duly did.'

Within weeks, their romance had become serious, which was bad news for Bill's Australian lover who worked for Qantas, and who had travelled to England to see him. But by now, captivated by Valerie, he had lost any interest in seeing the Australian woman again. In fact, Jack Belton went so far as to say that he had 'completely forgotten' about her while he contemplated a new life with Valerie. The biggest step towards their marriage was inspired by Valerie's young daughter Jane, whose innocent frankness with the couple pushed Valerie in the direction that Bill was already heading, recalling how much Bill 'hated living in a hotel room'; Valerie wrote that he: '. . . longed for a proper home life. I hadn't known him very long and one Sunday, when Bill had come to lunch, seven-year-old Jane, in the middle of the meal, suddenly said, "Bill, why don't you marry Mummy, she's looking for a husband." I could have sunk through the floor with embarrassment but Bill just said, "That's probably a good idea." Apparently he already had it in mind.'

Jane told me her reasoning was simple, 'I liked Bill – then.' Events proceeded quickly after that. Valerie was living at the time in a large, three-bedroom mansion flat in Hampstead that she had bought with the assistance of her mother. To help meet her bills, she had taken in a lodger called Mr Norris, a struggling freelance journalist who lived off baked beans, but once Bill came on the scene, Mr Norris was out.

Bill and Valerie were married on 3 March, 1960 at Hampstead Registry Office, followed by a reception in their flat. She had hoped that the event would be private, but Mr Norris lived up to the dictates of his profession by alerting some of the national papers. Not knowing of his liaison with the press, Valerie was astonished when she arrived at the Registry Office to find a row of motorcycles lined up on the pavement, each with two professionals, one of whom took photographs of the couple, the other who sped back to Fleet Street once the assignment was completed. 'Bill was used to this sort of thing but it was all very new and strange to me,' she wrote. One of the journalists who reported the event was from the *Daily Express*, and he spoke briefly to Bill before the short civil ceremony. 'The wedding will be very quiet. In fact I have been trying to keep it as quiet as possible,' Edrich told him, adding that 'the girls have met my son and they get on very well together'. The *Daily Mirror* was also present and Bill snapped when its reporter asked about his vow not to marry again, 'Of course I said that but a chap has the right to change his mind.' The reporter also enquired about his new wife's interest in cricket. 'She's not knowledgeable but she likes it,' he replied.

After a honeymoon in Tenerife, the couple returned to London and Valerie went back to work with AMP. But soon a problem arose between them. Edrich was involved in several enterprises in the early 1960s with Jack Belton and his former England colleague the wicket-keeper Godfrey Evans, but none of them had yet taken off and he had plenty of free time on his hands. Moreover, he had developed a jealous, possessive streak towards Valerie, not a very consistent quality in a lifelong seducer. Feeling threatened by her male, often younger clients, he tried to insist on accompanying her to her meetings with them. This was, wrote Valerie, 'quite impossible when discussing private finances so I had to resign. AMP were not too happy,' she recorded. Another part of Valerie, however, was gratified by the intensity of Bill's devotion. 'When I first met Bill, after having been neglected and finally rejected by John, it seemed wonderful that he wanted me to be with him all the time, and I was quite happy to be "possessed".' But practically it was not the easiest start to their married life together, for not only did they have to find a way of replacing Valerie's lost earnings, but also their family was growing so they needed more space. In addition to Jane and Judy, Valerie gave birth to Justin on 17 January, 1961, who was to inherit much of his father's talent for cricket. What made the legal side of Bill's relationship with Jane and Judy interesting was that he formally adopted them, so he was more than a stepfather. 'We were not his stepchildren. We wanted to be adopted because our father had disappeared. I remember being asked in the judge's chambers if we were happy and I said, "yes", I did genuinely want a daddy,' Jane said. She further recalled how, 'when Justin came along I spent a lot of time with him, though I don't really remember Bill engaging with us. He was very hands off with us but he adored Justin and that always annoyed me because Justin got whatever Justin wanted, Jasper we saw only briefly on the occasional weekend because he was living with Jessy or was at Gresham's boarding school.' Jasper's recollection was of a less harmonious home. 'Dad used to tell Jane that she looked horrible with her straggly hair. He did not really like Jane or Judy; he gave them a hell of a hard time because they were in the way. I had a lot of respect for Valerie. In those days at the London flat, she and Bill were in love.'

But their days in the capital were numbered. Bill felt he had found the solution to their difficulties when he met a man in a pub who wanted a quick sale on his large house in the village of Shepreth near Cambridge. On visiting the property, which was called The Chase, the next day, Bill and Valerie felt it was perfect: in good condition, with lots of space, a low purchase price, cheap to run, and the potential to keep livestock and make some money. Apart from apparently meeting their needs for more space and a potential income, The Chase also appealed to Bill because of that streak in him that always cherished rural life. According to Valerie, Bill was 'a real countryman at heart and hated London'. Bill's older brother Eric had kept rabbits commercially, so once the family was settled into The Chase, Bill and Valerie decided to do the same. Guided by Eric, they were quite successful at rearing litters, many of which they sold to Alfred Moss, the father of the racing driver Stirling Moss, who was a successful trader in the business. Transporting the rabbits to Alfred Moss's base in Tring was the duty that Valerie disliked the most: 'I had to forget that they were going to be turned into lovely tender meals but it was difficult. I don't think we ever ate any ourselves and we kept the eventual destiny secret from the girls.'

Rabbit production was just one angle that Edrich pursued in the years immediately after his retirement from Middlesex. 'When it came to business, he was always having a dabble,' said Peter Parfitt. 'My dad had a very inventive mind, a sharp brain and was full of enterprising ideas,' recalled Jasper, who also said of Jack Belton, 'They drank a lot of beer together and used to have a good laugh. Jack had black, greasy hair and was quite affable, but he was not as rural as my father. Bill was a farmer at heart whereas Jack was a townie.' Apart from the production of instructional coaching films and the sponsorship of his own brand of cricket boots, the first real commercial enterprise in which Edrich had been involved was Concrete Pitches Limited, run by his old friend from Acton,

Ted Ward. Both Bill and Denis Compton were co-directors of Ward's firm, which boasted that it was the 'sole manufacturer of the pre-cast concrete pitch'. But after a wave of enthusiasm in the late 1940s for such surfaces, interest fell away in the 1950s, the decade that also saw the beginning of the end for Latham Paints under Baring, who had been too inclined to treat the firm as a vehicle for his own entertainment. Nor did Edrich's work with the Wellingborough firm Rubber Improvement Limited yield any dividends, despite its development of a new type of plastic cricket ball, partly because problems with the seam were never resolved.

But Edrich had higher hopes when he set up a marketing company with Belton and Evans called BEE, which he thought could make his fortune by promoting ground-breaking new products. During his interview about the break-up of his marriage with Jessy in July 1959 he mentioned BEE and said, 'I think it's going to prove a great success.' Less than a year later, the *Daily Mail*, under the headline 'It's all business for Evans', reported that the former England wicket-keeper had 'a tie-up with Bill Edrich in a sales promotion firm'. Somewhat predictably, given their lack of commercial experience, their very first initiative turned out to be a flop. Edrich and Evans had set up a demonstration in Hoddesdon for the press and police of a new anti-theft device invented in Germany for which they had secured the selling rights. Fitted to a cashier's bag, the appliance had a container packed with a chemical dye, which in turn was connected to an electric cable. In theory, if there were an attempt to snatch the bag, the electric current in the cable would be activated, releasing 400 cubic feet of purple smoke, which would stain the thieves' clothes and the cash. But to their embarrassment, when Edrich and Evans gave their display, the gadget failed to work three times in succession. On the first occasion, the German inventor blamed a worn-out battery; the next two failures were put down to a fault in the cable. Evans was seen angrily remonstrating with the inventor, 'the bag did not go off when it should have done so it is not foolproof. We must have an explanation,' he said. The inventor promised that it would work the fourth time, and it did, but by then the damage had been done. The incident became a metaphor for the wider failure of BEE, which never made the commercial breakthrough that was Edrich's dream. More prosaically, Edrich then managed to get some marketing work with an East Anglian company called Air Products, a move that pushed him into sewage. In 1963 he began promoting a new mobile treatment plant for processing waste, one of the early examples of which was installed on a new housing estate in the Norfolk village of Dersingham near King's Lynn. Called the Oxygest, this plant was designed in the USA and built in Wrexham. Showing commendable if surprising enthusiasm for its capabilities, Edrich boasted that it could be installed in less than a day and was ideal for any site 'in outlying areas without municipal sewer facilities', as he explained to the *Lynn Advertiser.*

The study of municipal sewage facilities was not what Edrich had in mind for his post-Test and post-first-class career. Given his love of cricket, it might have seemed obvious for him to go into the press box, following the path taken by so many other ex-players, including Compton. But his tour to Australia in 1958–59 could not be regarded as an unqualified success, partly because of the explosive rows he triggered over his articles in the *People* about Hutton and Wyatt. Too enveloped in controversy, he failed to inspire respect as a measured pundit, while his heavy drinking led to the view that he was unreliable, incapable of sustained work and deeply hypocritical when he denounced the indiscipline of other Test cricketers. In his own 1960 book *Over to Me* the Surrey off-spinner Jim Laker revealed the low opinion of both Edrich and the South African off-spinner Hugh Tayfield during this tour, claiming that they were regarded with even more contempt than the notorious Johnny Wardle of Yorkshire, whose capricious peddling of his grievances against club, country and colleagues had left him ostracised in English cricket. But Laker reserved some of his harshest words for Edrich:

There are two sorts of pressmen on tour: professional journalists and famous players of the recent past, such as Wardle, Tayfield and Edrich. Just how well they did is for others to judge. What people seem to overlook is that it takes some skill to do the job well and that some cricketer journalists can barely type their own name. I have already mentioned Wardle. Although he was obliged to indulge in personal criticism, he was at least at the cricket. As far as possible we avoided Edrich and Tayfield, which gives you some idea of what we thought of the truth and relevance of their writings. In many ways it was odd to see two of cricket's most turbulent characters attacking one of the mildest-mannered parties of which I have ever been a member.

Edrich was outraged by these comments, which he felt were a slur on his integrity. His resentment was augmented by a sense of commercial betrayal, for Laker's publisher, Frederick Muller, had also produced his book *Round the Wicket*. On his instructions his solicitor, the former Surrey captain Monty Garland-Wells, sent a letter to Muller demanding both an apology and amendments to the offending passage. Desperate to extinguish the flames of acrimony Muller capitulated instantly, promised to alter future editions, agreed to pay Edrich's costs and issued an abject apology: 'The publishers wish to state on behalf of themselves and Mr Laker that Mr Edrich is in their opinion a highly responsible and skilled cricket journalist and that the text of *Over to Me* has now been amended to remove any possibility of misunderstanding.' Laker's encomium was too brazenly insincere to do Edrich any good. Indeed, his foray into cricket writing at the end of the 1950s had shown that he was not cut out for this craft. It was not just the establishment that disliked his style. Among the adjectives used by members of the public to describe his material were: 'scurrilous', 'obnoxious', 'tittle-tattle' and 'foolish'. One reader from Hounslow said that 'the ability to play cricket does not, ipso facto, endow a person with the ability to write'.

Muller's clash with Laker was not the last of the rows that erupted in the fallout from the disastrous Ashes tour of 1958–59. In his book published that summer called *Round the Wicket*, large sections of which were about the trip, Edrich made a savage personal attack on Wardle, accusing him of disloyalty to Yorkshire, demeaning county fixtures by his 'clowning' and publishing 'ill-advised' articles. Wardle, wrote Edrich, always 'creates the uneasy feeling that he might leap into print at the drop of a glass of beer at a late-night party' and was deeply unpopular on the cricket circuit. In keeping with the tone of the feud, Wardle delivered a blistering response in the *Daily Mail*, having a go at Edrich's character and record. 'I live for cricket while others just live for a good time,' he said, adding that many of Edrich's words were rich 'from a man whose own party habits have got him into trouble. At the drop of whose glass of beer? It is more likely to be Bill Edrich's glass than mine for it is doubtful that I would be at that late-night party.'

The feud between the two men was to carry on for years, and was played out in the comparatively obscure setting of the Minor Counties Championship during the 1960s as Wardle appeared for Cambridgeshire and Edrich for his native Norfolk. Their seething animosity made the fixtures between the two clubs highly charged, especially because Edrich also had little time for the Cambridgeshire captain Maurice Crouch. But on another level, Edrich's takeover of the Norfolk captaincy in 1959 was exactly what he needed to keep him connected to cricket, give him a sense of purpose and impose his personality on a new generation of fans. Instead of fading into the darkness, he enjoyed a long Indian summer, which pushed back some of the shadows that had crept across his reputation. Where the Edrich of the press box often sounded sour, vindictive and self-serving, the Edrich who captained Norfolk was lovable, gracious, amusing and loyal. The wheel had come full circle, and he was back in a cricket culture that cherished him.

His return to Lakenham in 1959 had an immediate impact. Derek Godfrey, a young Norfolk fast bowler who was just 17 at the time, recalled that Edrich was 'a real leader, a real character, a very impressive person. He inspired people. He had a natural authority about him. I was a bit awestruck.' Apart from Edrich's leadership, Godfrey also found that he was still a fine cricketer, who, even at 43, was a cut above most other players in the Minor Counties. 'He bowled off-spin and got lots of wickets. He was not a big spinner of the ball, but he was consistent and put it on a length. His fielding was excellent. His reflexes were still pretty good and very rarely did he drop a catch. As a batsman he was fearless, never took a step backwards and was always looking to attack.' Henry Blofeld was another who played under Bill from 1959. Having been a prodigy at school, Blofeld's first-class career was restricted by the legacy of severe injuries he had suffered in a road accident in his last year at Eton, but he was still good enough to win his Blue for Cambridge University and spend nearly at decade with Norfolk until 1965 when the demands of his flourishing career in journalism became too great. As he recounted, it was a fascinating experience:

Bill was a considerable figure, a great character. He was bright, but at times did his best to disguise it. He was not altogether popular with the authorities; Freddie Brown would not have him at any price. He did some silly things, but there was something essentially honourable about him. The thing I remember most was his great sense of humour. He loved to laugh and he was always fun in the dressing room. On the field, I kept wicket and he was at first slip. He talked a lot, often about playing for England or Middlesex. There would be an incident, or someone would play a strange shot. It would trigger a memory and he'd be off. In fact, there were times when the umpires stepped in and said, 'Will you stop talking?'

Blofeld thought that, though Edrich bowled his 'little off-breaks very well indeed', he was no longer an outstanding force as a batsman: 'He made his runs, but he was very much a leg-side player, not very graceful.' Blofeld also recalled the friction in matches with Cambridgeshire, because of Edrich's antipathy towards both Wardle and the skipper Maurice Crouch: 'Maurice was a fairly lively Cambridgeshire farmer and as captain he had carried all before him, doing exactly what he wanted. Then suddenly he found himself up against Bill who was going to do things his way, so naturally there was a bit of friction. There was a match at Lakenham where Maurice made the first pair of his career and in the second innings I caught him behind. But Maurice refused to walk and Bill had a very lively conversation with him until he left the crease. Bill believed in walking.'

As a captain, Bill commanded respect because of his distinguished record, which he was not shy to emphasise by wearing his England pullover or his MCC tour blazer. But he was also an innovator. The Minor Counties Championship was a two-day competition which, for much of its recent history, had been infused with a defensive mentality that focused on avoiding defeat, grinding down the opposition and treating a first innings lead as an end in itself, all traits that were worsened with the improvement in the quality of pitches. But Edrich, whose role model as captain was the dynamic Middlesex leader Walter Robins, brought a very different approach, one that prioritised decisive results and the entertainment of spectators. At the centre of this bolder strategy was the creative use of declarations, where he frequently proved himself willing to risk defeat for a greater chance of victory. 'Tactically he was brilliant. He was always trying to get results and was never satisfied with draws. He was happy to declare when we were just ahead on the first innings,' recalled Derek Godfrey. Nor was Edrich hesitant about using his prestige and charm to pressurise opposition captains into setting reachable targets for Norfolk. In a sense, he was deploying the methods of limited-overs cricket before its arrival in the English game. To Henry Blofeld: 'His authority as a cricketer was awfully good news for us. I think we got quite a few declarations where Bill rather conned the opposing captain. He was a great enthusiast. I remember a match against Suffolk at Lakenham that Bill was determined to win, which we did. I slogged around 30 very quickly and Bill gave me my county cap on the steps of the pavilion, which was a great moment for me.'

In 1959, Norfolk had their best season since the war, finishing in seventh place. Edrich also proved himself a valuable all-rounder, averaging 20 with the ball and 46 with the bat. Even better followed in 1960 when Edrich led Norfolk to the top of the Championship table, though under the unsatisfactory system in place, the destiny of the title was decided, not by this position, but by a challenge match over three days between the two leading teams. The runners-up in the table that year were Lancashire Seconds, and they duly won the encounter by nine wickets. Any sense of disappointment at this outcome was counter-balanced by the recognition of the transformation that Edrich had brought about at the club. A major feature in *The Cricketer's Winter Annual*, headlined 'Norfolk Show the Way', praised Edrich for developing 'a spectacular new approach to two-day cricket', in which 'almost everything is subjected to getting a result by 6.30pm on the second day and once the final challenge has been made at the close of the third innings there is no thought of backing down to a struggle merely to save the game'. The magazine explained that Edrich's success was founded on four principles: a preference for batting second so that Norfolk chased rather than set the target; the avoidance of shutting out the opposition so that they only had a draw to play for; an all-round abhorrence of time-wasting and negative tactics;

and quick runs, with 'no thought at all for personal averages'. Nevertheless, Edrich's figures were excellent in 1960, with 852 runs at an average of 53, and 43 wickets at 16 apiece.

One simple physical reason for this significant improvement in his play was his greater physical fitness as a result of drastically cutting down on his alcohol consumption. Valerie had made it a condition of their marriage that he should be more abstemious and he had accepted, resulting in the incongruous sight of Bill drinking shandies during the season. It was not until baby Justin's arrival in early 1961 that he deviated from this regime, though with Valerie he was never to plumb the depths of excess that he reached at times in his later years. The quality of Bill's leadership and standard of play was further enhanced by the convenience of living in the East Anglia countryside after their move from London. In geographical terms, he grew even closer to his native county when the couple sold The Chase in Shepreth and bought a large period farmhouse in the Suffolk village of Wyverstone near Stowmarket. Called Knight's Court, the property had three acres of land and several outbuildings, some of which were to be used for another new commercial venture: to the list of occupations that Bill had tried, he now added that of poultry farmer. His older brother Eric had made the switch from keeping rabbits to chickens and he persuaded Valerie and Bill to do the same. It was a major undertaking that involved looking after a flock that could have over 12,000 birds so they had to employ two assistants from the village. According to Valerie, they made 'a reasonable income' and 'Bill, ever the countryman, loved it', though Jane had exactly the opposite memory: 'Bill hated it and it did not really succeed.'

Life at Wyverstone also had some advantages for the children. There was space in the grounds for Jane and Judy to have a pony each, and room in the garden for a concrete cricket pitch. Even as a small child, Justin displayed both a skill and an interest in the game, much to his father's delight. Jasper was less fortunate. He too loved the sport but a problem with his eyesight limited the level he could attain. 'I was very short-sighted. Even so, I was not that bad. I captained the Under-13s at school. Anyway, I did not let my eyesight get in the sway of my enjoyment of cricket,' he said. Justin recounted the pride that his father took in the early signs of his potential. 'It was very important to my father that I had a talent for the game, though that was obviously hard on Jasper. The concrete pitch at Wyverstone was covered in coconut matting so we could practise. He never over-coached or went into too much technical detail. He wanted it to remain fun. He would just bowl at me and I would hit it.'

Sustained by cricket, family and the farm, Edrich appeared to be becoming a figure of substance in his locality. He opened fetes, spoke at dinners, judged beauty contests and supported charities. The young blade about town of the 1930s had turned into a country squire of the 1960s. 'He went shooting quite a lot,' said Jane, 'and would bring these wretched pheasants home and hang them in the larder till they got very high. Then he would pluck them, puffing away on his pipe.' He also enjoyed being the host who could preside over abundance. Jean Beecroft, Eric's daughter, recalled the generosity of his welcome when she visited Knight's Court. 'It was always lovely. Bill was very hospitable and always kind. Valerie was really pleasant to us as children, a really nice, charming lady. She and Bill made a good couple.' Confirmation of his status came in May 1964 when Bill topped the poll in the election for Wyverstone Parish Council. Although he was a Conservative and occasionally attended Tory events like fund-raising galas, his role as a parish councillor in the village was civic rather than political.

But by far the greatest element of his local fame came from his leadership of Norfolk. His form in 1961 was better than ever as he topped both the county's bowling averages at 24.22 per wicket and batting averages at 79. In one astonishing performance at Lakenham against Staffordshire, he became the first Norfolk player to make a century in each innings, hitting the winning runs in a daring chase during the last over. Clive Radley, another of Norfolk's great Middlesex and England batsmen, along with Parfitt and Edrich, made his debut that season. 'He was not afraid to lose a game if he had a chance to win it. He led by example, chasing anything and set interesting declarations,' Radley told me as he went on to explain that, like the case of Peter Parfitt, Edrich was instrumental in his move to Lord's. 'He recommended me to the club. They gave me a three-year contract on the strength of that recommendation. I did not have a trial, did not even have to go up to London.

The committee must have respected his judgement.' But Radley admits that judgement was questioned by some of the senior players, like John Murray, known as JT because of his initials, and spinner Fred Titmus. On a freezing cold April day, Radley had his first net. 'I remember standing at the back were JT and Fred Titmus. They were just shaking their heads because I could not lay a bat on the ball. It was going past the outside edge or whacking into my thigh.' Five years later, when Radley was established in the team, he spoke about the incident to Titmus:

'Do you remember the first net I had? What were you saying to JT?'

'What I said to JT was this: "I had always thought that old Bill was a bloody good judge of a cricketer, but he's cocked this one up."'

Edrich's form dipped slightly in 1962 but he still averaged over 40 with the bat. Fast bowler Michael Oxbury, who went to school with Clive Radley, made his debut that season against Hertfordshire. In his typical fashion Bill Edrich, resplendent in his MCC blazer, met Oxbury on the steps of the pavilion and said to him:

'We're here to play cricket and enjoy it. I don't want you to be nervous. Just call me skip.'

I played in 10 of the 12 Championship games that year and most were under his captaincy. What always impressed was the fact that this great man, who was such a good batsman and bowler, had a wonderful gift for captaincy, certainly at minor county level. He wanted to win, but also to entertain.

Oxbury recalled a game against Lincolnshire, in which Edrich bowled him for 21 consecutive overs in the second innings, while he bowled 21 at the other end:

We won that match because he bowled tight and he told me to keep the ball well up, with no extra cover. I kept being driven and that kept Lincolnshire in the game while he was getting wickets at the other end. He had worked out that this was the way to win the game. He was very astute. He had a brilliant brain, a cricket brain. You knew skip was at slip. His experience of first-class cricket meant that his hands could always manage to grab the ball. He was an excellent fielder, hardly anything got past him.

Oxbury concluded, 'he was a big personality. He did not give speeches or pep talks. Somehow he just had a gift for getting the very best out of young cricketers. He made you feel that you could do things that you hadn't realised you could.'

12

FADING LIGHT
1963–1971

'He tried to sell it to one or two of us, but I didn't have any money then
so it did not make any difference to me. Nobody was taken in by it.
I don't think Bill was very good at selling insurance really.'

Paul Borrett

The shandy regime was a passing interlude. Edrich had not been
fundamentally changed by a new marriage, a new home or a new cricket
club. The existential hedonist, living for the moment, remained a powerful
facet of his character. Even as he reached his fifties, his social appetites were
unsated and his stamina for pleasure-seeking was undiminished. Age,
responsibility and experience did not alter the pattern of his life which had
been set when he first joined Lord's.

Just as at Middlesex, his teammates at Norfolk were amazed at this capacity
for late hours. Men 30 years younger struggled to keep up with him when the
club was on away trips, where Bill felt free of domestic ties. 'I was 23 when I
first played with him and I found it pretty exhausting. I am not exaggerating
when I say we never went to bed before 4 o'clock,' said Ted Wright, who played
with him at the end of the decade. Similarly, Paul Borrett, the son of Jack
Borrett, one of Bill's closest Norfolk friends, recalled that 'it was quite difficult
but a lot of fun' when he started out in 1967 under Edrich's unorthodox
leadership:

He would not let you get to bed. He would sing all night. One of his
favourites was 'A Nightingale Sang in Berkeley Square'. He did not hold

205

his drink particularly well but he did drink a lot. The last game of the season was usually at Beaconsfield, where he had a great friend called Cliff Jardine who ran a pub there. One night, when it had got to about four in the morning, we went off to bed but he and Cliff carried on. Then they found that they had run out of lager, so he and Bill went down to the cellar to get more. Cliff went down first. Bill immediately followed, falling on top of Cliff and breaking his arm. Cliff had to be carted off to hospital in an ambulance. I remember Mrs Jardine at breakfast the next morning:

'Mr Edrich, you're never staying in this place again, ever.'

Barry Battelley, who bowled left-arm spin, thought that Edrich had 'quite a good voice', though its quality depended on how much he had drunk. 'He just liked entertaining, a wonderful chap.' Bill's fame at Norfolk in the 1960s, however, did not match that of his golden years immediately after the war, as Battelley found when the team went to a Norwich night club: 'Bill liked that sort of place – and then in walks Gordon Banks, the England goalkeeper. Bill went up and shook his hand and Gordon Banks did not know who he was at all – or at least he did not recognise Bill. The look of puzzlement on Gordon's face gave us all a laugh.' On occasions, Edrich's unstoppable eagerness to celebrate could affect the discharge of his duties. The Warwickshire professional turned commentator Jack Bannister cherished an incident at the beginning of a local derby between Norfolk and Suffolk when Edrich turned up just before the start, 'giving every indication of having been at an extended party which had not long ended. As home captain, he should have had a coin but had to borrow one from his star-struck counterpart, to whom Edrich had been a boyhood hero. Imagine his reaction when the coin was handed over and then flung, discus fashion, towards mid-wicket, before Edrich told him, "If you can find it, you can bat."'

Inevitably, the search for amorous diversions was an ingredient of this hectic socialising, especially when Valerie was not around. 'She was often in attendance and made her presence felt,' said Henry Blofeld of Norfolk's home games. But it was a different story on the road. 'I witnessed his charm with women because we all had to stand aside if there was a smart lady at the bar. He would always make a beeline for any attractive woman,' recalled Paul Borrett. The Essex and Norfolk batsman Graham Saville, to whom Edrich acted as a kind of mentor in the 1967 season, told me that:

Bill had a wonderful way with women. He had a really good personality. I remember we played Herts and we stayed at a hotel just outside Bishop's Stortford. We went to a pub in the evening, where one of the lads knew the landlord and landlady, who had previously lived in Norfolk. We all went there as a team. 'Come on, everyone's going,' Bill said. Now the landlady really was very, very attractive. Bill's eyes just went round and round and round. She would have been in her early thirties and Bill was flirting with her the whole night. The next day, one of us asked, 'Did you succeed last night?'

'No – I could have done but her husband's a nice man, isn't he?' Bill replied.

And I thought to myself, 'Blimey, that's never stopped you before.'

Bill showed less restraint one time he gave a lift to the young Norfolk player Geoff Fiddler on an away trip. Geoff recounted the story to his teammate Robin Huggins, who shared his recollection of the events with me: 'They met at the Bell Hotel in Norwich. Before driving off, Bill said to Geoff, "I've got to make a bit of a detour on the way." Soon they arrived at a house whose door was opened by a lady. Bill and Geoff were ushered inside. Then the lady said, "Geoffrey, I have got some sandwiches and tea for you," before adding, "Mr Edrich and I have some business to attend to." End of story. Bill and the lady went upstairs while Geoff enjoyed his sandwiches.'

On the field, even with this exhausting schedule, Edrich continued to weave some of his old magic, both as captain and player. In 1963 he topped the Norfolk averages with the bat at 41.92 and also took 45 wickets with his off-spin at 16.66. The next season he headed the county's batting averages again at 39 as he took Norfolk high in the top half of the Championship table. His skill and encouragement to others was captured by Robin Huggins in a recollection of an away game against Hertfordshire, whose attack was headed by Bill's former Middlesex colleague Henry Tilly, a highly effective fast-medium bowler:

> It was a green wicket. We lost the toss and we were put in to bat. Pretty quickly Henry Tilly had us four wickets down and I walked out to join Bill, the not-out batsman. I'll never forget how he came up to me and said, 'Don't fucking get out.'
>
> I was sort of petrified. Henry was moving the ball all over the place, off-cutters, leg-cutters. I played and missed, nicked through the slips, but somehow made 16 and Bill and I put on over 70. Anything short, Bill just murdered. He would pull even from a ball outside off stump. He was fantastic. Anything short he picked up very early and just whacked it through mid-wicket. It was amazing. More through luck than judgement, I hung around for about 90 minutes. During the innings, he kept coming down the wicket to say 'well played' even if I had missed three balls in the over and nicked two of the others. I did not play many attacking shots, and just took ones and twos where I could. He was encouraging when you batted with him. But he also laid the law down.

It was Edrich's courage that deeply impressed David Pilch, who played 23 years with Norfolk up to 1984: 'He never wore a thigh pad, but instead took a handkerchief out of his right-hand pocket and put it in his left-hand pocket. The other thing I never understood is how, having faced people like Lindwall and Miller, all he ever wore was a pink plastic box. That personally terrified me. I had a metal one. It got bashed about but at least it bloody survived. The pink plastic one shattered. Bill was a very, very good player. I don't feel that nationally, Bill was as respected as he should have been.'

Ted Wright, who played with Edrich at the end of the decade, also recalled that Edrich 'was not frightened of anything. We did not wear much protection in those days. I had a pair of batting gloves with green spikes and everyone was taking the mickey. He turned round and said, "Those were plenty good enough for Lindwall and Miller."'

As a batsman, Edrich prided himself in playing cricket in the right spirit, which is why he insisted that players in his side walked if they edged the ball. But as so often with him, there was a strange dichotomy, for he did not apply the same moral code when he was bowling. On the contrary, he was all too happy to use his wiles and repeated appeals to earn his wickets. In this way, a spell from him could take on a theatrical quality, full of histrionic gestures, muttered asides and knowing looks. Robin Huggins recalled, 'As a spinner, he was a bit of a con artist. He was not a great turner of the ball, but if one deviated a bit he'd say, "I'll go round the wicket, umpire, it's really turning." Because of his reputation, umpires succumbed to him.' The contradiction was noticed by Graham Saville. 'Bill was a stickler for playing the right way. "You know you're out, you go," he would say of batting.' Yet as spinner, 'he would stand there, looking at the umpires, trying to intimidate them. He got a fair few decisions for Norfolk.' The Suffolk player Tony Warrington was on the receiving end of some of Edrich's manoeuvres:

There was a Minor Counties umpire, nice fellow, slightly overweight, called Stan Moore. Norfolk had cricket week at Lakenham and had three two-day games then, with the same umpires for all three games. Bill being Bill, he would get to know the umpires very well, chat them up, buy them drinks, that sort of thing. In one of those matches, Bill was bowling off-spin from Stan Moore's end. As the non-striker I was at the same end, and I watched one of Bill's deliveries hit the batsman on the pads. As he turned and walked back, he said very quietly, 'How's that Stan?'

'That's not out Bill.'

A few overs later he again hit the batsman on the pads.

'How's that Stan?'

'That's not out Bill.'

I thought to myself, 'Hang on, the third time it will be out.' Sure enough, soon a much louder appeal went up, 'How's that Stan?' with a wry smile on his face.

'That's out Bill"

It was his reward for buttering up the umpires.

Another time we were playing at Lowestoft, which is right on the border with Norfolk. We got big crowds for these games. Towards the end of the first day we were getting on top, and the sun had started to drop behind the sightscreen at one end. All of a sudden he was chatting the umpire up, claiming that because of the sun, he could not see the ball.

'Well, I can see it,' said our keeper.

But Bill persuaded the umpires to come off for bad light. It was very sunny. It wasn't affecting our slips or our keeper, so how was it affecting Bill? He was very crafty. He was using his personality to get on the umpires' side.

Edrich could be headstrong, especially where Wardle and Maurice Crouch, his two enemies from Cambridgeshire, were concerned. Graham Saville remembered during the tea interval a ferocious public row between Edrich and Crouch in the President's tent at Lakenham during a festival match:

We had been fielding and as we walked to the tent we could hear their voices.

'I suppose you've declared,' said Bill.

'Are you now captain of Cambridge?' replied Crouch.

'No.'

'Well, I'll declare when I want to.'

Paul Borrett felt that Edrich 'had no side to him but he could be a bit awkward with some people who rubbed him up the wrong way. He could certainly stand his corner. I remember one game in which he did not want to come off the field during rain because he was hoping for a finish. So he took a deckchair out and sat in front of the pavilion in the pouring rain. He was certainly a character. We were in awe of him.' Awe was also the emotion felt by Gordon Bland when he first played for Norfolk in 1965, having hero-worshipped Edrich as a boy. 'I recall he was bowling his off-spinners and I was fielding at mid-on. The ball came to me and I had to toss it to Bill a mere ten yards away, but I was so in awe that the ball would not come out of my hand properly. So the ball bounced in front of him and he flicked it up into his hand with his boot.'

By the mid-sixties, Edrich's lustre was beginning to fade, particularly in his batting, where his average fell to 20 in 1965, and remained below 30 in the following two seasons. By then, his cousin John Edrich had emerged as a Test star of even greater quality than Bill. In 1965, John scored an extraordinary unbeaten 310 against New Zealand, hitting 57 boundaries, still the most in any Test innings, and that winter he had a successful Ashes tour of Australia. Of Bill's brothers, Geoff had become a coach at Cheltenham College after a spell with Cumberland, having been sacked in 1959 as Lancashire's Second XI coach after accusations of indiscipline in his young team and a conviction for drink-driving, a punishment that exacerbated his depression. Eric, working in the poultry industry, had long retired from the game, though the youngest brother Brian, now a coach at St Edward's School in Oxford, continued to turn out for Oxfordshire. Thanks partly to the Test exploits of their cousin John, interest in the Edrich cricketing family remained high. On occasions, the annual charity match between the Edrich XI and the Lord's Taverners, held in the village of Ingham and organised by Paul Borrett's father Jack, was even televised on the regional network because of the big stars it attracted. A distant cousin, Keith Edrich, enjoyed watching these events and was struck by Bill's commitment to this fixture, 'He used to try harder than some, but it was all fun. John was my next-door neighbour. He was quiet compared to the others.' For Keith, having the Edrich name turned out to be 'a mixed blessing. When you are an ordinary player just at village level, the name leads people to think you ought to be better. It has been a double-edged sword for me.'

But the image from Ingham of gentle harmony on and off the field was misleading. Bill's gift for generating controversy and chaos had not deserted him in the twilight of his career. In fact, it was about to be turned on full blast, both in his married life and in his paid occupation. Unsatisfied with his income, still hankering after the opportunity to become rich, Edrich turned to the world of insurance that had brought him and Valerie together. He had always been good at arithmetic, and confident with people, so in the late sixties he became a salesman for a new company that seemed to have found the financial holy grail of achieving colossal returns while enabling the promoters of its policies to earn huge sums in commission. This company, called International Life Insurance, was the British subsidiary of the global conglomerate Investors Overseas Services, which had been founded by the American financier Bernie Cornfeld. Born in Istanbul, he was the son of a Romanian-Jewish actor who emigrated to the USA when Bernie was just four but died only two years later. The poverty of his New York childhood pulled him in two opposite directions. On the one hand, he was a fierce critic of capitalism, a stance that led him both to become a social worker and a member of the Trotskyite Socialist Youth League. On the other hand, Cornfeld wanted to break free of his background by making money, and his fertile, ambitious mind focused on the sale of mutual funds to achieve that goal. In 1956 he set up Investors Overseas Services (IOS), incorporated outside the USA for tax reasons, and, with its promises of soaring prosperity for both clients and sales representatives, it was a roaring success. Cornfeld was soon nicknamed the 'Billy Graham of Investment' or the 'Prophet of Profit'. Within ten years, IOS was reported to have 140,000 sales staff worldwide and offices in more than 100 countries. According to a report in the *Daily Mirror*, the IOS office based in Geneva had 'its walls covered with velvet and filled with beautiful mini-skirted receptionists'.

Despite all the traditions of the City, International Life Insurance, the British arm of IOS, had been part of this dramatic expansion. At the heart of the boom was the company's aggressively promoted 'Dover Plan' scheme, a unit-linked insurance policy that offered far bigger returns than the annual bonuses of conventional 'with profits' policies. The plan had nothing to do with the port in Kent but was simply named after a Mayfair street near the company's British headquarters. Some sales staff were boasting that, after training, they could make more than £5,000 a year from the Dover Plan, while generous rewards beckoned for other employees. 'Girls, money is exciting. We have made it that way through the Dover Plan. If you think insurance investment and the world of finance is boring – you're wrong. Here is your opportunity to find out why so many girls enjoy working with us', ran an IOS advertisement for typists, administrative assistants, key-punch operators and stock clerks in January 1970. By June that year, 153,000 Dover Plan policies had been sold in Britain.

In support of Dover Plan, a vast new empire had been created – and Bill Edrich was part of it. His role in pushing the policy has never been mentioned before but it was a crucial part of his livelihood in the late sixties and early seventies. Edrich was more than just a salesman for International Life Insurance; he was also a front man for the company in the East Anglian region, as can be gleaned from two adverts that appeared in the autumn of 1970. One, in the *Cambridge Evening News* on 23 October, explained, 'I have recently been appointed the Eastern Regional Recruiting Manager for International Life Insurance (UK) Limited. I have to offer responsible gentlemen an exciting career with this dynamic company. Very high earnings potential. You have probably heard of me from other fields. To arrange an interview, ring this number and ask for Bill Edrich.' The other advert was run in the *Eastern Daily Press* on 3 November and opened, 'Would you be prepared to say, "Madam, I think this financial plan would be too much of a burden at this time?" It's not easy to be so generous, not when you're working on commission. But when you are selling OUR plans, advice is all part of the service.' It went on, 'With us, you would be selling our highly successful Dover Equity Plan, which as well as giving full life cover, offers high maturity values through the investment of policy-holders' premiums in equities and securities.' The advert promised that it 'is a sound plan and it sells so you can expect to be earning £2000 in your first year with us and if in 4 to 5 years you are earning double that, we'll not be surprised. International Life Insurance is a British Company active throughout the UK. At the moment we need salesmen in the East Anglia area. These are career openings with good prospects of promotion to management status. Please telephone Bill Edrich in Norwich on this number.'

In fact, Edrich's recruitment drive did not represent the triumphant advance of a flourishing company but rather the panicky response of an organisation in severe trouble, whose reputation and sales force were collapsing amid intense scrutiny from regulators and politicians. IOS and its British arm had been built on the promises of wealth, yet now a huge number of ordinary people faced severe losses after investing large chunks of their savings in the dubious Dover Plan. As far back as the mid-sixties, experts had expressed doubts about both the sustainability and extravagance of the IOS structure. Those concerns were realised in the financial downturn at the beginning of the new decade, as the journalist Tony Bridgland explained in *The Telegraph*, 'when the stock market dived in 1970, the shortcomings of unit-linking were cruelly exposed. Unlike with-profits policies, there were no reserves to prop up the returns in bad times, and investors' hopes of riches evaporated.' The collapse of IOS created a huge international scandal that dragged on for years. Bernie Cornfeld was arrested in 1973 on corruption charges and jailed in Switzerland, though he was released on appeal within a year. He was reckless and cavalier, but he was not in the same league as the genuine crook who took over IOS when it ran into trouble, the drug runner and mobster Robert Vesco, who was soon on the run from the American authorities. He holed up in Cuba, only to end up in prison there on fraud charges.

Fortunately in Britain, International Life Insurance did not suffer such a grim fate. It was bought by a series of reputable City firms, eventually becoming part of the Allied Hambro insurance giant, for whom Bill Edrich worked during his final years, retiring only a few months before he died.

Indeed, Edrich suffered little lasting damage from the scandal, even though the saga was one of his less edifying achievements. If, in the autumn of 1970, he genuinely thought that the Dover Plan was 'sound', he was deluding himself. If not, he was deceiving the public. One observer, who saw his salesmanship of the Dover Plan in action, felt that 'it was a bit embarrassing that he would push it shamelessly. In Lord's Taverners games, he used to field at slip with it in his pocket and impose it on people like Brian Johnston who were too nice to say no.' Yet despite his fame and high profile in the IOS's recruitment campaign, his name did not feature in any of the explosive debates about the affair. Neither his sister Ena nor his wife Valerie mentioned the Dover Plan in their private memoirs, even though the latter had worked at a high level in insurance. Edrich himself was silent on the subject for the rest of his life, and continued to work in the industry without ever being challenged about his role.

Yet the scandal undoubtedly cast a shadow over his final period with Norfolk, largely because he had been using his unique position at the club to sell Dover Plan policies. As Robin Huggins recalled, 'I was going to invest in one through Bill – he must have mentioned it in the dressing room – but I was warned off because of the publicity. I was very young then.' Paul Borrett was in the same position. 'Dover Plan was quite controversial. He tried to sell it to one or two of us, but I didn't have any money then so it did not make any difference to me. Nobody was taken in by it. I don't think Bill was very good at selling insurance really.' But it seems that Bill sold a policy to Paul's father Jack, his great friend, who was said to have lost a substantial amount in the scheme. 'My father never mentioned anything about it. I don't think he would have put much in, but he may have put in some. But there was no sign of any friction between them and they remained friendly. In the Norfolk dressing room people were a bit circumspect. Bill thought it was a jolly good idea but no one else did.'

The cricketer who felt strongest about the issue was Richard Jefferson, who took over the captaincy of Norfolk in 1968 when Bill stepped down at the age of 52. A fine medium fast bowler who had played for Surrey and Cambridge University, Jefferson seemed the ideal candidate to take charge, but he soon found that the job was a poisoned chalice, not least because of Dover Plan:

I had played under Bill and captained the side a couple of times when he was not available. Before the 1968 season, he retired, was given a fond farewell and sailed off into the sunset. But then in the winter, he rang me up to explain that he had got a new job, selling insurance with Dover Plan. I actually invested a small sum, about £500, and made some money. But other people who put in considerably more lost money when the plan went pear-shaped. I don't think Bill was ripping people off but Dover Plan failed. It went down and took a lot of people with it.

These financial problems contributed to an uneasy atmosphere at the club. Jefferson also felt that the presence of Bill undermined his authority, especially

Bill's determination to maintain the nocturnal chorus of approval from the newer recruits. 'I was aged 28 and Bill was 55 and was a legend. Everyone in Norfolk was in awe of him, not surprisingly. Bill was keeping a group of cricketers up until two o'clock in the morning, telling stories of bombing Germany. This did not go down 100 per cent well with me as captain, that Bill was leading these young players astray.' Even with these difficulties, the county continued to perform well on occasions, as in 1969 when they reached the Gillette Cup against Yorkshire. Edrich could still hit some glorious innings, like the 93 not out he made against Hertfordshire at Lakenham in 1970 when chasing down a target of 160, as Paul Borrett remembered. 'It was a flash of his old genius. We had been set an almost impossible target. But he smashed it everywhere and we just failed to get them by one run, having needed two off the final ball. That was an amazing performance for someone in his fifties.' That same year Norfolk played against Middlesex in the Gillette Cup in 1970 at Lord's, the match serving as a cue for an outburst of nostalgia over the return of the old warrior. 'Lord's Greets Old King Bill', ran the headline in the *Daily Express* above Crawford White's interview with Bill, who confessed that the 'bowlers seem a bit quicker than they used to be but I am still enjoying it'.

Less enjoyment was derived by Richard Jefferson, who was infuriated that he could not have the team he wanted for the game. Instead, he sensed that the selection was effectively dictated by Bill:

There was a great argument over who was to get the last place in the side for that match. There were five of us and I was outvoted. Two of us wanted my candidate, the other three wanted the alternative, the son of a leading figure at the club. Bill's influence got the voting going against what I wanted. After the game I resigned the captaincy, and I stopped playing. As captain I felt that I should be able to take the side into the field that was my side. We did not have a row about it. I felt my captaincy was compromised. I have no animosity towards him but I was put in an impossible situation – the situation of Bill being a God in Norfolk cricket.

The match against Middlesex did nothing to challenge the process of deification. Norfolk were heavily defeated by 147 runs, but, in Peter Laker's report for the *Daily Mail*, Edrich 'emerged defiant from the wreckage' with his 'pugnacious 36'. In his report for *The Times*, John Woodcock wrote that 'it is difficult for a small man to stride but Edrich still manages it. He arrived at the wicket at just after four o'clock and by a quarter-past five he had got his pulled drive into working order. That and the hook and the cut always brought him his livelihood.' It was the last important innings he played for Norfolk. Edrich bowed out the following season without any fairy-tale ending. He averaged just 11 with the bat, did not take a wicket and Norfolk finished bottom of the table.

13

CLOSE OF PLAY
1971–1986

'No game in which he took part could ever be restful. He was full of
bounding energy and vibrant courage: he needed action.'

John Arlott

The distinguished journalist Peter Hayter, son of Britain's first sports agent Reg
Hayter, recalled the warmth of Bill Edrich's visits to the family home in Stanmore
on Friday or Saturday nights: 'One thing he always used to do was to insist that
he wasn't drunk so he would drive home. Obviously this was a ludicrous notion
but we went through the pantomime every time of saying: "OK, Bill, mind how
you go." The next morning I would walk about 20 yards away from our house
and would see his car parked outside, with Bill fast asleep inside. He never did
actually attempt to drive home. He was sensible enough for that.'

But in truth Bill was not always that sensible, as his conviction in 1954 for
dangerous driving proved. He was caught out again in June 1971, when he lost
his licence in a near-farcical manner. Without comment, *The Daily Telegraph*
reported the bald facts of the case: 'Cricketer Fined: William John Edrich, 55,
the former Middlesex and England cricketer, of Knights Court, Wyverston,
Suffolk, was fined £50 and disqualified from driving for a year yesterday by
magistrates at Baldock, Hertfordshire. He pleaded guilty to driving with an
excess of alcohol in his bloodstream.' Jasper, the eldest son, gave me the family's
version of what happened:

The story is that he stopped on the way home from London to Suffolk
because he was a bit tired. He decided to have a kip by the side of the road.
The police saw him, stopped their car and asked him if he was all right.

Then the officer smelt his breath and said, 'Well, sir, you had better keep sitting there because you're drunk and if you drive on you will be a danger to other users and you will be arrested.' My dad didn't listen. He couldn't get back to sleep. So 15 minutes later he drove on, but the police were waiting for him round the corner. They picked him up and charged him. He was banned for a year.

A few months earlier, Bill, contemplating his imminent retirement as a player, had professed himself content with his rural life, alongside his family and his various business ventures. Following an interview with Bill for the *Diss Reporter* in October 1970, John Jones wrote that he: '. . . now deals in poultry and insurance and if you think that's a mixed bag for one man to tackle then you have never met this pipe-smoking, congenial man who seems to have an air of authority on every subject and a likeable manner that has served him well through the years. Hair greying in the odd place, the face a little more weather-beaten than most Middlesex fans would remember it, Bill Edrich has aged without growing old.'

The profile went on: 'The man and the house, the countryside, the two dogs and his wife now seem at home in Suffolk, a long way from the cheering crowds and the hero worship that made him every boy's idol in the post war years. "We like it here and it suits me for business purposes to be in this part of England. Now I'm here I don't think I could ever go back to London despite the many memories it holds."'

Of Justin, he told the reporter, 'I certainly won't push him into cricket but he seems to be going that way himself. If he makes the grade all well and good but if he doesn't or chooses not to, I shan't complain.'

Yet contentment was far more elusive than Edrich could admit to the journalist for the *Diss Reporter*. In reality, in his characteristic restless fashion he was wearying of his wife Valerie, his adopted daughters and the routine of rural life. He could not claim to have made a success of his brief attempt to become involved in Suffolk local government; embarrassingly, he was the only sitting Wyverstone parish councillor not to be re-elected in May 1967. At home, the first flush of love had passed, leaving him irritable, as his stepdaughter Jane remembered:

Unfortunately, I am the spitting image of my birth father and Bill didn't want reminding that we weren't his. He had a lot of masculine pride and could not really relate to girls. He didn't really engage with me and Judy. I cannot remember him helping with any schoolwork. His own father took him to task several times about me, because he adored me the way I adored him. I put his moods down to his chequered history with women. If he wasn't being idolised he was not really happy. He was very needy and drink sometimes substituted.

Judy, Jane's younger sister, had just an awkward experience of living with Bill:

The job of a stepdad is not easy. He tried and failed but I didn't let him into my life. It's a great shame, our relationship. I feel quite sad that I did not want to get close to him. I did not see the secret of his charm with women but how would I? He certainly expected a lot of my mother. He felt she should be there at his beck and call. I remember once at the dinner table, he asked my mother to pass him the salt, even though he could easily reach it. I said to him, 'My mother is not your slave.' I was sent to my room. I probably said something nasty on the way. Bill was very possessive of my mother; he expected her to be there for him. She was very intelligent and quite independent.

The most drastic change in the dynamic of Wyverstone occurred in 1971 when Bill grew close to a friend of Valerie's called Margot Kyle, who lived in the village of Cotton three miles from Wyverstone. A medical secretary who, like Valerie, was both independent-minded and professional, Margot was dissatisfied in her own marriage. When Valerie learnt of the affair, instead of being outraged, she showed remarkable forbearance, perhaps because part of her hoped that Bill might be more distracted at home and therefore his relentless, demanding presence would be mitigated. That is certainly what Jane thought: 'Deep down she was relieved because Bill was quite difficult to live with.' Jasper could see why his father was drawn to Margot but had his doubts about her intentions: 'She was tall, had shortish hair, high cheekbones and was very attractive but a bit superior. She came from an affluent background and was always trying to impress.' In her memoir, Valerie wrote that she had been 'content to go along with the affair provided they were totally discreet so that I was not embarrassed'. But as Valerie put it, discretion was 'not one of Bill's strong points' with the result that Margot's husband found out about the affair and so demanded a divorce, which unfairly put Valerie in a difficult position. 'Since Bill had been partially responsible for this predicament, he decided that the honourable thing would be to marry her, and asked me for a divorce.' Knowing Margot well from their long friendship, Valerie was certain that she would not be interested in marrying Bill, so she tried, for the sake of Justin, to persuade Bill to stay and see Margot. 'I should have known better – he was adamant that if he was divorced she would marry him, so eventually I had to agree. He bought a very nice flat for her in Belsize Park in London where, despite several abortive attempts to persuade me to take him back because he was unhappy, he lived until he fell for someone else.' For her part, Valerie had to leave Knight's Court and move to the Suffolk village of Eye.

Judy, understandably, felt bitter towards Bill. 'He left my mother, I was not going to stay in touch.' Jane had a particular grievance against him, in that, when he was temporarily banned from driving, he had instructed her to take him in his beloved Rover 2000 to see Margot, a profoundly insensitive request at which she indulged in her own minor act of revenge. 'When I got into the car, I would throw away the cushions and push the seat right back so if he got into the car the next day with a client, he would have to move the cushions and adjust the seat and he hated that. So he bought me a Mini.' Two years later, when Jane was getting married herself, she asked her own father to give her away. 'I wanted my own father because I did not like what Bill was doing to my mother. Bill was really angry about that and went away for the weekend. By that point I had moved out, and was living in Ipswich as I trained to be a nurse. There were no cosy chats. He did not keep in touch with mother much.' Justin said that he 'did not harbour resentment' at his father and 'did not blame him' for 'fundamentally he was a good man'. But he admitted that, as he went back to boarding school, 'it was incredibly hard for me at that age'. He also reflected that Bill and Valerie were very different personalities: 'She was stiff upper lip, and stoical, very different to his more passionate personality.'

The breakdown of his marriage to Valerie also caused pain to other members of the family. When Bill visited his parents to break the news, he took along his great friend Jack Borrett, Paul's father, for moral support. According to Paul:

He rang up my father and said, 'Jack, come and have a drink with me, I've got to tell my parents that I'm getting a divorce again.' So he went with Bill and when they arrived Jack said, 'I won't come in. We can have that drink afterwards.' His parents were a lovely couple. When Bill came out, Jack asked him:

'Well, how did that go?'

'My mother cried, she was sobbing. She didn't take it very well at all.'

'What about your father?'

'He just asked me, "Who do you think is going to win the National this year?"'

The feelings in the family were captured by Bill's sister Ena in her memoir, where she wrote: 'My mother had taken it very hard and father had shrugged it off but we all felt this new relationship to be foolish in the extreme. It seemed that Bill would never grow up. "That bloody Bill," Geoff said. Eric, when he heard, said, "Well, bugger me!" A member of the family derided Bill to Brian, but, ever loyal, Brian gave him short shrift. When Bill was criticised to my mother, she replied, "Well, he's my son and he hasn't killed anyone yet." Bill seemed incapable of staying in the mundane. Everything needed to be new and exciting.'

Four failed marriages had taken their toll on Bill's natural ebullience and his bank balance, so there was no question, even as approached the age of 60, of his giving up his work in the insurance industry for Allied Hambro. Indeed, as with International Life Insurance, his fame made him a useful point of public contact for advertising campaigns, like that in 1982 for the Allied Hambro Financial Management Programme, which stated, 'for more information, apply to Bill Edrich, Brummel House, Savile Row, London'. Opinions vary about the importance and quality of his work for the company. Colin Webb, his former manager at the Oxford Circus branch in London, told Edrich's previous biographer Alan Hill that 'Bill was a very good door opener, technically not brilliant but admirable in spotting an opportunity. He could grasp the essentials very quickly before calling in the expert.' Rodney Edrich was more doubtful, 'He used to say to me, when we were in London, "I must be back in the office at 4.30pm to sign the letters." This was when he was an insurance supremo.'

He was still deeply involved in cricket. Even Bill's advancing years could not halt his participation in charity games, as Sir Tim Rice remembered: 'I once played with him in a match at Blenheim Palace when he must have been in his sixties. But he was still a determined player who knew how to look after himself. I think I managed to bat about eight overs. At one point I hit the ball into the deep, almost to the boundary, and as we trotted past each other in the middle, he said to me, "One's enough, old boy." Yet a few balls later, when he stroked one into the outfield, he seemed to have recovered his stamina, calling me through for three.'

The historian and writer David Frith also played a match for the Lord's Taverners under his captaincy when Edrich was 60: 'He scored 61, one more than his age. It was a rugged innings. Not naturally graceful, he was often very effective. There was an affectation about his batsmanship, as with his speech, and it is noticeable how close he comes to toppling over in demonstrating the forward defensive in a coaching film.'

On his retirement from playing first-class cricket, he sat for a spell on the Middlesex Committee, 'He was a good attender and he knew the players, knew the game. He followed cricket closely and was a good judge of a cricketer,' said Mike Murray, though Charles Robins did not find him 'eloquent'. Occasionally, he caused embarrassment in the corridors and car parks of Lord's, as when he turned up drunk at one meeting, knocked over a chair, and then collapsed on the floor. Another time he had to be helped from his car because he could barely stand upright. His perceptive analysis of players made him a popular adjudicator for the Man of the Match awards in one-day cricket, and such was the respect for his views that there were no accusations of bias when he had to choose his own cousin John Edrich, the great Surrey batsman, as the winner. But Robin Huggins from Norfolk remembered a moment when Bill almost incapacitated himself from performing his duties:

> Bill was doing a Man of the Match presentation in Norwich for the Minor Counties knock-out competition. The sponsor was the English Estates. There was obviously plenty of wine and beer at the lunch. Bill was basically drunk when he did the presentation, and was slurring his speech. He then went into the bar in the clubhouse and right at the end there was a brick wall that he was leaning against. I was talking to him and he gradually slid down the wall and ended up sitting on the floor. It was extraordinary. He basically subsided to the floor.

Embarrassment of a different kind was felt at Lord's in 1983 when Compton and Edrich, in league with the right-wing Tory MP John Carlisle, launched a campaign to force the MCC to restore sporting links with South Africa. The trio organised a petition that garnered sufficient support to require the MCC both to hold a special emergency meeting and to conduct a full ballot of the membership to decide whether the club should organise its own tour, in defiance of the international sporting ban. Just one year earlier Geoff Boycott and Graham Gooch had led a rebel tour of South Africa, and both had received substantial bans from playing for England. But the belief held by Compton and Edrich that there was widespread outrage over decisions like that was a delusion. In truth, despite nostalgic affection for the two old warriors of 1947, the overwhelming feeling within the English cricket world was one of dismay at their stance, not only because of widespread repugnance at the apartheid regime and a recognition that sanctions were beginning to work, but also because any decision by the MCC to defy the boycott would turn England into a sporting pariah. Even Margaret Thatcher waded in heavily against them, pointing out that their demand would breach the 1977 Gleneagles Agreement that introduced the boycott, thereby potentially tearing apart the Commonwealth. The Lord's establishment won the votes in the ballot and the special meeting easily. The pair were left isolated. Even Justin disagreed strongly with his father on this point. 'He was pretty right-wing and felt South Africa should be allowed to play Test cricket. I argued that because South Africa was a sports-loving country, the ban was helping to end apartheid. He was having none of that. We would go at it pretty strongly, usually fuelled by alcohol.'

A more public instance of intoxication occurred during the celebrations for the centenary of Test cricket in March 1977, when every Englishman who had played in an Ashes Test was invited to Australia for a historic anniversary game at the Melbourne Cricket Ground. Inevitably, Edrich had over-indulged before he even reached the plane and was soon dragged into a sensational mid-air incident involving Britain's most famous cricket writer. The most authoritative version of what happened came from Peter Watson, then the Sports Editor of the *London Evening News*, who witnessed the entire scene:

> Bill seemed to be flying higher than the plane before we took off from Heathrow. Champers flowed throughout the flight and Bill, always the life and soul of any party, became rowdier and rowdier. He was walking up and down the aisle trying to get us all to join in a sing-song. John Arlott was dozing in his seat just across the aisle from me. He had fallen asleep with headphones on and was tuned into a classical music tape. Bill stopped alongside him and turned up the volume to full pitch. Arlott jumped out of his seat and lashed out – perhaps deliberately or purely instinctively – and thumped Bill right in the eye. It was all over in seconds and not a fist fight as reported in some quarters. What I found very touching was the way Denis Compton took command of the situation. He guided the worse-for-wear Bill to the toilet, cleaned him up, brought him back to his seat and looked after him like a brother.

In Bill's own account quoted in Norman Giller's biography of Denis Compton, he admitted he had been in a party mood even before take-off, and could not remember much about the incident. 'What I do know is that I had ten of the greatest days of my life, meeting old friends from my cricketing and RAF days. When we landed at Melbourne everybody wanted to know about my shiner but I just laughed it off.'

Cricket was also at the heart of the trips he took to Corfu, courtesy of Ben Brocklehurst, the former Somerset captain, and his wife Belinda. They were the proprietors of *The Cricketer* magazine, which organised holidays to the Greek islands, and Belinda has only happy memories of his times there:

> Bill was very popular, a fantastic character. He loved the Greeks and they loved him. He was tremendous company, such a warm-hearted, decent person. I remember one lovely occasion we were having lunch in a Greek restaurant, having a jolly time with huge bottles of wine on the table, and a young man came over wanting to talk to him about cricket.
>
> 'Tell me, were you ever intoxicated when you were in the field?'
>
> 'My dear chap, I never wasn't.'
>
> He certainly drank too much and sometimes got paralytic, but he was never unpleasant with it and never got sick. He was not a great reader but once we had a big Scrabble competition and Bill won. He was much more 'wordy' than people realised. In the 1970s he was with Margot. She was terrific and he adored her. I never saw him flirting with other women and when he had Margot there they were like a married couple.

Belinda's son David said of Bill's visits to Corfu, 'He came out and played some cricket with *The Cricketer* XI. I saw the old magic. He still had a very good eye, saw it early.' Henry Blofeld was another visitor to Corfu and enjoyed a century partnership with Edrich in one game at a ground that had Bill's approval, since the tables at one side were laid out with ouzo and wine. 'I don't think in Corfu he ever drew a sober breath in the evening,' said Blofeld. One holidaymaker, Edward Handley, who went on a *Cricketer* trip with his wife, remembered how:

> . . . he used to come down to breakfast and have his first ouzo of the day. He said to me at one point, 'Do you know that when I'm batting after I have consumed a lot of alcohol, I often see three balls coming towards me. I generally go for the middle one and it seems to work.' One evening Bill was drinking with my wife Lynn and me. Suddenly he said, 'Do you know that I have sired a child in every continent of the world?'

Quick as a flash, Lynn replied, 'No you haven't, Bill, not in Antarctica.'

'You may be right there.'

John Arlott said of Edrich, 'he had any amount of courage and could be furiously argumentative. He was convivial but could be intemperate.' The former Glamorgan and England captain Tony Lewis, who became one of the game's best-known writers and broadcasters, recalled in his *Sunday Telegraph* column in June 1996 witnessing an example of Bill's endearing eccentricity:

He walked into the Tavern pub alongside Lord's and ordered six large gin and tonics and said, 'Help yourself'. He then walked over to the juke-box, inserted a coin, and returned to take Mrs Lewis's hand to his lips before whisking her away in true *Come Dancing* style, knocking over the occasional chair as he sung loudly and pleadingly into her eyes. 'You are the sunshine of my life.'[2] It was 11.30 in the morning. There were no cameras.

But when he was editor of *The Cricketer* and had a frosty relationship with Brocklehurst, David Frith saw another, more 'snarly' side to Bill. In Frith's account, Edrich came up to him at a cocktail reception and asked: 'What did you do in the war?' 'I was an infant but my father was a fireman.' He sniffed. He wasn't finished. 'Anyway,' he said with eyes half closed, 'you're a bloody rotten editor.'

Robin Marlar said to me that Edrich could 'get out of anything', even a lively night with the Lord's Taverners when Marlar gave him a lift home far later than Bill's partner was expecting. 'She was coming down the pathway with a hatchet, a real one, but he charmed his way out of that.' There was, however, no way of smoothing over the fall-out from the latest twist in his domestic life, when in early 1983, after frequently asking Margot to marry him during their eight years living together, he suddenly told her that he was leaving. 'Of all the dirty, rotten tricks,' she said of his unexpected departure in an interview with *The People*. 'We had planned to marry. I lost count of the number of times he proposed. But given his past record, I wanted to be absolutely sure it would work. Bill has had a terrific number of lady friends over the years. He is very romantic. But he's also a little

---

[2] Extracted from Tony Lewis' 'Final Word' column in the *Sunday Telegraph*.

boy who needs an enormous amount of attention.' Margot admitted their relationship had become strained when Bill acquired a taste for expensive London nightspots. 'Bill would sometimes not come back until five in the morning. We'd been together so long most people looked on me as Mrs Edrich.' Rodney Edrich, though generally supportive of Bill, thought his treatment of Margot was 'scandalous. It showed she was wise not to marry him. She was a wonderful woman.' According to Rodney, she came home one day to find him packing: 'Hello dear. Are we going on a trip somewhere?' 'You're not, I am.'

The new woman in Edrich's life was Mary Somerville, a divorcee who ran a hairdressing salon in the high street of Chesham in Buckinghamshire. They were married on 4 September, 1983. Margot was still full of anger and sorrow at what Bill had done, when she spoke to a reporter of the *News of the World* on the wedding day: 'I still miss him terribly. I feel so empty without him. I never realised I could feel so lonely but I am not one to shout or scream or create a fuss. The night he left his last words were, "I hope we can still be friends." I thought that was a bit much as he had just sort of kicked me in the teeth. The most hurtful thing of all was that one day he came back to collect the rest of his things and he did not even have the decency to tell me that he was getting married. I read about it in the paper the next day.'

It was at the wedding between Mary and Bill that John Warr, the former Middlesex captain, uttered the most famous line of all about Edrich's matrimonial record. When asked if he would like to sit with the bride or the groom's side, Warr said, 'Put me wherever you like, old chap. I have a season ticket to these events.' In the same vein, Warr was at a meeting of the Middlesex Committee when there was a discussion about wedding presents for first-team players. There was what the minutes described as 'prolonged laughter' when Warr said, 'Well, thinking of Bill Edrich, for heaven's sake let's not make it retrospective.'

For all such humour, there was a bleak sense of foreboding about his marriage to Mary, which he called his 'Fifth and Final Test'. Apart from the disappointment for Edrich, keenly aware of social status, of having to live in a small flat above his wife's hairdressing business, a far more serious problem was that Mary, who was 26 years younger than Bill, had a drink problem of her own and she dragged Bill deeper into the grim valley of addiction. There were indications that her fondness for the bottle may have precluded other forms of intimacy, reflected in the fact that in the bedroom of their flat in Chesham their two single beds were far apart. Trapped in their little flat, the emotional gulf between them became ever wider. Justin noted that 'theirs was not an ideal relationship. She was an alcoholic and he was a borderline alcoholic. At the end, he and Mary would knock back a bottle of vodka every night between them.' Other family members witnessed the destructive influence of their mutual dependency. Jane Edrich, the widow of Bill's brother Brian, said to me, 'It was a bit of a rocky marriage. I don't know if he and Mary were happy. I think their marriage was quite often down because they both drank a fair bit and inevitably they got into arguments.' Rodney Edrich felt that Mary bore a heavy degree of responsibility for this friction: 'I formed the impression that it was a very unhappy liaison. The family indicated to me that it was she who encouraged Bill to drink again because she was an alcoholic. I think before then he had moderated his drinking.'

Jasper, by now married and living in South Africa, found Mary difficult to handle when she came out with Bill to see him. One night Jasper and his wife threw a big party at their house, but Jasper's wife became deeply upset at Mary's behaviour. 'Mary was drunk and getting very friendly with me, lots of banter. My wife did not like it all. In fact, she hated Mary.' Similarly, when Bill brought Mary with him on a *Cricketer* trip to Corfu, Belinda Brocklehurst said, 'it didn't really work so well. People did not warm to her. It was very, very sad.' That sadness often came through the long, rambling phone calls that Bill made to his relatives, late at night, desperate to hear a reassuring voice in his maudlin loneliness. Penny, Jessy's daughter, recalled: 'I think maybe he was a rather sad person. He would ring us all up for a chat, even me. I don't think he liked to be on his own.' At times there was almost a valedictory tone about his conversations, as when he told Ena, now in Australia, that 'I do love you', and he thanked her husband for 'looking after my sister so well'. The same sense of an era coming to a close in the family was experienced by Justin, who took his father out to lunch in April 1986, during which they had 'a massive argument. I dropped him home afterwards. He got out, walked about ten yards, then came back to the car, made me wind down the window and said, "I do enjoy our little arguments." I did feel he was challenging me, testing me.'

That spring two significant social events were held in London that emphasised the public's continuing, devoted embrace of Bill Edrich. The first was a gala black-tie dinner at the Berkeley Hotel, in honour of his 70th birthday, to raise funds for the Lord's Taverners, with tickets costing £100 per head. In the *Daily Mail*, Ian Wooldridge, an eloquent fan of Edrich, wrote that the event would be an 'occasion of unashamed nostalgia and thanksgiving for the unlikely arrival at the milestone of three score years and ten of a gentleman named W.J. Edrich'. Wooldridge concluded on a bright note that it was 'too early in the life of Bill Edrich to deal in epitaphs'.

The second event was a special patriotic lunch at the Grosvenor House Hotel on 23 April to mark St George's Day. As an English traditionalist, Edrich was in his element. Both tears and champagne flowed as the band of the Blues and Royals played 'Land of Hope and Glory', and he was profoundly touched when Air Vice-Marshal Sir Ivor Broom, the chief speaker who had flown with him in Bomber Command, mentioned in his post-prandial speech Edrich's courage, which had won him the DFC. Peter Parfitt was also one of the guests and he remembered Bill being 'on excellent form that day'. Parfitt's Middlesex and England colleague John Murray was also struck by the animation of Edrich. 'Everything was so England. Bill could not contain himself. Before long, he was among the bandsmen, still holding a glass of champagne and marching with them on the ballroom floor.' After this happy, stirring lunch, he was driven back to Chesham in a chauffeur-driven Rolls Royce, provided by one of the wealthy sponsors of the lunch. Well-oiled but still functioning, he arrived home at about seven o'clock. After he and Mary had some tea, they settled down, as was their custom, with a few drinks. Then at midnight, Bill said he was going to bed. According to Mary's account, he left the lounge and then she heard him climbing the stairs. But after he had reached the top, there was a loud bump. She rushed out of the lounge to find her husband unconscious at the bottom of the stairs. An ambulance was called, but Edrich had died before he could be taken to hospital.

Bill Edrich once told his friend David Brocklehurst that 'he wanted to die on the job, making love to a gorgeous woman'. Reaching his end after a magnificent, patriotic event, where he had been surrounded by admiring ex-RAF and England colleagues, was perhaps the next best way to go. But there has been speculation that perhaps there was a darker side to this accident, which made it both more sinister and more tragic. Such concerns were partly triggered by the inconsistent coverage of how Edrich's death had unfolded. The first reports suggested that he had died in his sleep, alongside a quotation from Mary that he 'had just conked out'. The *Buckinghamshire Advertiser* added fuel to the flames of doubt by running a story that was headlined 'Mystery over death of Cricketing Legend'. Having revealed that there would be a Coroner's Inquest, this report then said that 'a spokesman for the Thames Valley Police confirmed that Mr Edrich had not died of natural causes but refused to comment any further on his injuries'. The paper also said that his 'fifth wife and other friends refuse to speak about his death until the inquest is heard'.

Any such suspicions remained firmly in the background as the local coroner, John Roberts, conducted the inquest. His report, issued on 24 May, 1986, concluded unequivocally that Edrich's death was an accident caused by a fractured skull as a result of a fall down the stairs. Crucial evidence had been provided by the pathologist Winifred Gray, who had stated that, although Edrich was 'very fit' for a man of 70, his blood alcohol count was 358 milligrams, the equivalent of being more than four times over the drink-driving limit. Furthermore, his balance may have been affected by the two artificial hips for which he had undergone major surgery. Roberts's verdict was that alcohol had 'caused some impairment to Mr Edrich's co-ordination', leading to the accident. During her appearance at the inquest, Mary had broken down and once the hearing was over, she revealed the extent of her grief. 'I've never felt so lonely. I am so unhappy. It is such a tragedy that he died because he had been enjoying himself so much.' Deeply distressed by what had happened, she joined Alcoholics Anonymous, gave up drinking, and placed a new focus on her business. In the local elections of 1987 she stood unsuccessfully in Chesham for the Conservative Party.

But then a further tragedy struck. In April 1988, two years after Bill's death, Mary was driving on the A33 near Basingstoke on the way to see her brother for Easter. In the passenger seat was Sara, her daughter from her previous marriage, who was now a pupil at Lowndes School in Chesham. Reportedly, Sara felt that Bill was a terrible influence on her mother, as Jane remembered. 'She didn't like the way her mother was around him. She resented him and though I tried to talk to her, step daughter to step daughter, she wasn't having any of it.' The teenager was about to have far more to endure, as her mother's Mini was in a head-on collision with another car. Mary was killed instantly, but Sara, shocked and bruised, escaped from the wreckage. After the news of her mother's death, John Hunt, the President of the Chesham Chamber of Commerce said, 'We will always have fond memories of Mary, who was a personality of Chesham and very forthright.'

In April 1986 the tributes to her late husband had been on a much bigger scale. In the *Guardian*, John Arlott wrote that 'no game in which he took part could ever be restful. He was full of bounding energy and vibrant courage: he needed action.' In the *Daily Telegraph,* Jim Swanton said that 'Bill Edrich in all that he did on the field and in war was the personification of determination and courage, the very epitome of guts.' The *Daily Mail* described him as 'a five feet, six inches giant, a juggernaut in action in work and play', while *The Sun* called him 'the fighting cavalier'. Sadness was mixed with admiration in the accolades from a host of his cricketing contemporaries. Tom Graveney said that he was 'the most courageous cricketer I ever played with or against', and Trevor Bailey recalled that he played cricket 'with an unflinching nerve'. By a mournful coincidence, another England legend of the post-war era, Jim Laker, died just the day before, on 23 April 1986. In the *Sunday Times*, Robin Marlar wrote of 'Unplayable Jim and Unstoppable Bill, two mighty trees that fell in cricket's memory lane.' What Denis Compton remembered most about his Middlesex twin was Edrich's tremendous patriotism: 'His big thing, you see, was playing for England. He never got over that. "Playing for England, Denis," he used to say. "Just think of all the other buggers who'll never play for England."'

His funeral was held at St Mary's Church in Chesham, where the rector, the Reverend Robin Smith, praised his 'courage, skill and generosity', but added that he was 'a person who longed to be loved'. After his cremation, Mary was given permission by Lord's to put his ashes on the square, a very rare honour that showed the esteem in which Edrich was held. But there was also a slight element of farce at the occasion, which was conducted during the tea interval of a game between Middlesex and Essex. One observer present at the scene recalled that Mary 'had taken a lot of Dutch courage during the day', so when she went out with the MCC Secretary Jack Bailey to perform the rites, 'she was in a bit of a state'. As a result, instead of being scattered, the ashes were 'tipped in a pile in the position of gully'. Other witnesses, however, deny that she was intoxicated and argue that any agitation she showed was due to grief.

Later that summer a special memorial cricket match was held at Amersham between a Denis Compton XI and a Justin Edrich XI. The star-studded list of players and guests was a further reflection of Bill's standing in the game. As well as Compton, Len Hutton was there, along with the actors Michael Denison and Dulcie Gray. Among the players were Test players Fred Titmus, Clive Radley, Tom Graveney, Eddie Barlow, Richard Hutton and Don Wilson, while an often-hilarious commentary was provided by Brian Johnston and the comedian Barry Cryer.

An even more prestigious event took place in October when a memorial service was held at St Clement Danes, the RAF Church in the Strand. The *Bucks Examiner* provided a vivid description of the 'beautiful' proceedings, which were a 'mixture of the down-to-earth and the sacred, with a helpful touch of nostalgia and sentiment'. Bill's favourite singer Anne Shelton performed his favourite song, 'A Nightingale Sang in Berkeley Square', at the conclusion of which there was an evocative silence, broken only by the echo of her high heels on the stone floor, a sound and image that somehow captured part of the romantic essence of Edrich. There were readings from works by Neville Cardus, Raymond Robertson-Glasgow and John Arlott, in addition to tributes from Trevor Bailey, who said that 'Bill was always ready to provide his own cabaret act at a party', and Denis Compton, who described the incident on the 1946–47 Ashes tour when he told Wally Hammond that Bill had gone out for a run to cover-up the reality that he had not yet returned from an all-night bender. 'A great cricketer, a fearless fighter and one who loved life,' said Compton. As befitted a hero of Bomber Command, the music had a deeply patriotic flavour, featuring 'Land of Hope and Glory', 'Jerusalem' and 'I Vow to Thee My Country'. The *Bucks Examiner* concluded that 'after the blessing, the organist pulled out all the stops for the theme from the Dambusters by Eric Coates. As everyone filed out into the roar of London's traffic, someone said quietly, "Bill would have loved it."'

Jessy was one of the three wives present. Her daughter Penny recalled her mother turning to her at the end of this 'amazing, jolly event' and telling her, 'Bill would have sat up and said, "We're having a lovely time, aren't we?"'

BILL EDRICH'S STATISTICS

By Paul Dyson

TEST CRICKET

Key

M: Matches; **I**: Innings; **NO** or *: Not Out; **HS**: Highest Score
W: Wickets; **BB**: Best Bowling
Ct: Caught; **St**: Stumped

Era by era

	Batting							Bowling			
	M	I	NO	Runs	HS	Avg.	100/50	Runs	W	Avg.	BB
1938–39	9	12	0	307	219	25.58	1/0	293	6	48.83	2-27
1946–49	20	33	1	1,699	191	53.09	5/9	1,291	35	36.88	4-68
1950–55	10	18	1	434	88	25.52	0/4	109	0	–	–
Totals	39	63	2	2,440	219	40.00	6/13	1,693	41	41.29	4-68

Edrich's highest innings of 219 was made in Durban against South Africa in 1938–39. It remains the highest score made for England in the fourth innings of a Test match and has been beaten only three times for other teams, the highest being 223.

Against each opponent

	Batting							Bowling			
	M	I	NO	Runs	HS	Avg.	100/50	Runs	W	Avg.	BB
Australia	21	39	1	1,184	119	31.15	2/8	888	16	55.50	3-50
India	1	0	–	–	–	–	–	68	4	17.00	4-68
New Zealand	5	7	0	366	100	52.28	1/2	132	3	44.00	2-18
Pakistan	1	1	0	4	4	4.00	0/0	–	–	–	–
South Africa	9	12	1	792	219	72.00	3/2	524	18	29.11	4-77
West Indies	2	4	0	94	71	23.50	0/1	81	0	–	–
Totals	39	63	2	2,440	219	40.00	6/13	1,693	41	41.29	4-68

On each ground in England

	Batting							Bowling			
	M	I	NO	Runs	HS	Avg.	100/50	Runs	W	Avg.	BB
Lord's	6	10	0	266	189	26.60	1/0	222	6	37.00	3-31
Headingley	5	9	0	428	111	47.55	1/3	144	6	24.00	3-46
The Oval	5	6	1	219	100	43.80	1/1	177	6	29.50	4-68
Old Trafford	5	8	1	460	191	65.71	1/3	255	9	28.33	4-77
Trent Bridge	3	5	0	143	57	28.60	0/2	195	2	97.50	1-39
Totals	24	38	2	1,516	191	42.11	4/9	993	29	34.24	4-68

In each country abroad

	Batting							Bowling			
	M	I	NO	Runs	HS	Avg.	100/50	Runs	W	Avg.	BB
Australia	9	18	0	642	119	35.66	1/4	511	9	56.77	3-50
New Zealand	1	1	0	42	42	42.00	0/0	35	1	35.00	1-35
South Africa	5	6	0	240	219	40.00	1/0	154	2	77.00	1-9
Totals	15	25	0	924	219	36.96	2/4	700	12	58.33	3-50

FIRST-CLASS CRICKET

Batting and fielding
For each team

	M	I	NO	Runs	HS	Avg.	100s	50s	Ct	St
Middlesex	389	658	65	25,738	267*	43.40	62	133	381	1
MCC	74	119	14	4,001	150	38.10	11	20	55	–
England (Tests)	39	63	2	2,440	219	40.00	6	13	39	–
Other Teams	69	124	11	4,786	164*	42.35	7	33	52	–
Totals	571	964	92	36,965	267*	42.39	86	199	527	1

Edrich played in 20 English seasons from 1934 to 1958; he passed the 1,000-run mark in 15 and the 2,000-run mark in nine of these. His best season came in 1947 when he passed the 3,000-run mark, his figures for that year being:

M	I	NO	Runs	HS	Avg.	100s	50s	Ct	St
30	52	8	3,539	267*	80.43	12	15	35	–

There has been a total of 28 instances of batsmen scoring at least 3,000 runs in a season. Edrich's total of 3,539 is the second highest of these, his tally only being beaten by his Middlesex teammate Denis Compton who scored 3,816 (90.85 avg.) in the same season. Edrich's average of 80.4, has only been beaten by two other batsmen among the 28 – Herbert Sutcliffe (3,006; 96.96 avg. in 1931) and K.S. Ranjitsinhji (3,065; 87.57 avg. in 1900). Edrich scored 2,650 runs for Middlesex in that 1947 season, and this total places him in second position for the county, Patsy Hendren having scored just 19 more in 1923.

Edrich played in more matches at Lord's than on any other ground and his batting record there is:

M	I	NO	Runs	HS	Avg.	100s	50s	Ct	St
264	456	42	16,910	245	40.84	37	94	263	–

However, he holds a unique record among Middlesex players in that he is the only batsman to score at least 1,000 runs against each of the other first-class counties. His record includes over 2,000 runs against each of Northamptonshire, Surrey and Yorkshire. He also scored over 1,000 runs against the Players.

Record partnerships

Also in 1947, Edrich and Compton shared in a stand of 370 for the third wicket for England against South Africa at Lord's, and this remains the England record for that wicket. It was the first instance of two batsmen from the same county sharing a Test-century partnership on their home ground. This occurrence remained a unique record until Yorkshire's Joe Root and Jonny Bairstow shared a century stand for England at Headingley against New Zealand in 2013.

Edrich and Compton also hold the record for the highest stand for any wicket for Middlesex. They put together an undefeated 424 against Somerset at Lord's in 1948.

Bowling
Full career record

Balls	Runs	Wickets	Average	BB	5WI	10WM
32,914	15,956	479	33.31	7-48	11	3

Edrich passed 50 wickets in a season on three occasions, his best being 73 in 1946 when he took his best figures of seven for 48 for Middlesex at Worcester.

His record for Middlesex is:

Balls	Runs	Wickets	Average	BB	5WI	10WM
21,694	9,975	328	30.41	7-48	10	3

MINOR COUNTIES CHAMPIONSHIP

Edrich played for Norfolk in this competition for 18 seasons in two spells – from 1932 to 1936 and from 1959 to 1971. His full career figures are:

Batting							Bowling				
M	I	NO	Runs	HS	Avg.	100/50	Runs	W	Avg.	BB	5wi/10wm
171	276	47	8,034	152	35.08	9/50	7,956	414	19.21	7-45	21/4

Edrich passed 500 runs in each of six seasons, his best being 852 in 1960. His highest innings of 152 came against Hertfordshire at Broxbourne in 1935. His best bowling figures of seven for 45 came against Suffolk at Lakenham in 1962. As Lakenham was Norfolk's home ground, that was where he played most of his matches, scoring 4,384 runs and taking 230 wickets in 89 games.

In the family

Of the 12 members of the Edrich family who appear on cricketarchive.com, five played first-class cricket. Bill played against three of them – Eric and Geoff (both Lancashire) and Brian (Kent), who were all brothers. His career and that of fellow Test player John (Surrey), who was a cousin, overlapped by three seasons, but the pair never met on the field in the higher form of the game.

ACKNOWLEDGEMENTS

As a cricket fan, I had always been aware of the name Bill Edrich, but it was not until I started researching this book that I began to recognise what an extraordinary and colourful life he led. I have in the past written a cricket biography of Jack Hobbs, one of the true gentlemen of British sport. A teetotaller, practising Christian and devoted husband, he could not have been more different to Bill.

But the sharp contours of Edrich's personality are precisely what make his story so fascinating, and I am indebted to a huge range of people for helping me to build this narrative.

First, I would like to thank the excellent team at Bloomsbury, headed by Matthew Lowing and Caroline Guillet, whose wisdom, expertise and encouragement have turned this project into a reality. Indeed, it was Matthew who urged me to write about Edrich in the first place. I am also grateful to Richard Mason for his great editing job, Steven Lynch for his proofreading and to Xanthe Rendall and all the other Bloomsbury production, marketing and publicity staff for their efforts.

Many other people helped me with my research. I particularly appreciate the time generously given by Gail Armstrong to put me in touch with a large number of Norfolk cricketers who played with Bill. I was delighted that so many were happy to give me their memories, including Barry Battelley, T.G. Bland, Paul Borrett, David Pilch, Derek Godfrey, Robin Huggins, Richard Jefferson, Michael Oxbury, Peter Parfitt, Clive Radley, Graham Saville and Ted Wright – and Tony Warrington who provided a perspective from Suffolk. In addition, several friends like Sir Tim Rice and David and Belinda Brocklehurst gave me some thought-provoking material.

Recollections of Bill's first-class career came from Bill Higginson, Michael Murray, Charlie Robins, Eric Russell and Micky Stewart, while the late Robin Marlar gave me an interview shortly before he died. Other figures in the cricket world gave valuable insights, including Enid Bakewell, Henry Blofeld, Sir Geoffrey Boycott and Richard Hutton.

Equally helpful were a number of journalists and writers, among them Matthew Engel, David Frith, Norman Giller, Peter Hayter, Mark Peel, Christopher Sandford, Josephine Taylor, Giles Wilcock and Richard Whitehead. I also want to thank Richard and other distinguished figures, including Sir Geoffrey Boycott, Dickie Bird and Henry Blofeld, for their generous words about the manuscript.

Staff at archives, cricket clubs and libraries have been invariably courteous and co-operative with my requests for information, but several went far beyond the call of duty, most notably Alan Rees at the MCC Library and Hannah Fleming at Lord's. Indeed, with his courtesy, efficiency and profound knowledge of the MCC collection, Alan Rees could not have been more helpful, traits he also showed in granting me permission to quote from the papers I consulted.

I must also express my gratitude to Alexander Ward, Giles Baring's grandson, as well as Peter Ibbett, who helps to keep the memories of Bracondale School alive.

As usual, my trusted researcher Dr Kevin Jones performed wonders in the National Archives at Kew and the Imperial War Museum, uncovering great detail from Bill's war record, while vital background work was done in the Norfolk archives by Dr Gill Blanchard. During my research, other valuable advice, assistance and material came from Sue de Friend, Peter Emms, Michael Jeanes, Ian Jenkins, Andrew Radd, David Rimmer, Shaun Schofield, Jon Surtees and Derek Tomlin. Thanks also to my statistician friend Paul Dyson for his excellent statistical appendix.

But in deepening my understanding of Bill, my greatest debt is owed to the extended Edrich family who could not have been more considerate and frank in response to this project. Bill's two sons, Jasper and Justin, were outstandingly kind, but all those who spoke to me deserve my warmest thanks: Jo Bailey, Jean Beecroft, Jane Edrich, Judy Edrich, Keith Edrich, Jane Palley, Penny Cossins and Rodney Edrich. I am also grateful for permission from Justin to quote from his mother Valerie's private memoir and from Josephine Taylor, Ena's daughter, to quote from her mother's book *Girls Don't Play Cricket*.

As always, I am extremely lucky to have in Bill Hamilton one of the best, most reliable and shrewdest literary agents in the trade.

Being a writer gives me a powerful sense of purpose as I learn to live with Parkinson's, but none of this work would be possible without the support of my darling wife Elizabeth. Her wisdom and beauty remain a constant source of inspiration, just as her humour and kindness make the world bearable.

BIBLIOGRAPHY

Allen, D.R., *Arlott: The Authorised Biography* (Harper Collins, 1994)

Ames, L.E.G., *Close of Play* (Stanley Paul, 1953)

Arlott, J., *Test Match Diary 1953* (James Barrie, 1953)

Arlott, J., *Vintage Summer: 1947* (Eyre & Spottiswoode, 1967)

Bailey, T., *The Greatest of My Time* (Sportsman's Book Club, 1970)

Barker, R., *The Cricketing Family Edrich* (Pelham, 1976)

Barker, R., *Men of the Bombers: Crews Who Fought and Won the Campaign* (Pen & Sword Aviation, 2005)

Barnes, S., *The Ashes Ablaze: The MCC Australian Tour 1954–55* (William Kimber, 1955)

Bassano, B., *MCC in South Africa 1938–39* (J.W. McKenzie, 1997)

Bedser, A., *Twin Ambitions: An Autobiography* (Stanley Paul, 1986)

Bowes, W.E., *Express Deliveries* (Stanley Paul, 1949)

Bowman, M., *Daylight Bombing Operations 1939–1942* (Pen and Sword, 2020)

Brown, F., *Cricket Musketeer* (Nicholas Kaye, 1954)

Carew, D., *To the Wicket* (Chapman & Hall, 1950)

Cary, C., *Cricket Controversy: Test Matches in Australia 1946–1947* (Werner Laurie, 1948)

Chalke, S., *A Long Half Hour: Six Cricketers Remembered* (Fairfield Books, 2010)

Chalke, S., *At the Heart of English Cricket: The Life and Memories of Geoffrey Howard* (Fairfield Books, 2001)

Chalke, S., *Guess My Story: The Life and Opinions of Keith Andrew, Cricketer* (Fairfield Books, 2003)

Chalke, S., *Micky Stewart and the Changing Face of Cricket* (Fairfield Books, 2012)

Chalke, S., *The Way it Was: Glimpses of English Cricket's Past* (Fairfield Books, 2011)

Chester, F., *How's That!* (Hutchinson, 1956)

Compton, D., *In Sun and Shadow* (Stanley Paul, 1952)

Compton, D., *End of an Innings* (Pavilion Books, 1958)

Compton, D. and Edrich, W.J., *Cricket and All That* (Pelham Books, 1978)

Edrich, W.J., *Cricket Heritage* (Stanley Paul, 1948)

Edrich, W.J., *Cricketing Days* (Stanley Paul, 1949)

Edrich, W.J., *Round the Wicket* (Muller, 1959)

Edwards, A., *Lionel Tennyson, Regency Buck: The Life and Times of a Cricketing Legend* (Robson Books, 2001)

Evans, G., *The Gloves are Off: A Close-up of Cricket* (Hodder & Stoughton, 1960)

Fay, S. and Kynaston, D., *Arlott, Swanton and the Soul of English Cricket* (Bloomsbury, 2018)

Ferguson, W., *Mr Cricket: The Autobiography of W.H. Ferguson as Told to David R. Jack* (Kaye, 1957)

Fingleton, J. H., *The Ashes Crown the Year* (Collins, 1954)

Fingleton, J. H., *Cricket Crisis* (Cassell, 1947)

Foot, D., *Wally Hammond, The Reasons Why: A Biography* (Robson Books, 1996)

Frith, D., *Frith's Encounters* (Von Krumm Publishing, 2014)

Frith, D., *Paddington Boy* (CricketMASH, 2021)

Gill, M., *Growing Into War* (The History Press, 2005)

Giller, N., *Denis Compton: A Biography* (Andre Deutsch, 1997)

Gunn, P.B., *R.A.F. Great Massingham: A Norfolk Airfield at War 1940–45* (1990)

Hadlee, Sir R., *The Skipper's Diary: New Zealand's 1949 Cricket Tour of England* (The Cricket Publishing Company, 2019)

Hamilton, D., *The Great Romantic: Cricket and the Golden Age of Neville Cardus* (Hodder & Stoughton, 2019)

Hammond, W. R., *Cricket: My World* (Stanley Paul, 1948)

Heald, T., *Denis Compton: The Authorised Biography* (Aurum Press, 2006)

Henry, M., *Air Gunner* (Goodall, 1997)

Hill, A., *The Bedsers: Twinning Triumphs* (Mainstream Publishing, 2001)

Hill, A., *Bill Edrich: A Biography* (Andre Deutsch, 1994)

Hill, A., *Les Ames* (Christopher Helm, 1990)

Hollands, J., *Gran and Mr Muckey: The Fictionalised Memoirs of Sajit Contractor* (Edward Gaskell, 2003)

Howat, G., *Len Hutton: A Biography* (Heinemann, 1988)

Howe, M., *Norman Yardley: Yorkshire's Gentleman Cricketer* (The Association of Cricket Statisticians and Historians, 2015)

Hughes, M., *All on a Summer's Day* (Stanley Paul, 1953)

Hutton, L., *Cricket is my Life* (Hutchinson, 1949)

Hutton, L., *Fifty Years in Cricket* (S. Paul, 1984)

Hutton, L., *Just My Story* (Hutchinson, 1956)

Kay, J., *Cuts and Glances* (John Sheratt & Son, 1948)

Knox, M., *Bradman's War: How the 1948 Invincibles Turned the Cricket Pitch into a Battlefield* (The Robson Press, 2013)

Laker, J., *Over to Me* (Frederick Muller, 1960)

Lazenby, J., *Edging Towards Darkness: The Story of the Last Timeless Test* (Wisden, 2017)

Lee, H., *Forty Years of English Cricket: With Excursions To India And South Africa* (Clerke & Cockeran, 1948)

Leeman, D., *What's My Line? The Story of the Famous Programme* (Allan Wingate, 1955)

Lemmon, D., *The History of Middlesex County Cricket Club* (Christopher Helm, 1988)

Lindwall, R., *Flying Stumps* (Arrow Books, 1957)

Lodge, J., *Bill Edrich* (Association of Cricket Statisticians and Historians, 2003)

McCool, C., *Cricket is a Game* (Stanley Paul, 1961)

Marshall, M., *Gentlemen and Players: Conversations with Cricketers* (Grafton, 1987)

Mason, R., *Batsman's Paradise: An Anatomy of Cricketomia* (Hollis & Carter, 1965)

May, P., *A Game Enjoyed: An Autobiography* (Stanley Paul, 1985)

Midwinter, E., *Brylcreem Summer: The 1947 Cricket Season* (Kingswood Press, 1991)

Mortimer, G., *Fields of Glory: The Extraordinary Lives of 16 Warrior Sportsmen* (Amdre Deutsch, 2001)

Murtagh, A., *Touched by Greatness: The Story of Tom Graveney, England's Much Loved Cricketer* (Pitch Publishing, 2014)

Musk, S., *Michael Falcon: Norfolk's Gentleman Cricketer* (Association of Cricket Statisticians and Historians, 1988)

Overson, C., *Jack Robertson and Syd Brown: More than Just the Warm-up Act* (ACS, 2013)

Pawle G., *R.E.S. Wyatt: Fighting Cricketer* (George Allen & Unwin, 1985)

Paynter, E., *Cricket All the Way* (A. Richardson, 1962)

Peebles, I., *Patsy Hendren: The Cricketer and His Times* (Macmillan, 1969)

Peebles, I., *Spinner's Yarn: An Autobiography* (Collins, 1978)

Peel, M., *The Hollow Crown: England Cricket Captains from 1945 to the Present* (Pitch Publishing, 2020)

Phillips, B. J., *Arthur Wellard: No Mere Slogger* (Leisuresolve, 1996)

Quelch, T., *Bent Arms and Dodgy Wickets: England's Troubled Reign as Test Match Kings During the Fifties* (Pitch Publishing, 2012)

Raphael, F., *Going Up: To Cambridge and Beyond – A Writer's Memoir* (The Robson Press, 2015)

Rendell, B., *Frank and George Mann: Brewing, Batting and Captaincy* (ACS, 2015)

Rendell, B., *Walter Robins: Achievements, Affections and Affronts* (Association of Cricket Statisticians and Historians, 2013)

Richardson, A., *Because of These: Verses of the RAF* (Hodder & Stoughton, 1942)

Ross, A., *Australia 55: A Journal* (Legend, 1985)

Rowe, M., *The Victory Tests* (SportsBooks, 2010)

Sandford, C., *The Final Innings: The Cricketers of Summer 1939* (The History Press, 2020)

Sandford, C., *Godfrey Evans: A Biography* (Simon & Schuster, 1990)

Sandford, C., *Keeper of Style: John Murray, the King of Lord's* (Pitch Publishing, 2019)

Sissons, R., *The Players: A Social History of the Professional Cricketer* (Kingswood Press, 1988)

Snow, P., *A Time of Renewal: Clusters of Characters, C.P. Snow and Coups* (Bloomsbury, 1998)

Swanton, E.W. *Cricketers of My Time: Heroes to Remember* (Andre Deutsch, 1999)

Swanton, E.W., *Follow On* (William Collins, 1977)

Swanton, E.W., *Sort of a Cricket Person* (Collins, 1972)

Synge, A., *Sins of Omission: The Story of the Test Selectors 1899–1990* (Michael Joseph, 1990)

Taylor, E., *Girls Don't Play Cricket* (Linellen Press, 2008)

Tennyson, L., *Sticky Wickets* (Christopher Johnson, 1950)

Thomas, R. H., *Cricketing Lives: A Characterful History from Pitch to Page* (Reaktion Books, 2022)

Thurlow, D., *Ken Farnes: Diary of an Essex Master* (Parrs Wood Press, 2000)

Titmus, F., *My Life in Cricket* (Blake Publishing, 2005)

Trueman, F., *As It Was: The Memoirs of Fred Trueman* (Macmillan, 2006)

Turbervill, H., *The Toughest Tour* (Aurum Press, 2010)

Tyson, F., *In the Eye of the Typhoon: The Inside Story of the MCC Tour of Australia and New Zealand 1954/55* (Parrs Wood Press, 2004)

Waite, R., *Death or Decoration: A Vivid Account of One Bomber Pilot's War* (Newton, 1991)

Warner, Sir P., *Cricket Between Two Wars* (Chatto & Windus, 1942)

Waters, C., *Fred Trueman: The Authorised Biography* (Aurum Press, 2011)

Wilde, S., *England, The Biography: The Story of English Cricket* (Simon & Schuster, 2018)

Wilde, S., *The Tour: The Story of the England Cricket Team Overseas 1877–2022* (Simon & Schuster, 2023)

Williams, C., *Gentlemen and Players: The Death of Amateurism in Cricket* (W&N, 2012)

Woodhouse, D., *Who Only Cricket Know: Hutton's Men in the West Indies 1953/54* (Fairfield Books, 2021)

Wyatt, R.E.S., *Three Straight Sticks* (Stanley Paul, 1951)

Yaxley, P., *Looking Back at Norfolk Cricket* (Nostalgia Publications, 1997)

INDEX